## ArtScroll® Series

Rabbi Nosson Scherman / Rabbi Gedaliah Zlotowitz
*General Editors*
Rabbi Meir Zlotowitz ז״ל, *Founder*

MAKOVSKY FAMILY EDITION

# Living

Published by

**ARTSCROLL**
Mesorah Publications, ltd

# Chessed

Powerful stories and insights
to bring chessed
into our everyday lives

Rabbi Avrohom Asher Makovsky

FIRST EDITION
First Impression … February 2023

Published and Distributed by
**MESORAH PUBLICATIONS, LTD.**
313 Regina Avenue / Rahway, N.J. 07065

Distributed in Europe by
**LEHMANNS**
Unit E, Viking Business Park
Rolling Mill Road
Jarrow, Tyne & Wear NE32 3DP
England

Distributed in Australia & New Zealand by
**GOLDS WORLD OF JUDAICA**
3-13 William Street
Balaclava, Melbourne 3183
Victoria Australia

Distributed in Israel by
**SIFRIATI / A. GITLER — BOOKS**
POB 2351
Bnei Brak 51122

Distributed in South Africa by
**KOLLEL BOOKSHOP**
Northfield Centre, 17 Northfield Avenue
Glenhazel 2192, Johannesburg, South Africa

ARTSCROLL® SERIES
**LIVING CHESSED**
© Copyright 2023, by MESORAH PUBLICATIONS, Ltd.
313 Regina Avenue / Rahway, N.J. 07065 / (718) 921-9000 / www.artscroll.com

ITEM CODE: LCHH
ISBN 10: 1-4226-3286-5
ISBN 13: 978-1-4226-3286-4

Typography by CompuScribe at ArtScroll Studios, Ltd.
Printed in the United States of America.
Bound by Sefercraft, Quality Bookbinders, Ltd., Rahway NJ

$\mathcal{T}$his book is lovingly dedicated
in memory of

# Rav Avrohom Osher Makovsky זצ"ל
## הרב אברהם אשר ב"ר משה דוד זצ"ל
### נפ' ג' אדר תש"ט

better known to us as "Zaida."

$\mathcal{H}$e was the patriarch of our family. He arrived on American shores in the early 1900s. He was a tremendous *talmid chacham* who had learned for ten years at the Lomza Yeshivah and was privileged to receive a *semichah* for *shechitah* from Rav Chaim Brisker. He responded to an ad in a paper looking for a *shochet* in St. Louis, Missouri, and settled there with his family.

$\mathcal{B}$esides being a *shochet* and a *mohel* for most residents of St. Louis, he delivered a daily *shiur* in Gemara to *baalei batim*. Over a period of ten years, they completed the entire Shas and a gala *Siyum HaShas* was held for the entire St. Louis Jewish community.

$\mathcal{R}$av Avrohom Osher was among the staunch pioneers of Yiddishkeit in St. Louis. He, together with his noble wife, Fruma Devora (bas R' Elchanan Dov, who passed away on 14 Adar II 5692), with great *mesirus nefesh*, raised a large family to be *shomrei Torah u'mitzvos* at a time when, and in a place where, Torah and Shabbos observance were extremely difficult to adhere to.

$\mathcal{I}$t is our fervent hope that our family brings him continued *nachas* in the *Olam Ha'emes* as we carry on his legacy of living a life of Torah and mitzvos.

**Dedicated by his many
grandchildren and great-grandchildren
in appreciation of his hard work and *mesirus nefesh*,
which enabled the extended Makovsky family
the privilege of living a true Torah life**

# Table of Contents

# Acknowledgments

אודך ה׳ אלוקי בכל לבבי...

Words cannot do justice to the monumental debt of gratitude that I owe Hashem for allowing me to print a book on the topic of chessed.

Although chessed has been so close to my heart for so many years and I have delivered many *shiurim* on the topic, it never dawned on me to write an English book. In retrospect, I see clearly that it was the will of Hashem that I should print this book. Hashem sent me a special messenger to ensure that this project would come to fruition. This messenger is my dear friend, Rabbi Yitzchok Hisiger. When he first asked me to put my *shiurim* and stories on chessed in writing, I didn't take it seriously. Then he gave me the idea to make five-minute podcasts on chessed. He told me that all I had to do was record it and he would take care of disseminating it to the public. It was an offer that I couldn't refuse. After the podcast, Daily Dose of Chessed, took off very successfully, R' Yitzchok implored me to put the lessons and stories into writing. From the early inception of this book, and through every one of its growing stages, he advised and guided me constantly, giving selflessly of his precious time. This book never would have materialized without him. I will forever be grateful to him. It is truly amazing to watch all of the chessed he does on a constant basis. May Hashem grant him *hatzlachah* and *siyata d'Shmaya* in all of his endeavors.

I knew that in order to print a book that would impart the crucial message of chessed, I had to find a really good editor. Hashem sent me another unique messenger, Mrs. Chana Nestlebaum. She took every written page and turned it into a masterpiece. Her writing and editing skills are extraordinary. She never ceased to amaze me, as she always found the perfect words to express my ideas in the most effective and meaningful way. Klal Yisrael is lucky to have a writer of such a high caliber who uses her talents to be *marbeh kevod Shamayim*. May she be *zocheh* to continue to use her talents to benefit Klal Yisrael for many more years.

I was so fortunate to grow up in the home of my parents, Rabbi and Mrs. Reuven Makovsky, a home that was seeped in *chashivus haTorah* and *gemilus chassadim*. My father retired early and returned to doing what he loves most — learning full-time in the *beis medrash*, doing so with the passion and *hasmadah* of a young *kollel yungerman*. Over the years, many less fortunate people have found comfort, a listening ear, and delicious meals in their home. They constantly look out for others, feel for them, and help them. I learned from them what chessed is. May they be *zocheh* to continue enjoying *Yiddishe nachas* from their family with happiness and good health until one hundred and twenty.

My in-laws, Rabbi and Mrs. Moshe Hillel Glazer, raised their family in such a fashion that the children watched their father learn Torah day and night, with their mother by his side, as nothing besides Torah is important in their lives. They recently moved to Lakewood from Baltimore, where my father-in-law was a *maggid shiur* at Yeshivas Ner Yisroel for 50 years, inspiring hundreds of young *talmidim* to grow into *talmidei chachamim*. We are thrilled to have them so close by. They taught us by example how to live with outstanding *middos tovos*, as their home is truly a place of harmony where the *Shechinah* resides. May they be *zocheh* to many more healthy years, enjoying *Yiddishe nachas* from their beautiful family.

My relatives, Mrs. Donna Schneier, Dr. Debra Fink, and Dr. Randy Makovsky took it upon themselves to arrange the dedication of this book by the extended Makovsky family in memory of their *zeide*, R' Avrohom Osher Makovsky *z"l*, who was one of the founding pillars of *Yiddishkeit* in the St. Louis community. It was heartwarming to see their perseverance to make this dedication a reality.

A very special thanks to R' Shmuel Zaidman, who is the executive director of the "Lunch 'n Learn" program in Lakewood, New Jersey, where I have been privileged to deliver *shiurim* for over 10 years. He graciously sends out the email of the Daily Dose of Chessed podcast to all of its subscribers. Another special thank you to R' Nussie Guggenheim, who videos all the "Lunch 'n Learn" *shiurim*. He uploads these *shiurim* and also the Daily Dose of Chessed podcast to TorahAnytime. Thank you to both of them for enhancing my *harbatzas haTorah*.

A good friend of mine and a tremendous *talmid chacham*, Rabbi Shloimy Dickman, has always been there to help me in any way that was necessary. (I have noticed that I am not the only benefactor of his overflowing chessed, as many people seem to feel the same.)

The following people helped me in different ways with the publication of this book: Uncle Simcha Cynamon, R' Shloimy Cynamon, R' Dovid Cynamon, R' Doniel Glazer, R' Shimon Handler, R' Avrohom Newhouse, R' Itche Rosenbaum, and R' Yisroel Meir Shapiro. Thank you so much. .

The unmatched ArtScroll team did a phenomenal job, living up to their exceptional reputation. My thanks to Mrs. Judi Dick and Mrs. Rivka Fishbane for editing and proofreading the manuscript so expertly, and to Mrs. Estie Dicker and Chanie Ziegler for paginating the book so beautifully. Reb Mendy Herzberg stewarded the process to the finish line with true professionalism. R' Eli Kroen, whose talent is unreal, produced a most magnificent cover that truly enhances the book.

Last, but certainly not least, I cannot properly express my heartfelt appreciation to my devoted wife and wonderful children and sons-in-laws for their constant support and encouragement. Thank you. I couldn't have done it without you!

I fervently hope that this book will increase the passion for *ahavas chessed* amongst *Klal Yisroel*. May the merit of chessed protect us from *chevlei Moshiach* until the *geulah*, may it come speedily in our days.

Avrohom Asher Makovsky

To receive Rabbi Makovsky's chesed podcast via email, please send your email information to dailydoseofchesed@gmail.com.

# Foreword

## by Rabbi Yitzchok Hisiger

The book you are holding is not just informative and inspiring.

It is, in my opinion, life-changing.

I remember the first time that my dear friend, Rabbi Avrohom Asher Makovsky, shared his *shiurim* on chessed with me. I listened and was enraptured. I felt that he was speaking *to* me, not *over* me. His message resonated.

The message? It was surprisingly simple: Chessed is something we can all do — and *must* do. In fact, chessed is something we can all excel in. We might not be blessed with the acumen, or the wherewithal, or the diligence to become a Torah giant, but we all possess the abilities — and opportunities — to truly be giants in chessed.

And that's what I learned from Reb Avrohom Asher's *shiurim*.

I implored Reb Avrohom Asher to put his thoughts — the lessons, the observations, and the stories — into writing. I was honored to watch him do so, celebrating every step of the process.

People mistakenly believe that to be a powerhouse of chessed, one must be the head of a mammoth, world-renowned organization, such as Hatzolah, Bikur Cholim, Chai Lifeline, or Bonei Olam.

This couldn't be further from the truth.

The truth is that chessed opportunities surround us. They are ubiquitous.

We just have to train our eyes to identify them.

And that's what this book accomplishes in a powerful way.

A game-changer for me were the words of the *Pele Yoetz* (*os ches*), which Reb Avrohom Asher quotes in his introduction. The *Pele Yoetz*, in candid fashion, points out that many people spend money and go to all lengths to fulfill certain *minhagim* and *segulos*, while overlooking the Torah mitzvah of chessed that is so easily performed each and every day. These "small" acts of chessed are, in fact, regarded as giant achievements in the World That Counts.

As an aside, when we do chessed, we receive so much more than we give. It transforms who we are, making us happier, more content people.

Even if we don't have the money to give huge sums for *tzedakah*, there is so much that we can do in the realm of chessed.

Sometimes, if all we have is a hug to give someone in need of one, it can move worlds ....

*In May 2011, Dr. Itzhak Brook, a pediatric infectious disease doctor at Georgetown University in Washington, D.C., penned a most touching article in the Los Angeles Times. I was so impressed by what he wrote that I reached out to him and let him know what an impact his words made on me. I asked him if I may share his story here and he graciously acquiesced.*

Hypopharyngeal cancer, cancer of the lower part of the pharynx (throat).

Words no one ever wants to hear.

Dr. Itzhak Brook had discovered his illness somewhat differently than the average person finds out about such things. As a doctor, he had access to his hospital's laboratory results. After undergoing testing, he looked up his name in the pathology laboratory logbook.

What he saw shook him up.

*"Mildly differentiated squamous cell carcinoma."*

There it was, black on white.

How was it possible? Could it be an error?

Deep down, Dr. Brook knew that it wasn't. But just to be sure, the good doctor went to view the biopsy specimens under the microscope himself.

There was no denying it. The diagnosis was accurate.

Dr. Brook knew in a nanosecond that his life would never be the same. He had always felt impregnable and impervious to illness. Now his entire world was filled with unpredictability and apprehension.

Overtaken by despondency and incredulity, Dr. Brook walked slowly from the laboratory to his internist's office. He stammered as he broke the news.

The internist didn't say a word. Instead, he slowly stood up and walked over to Dr. Brook. He then gave Dr. Brook a warm, caring embrace.

It was a hug that Dr. Brook has not forgotten.

He felt so good knowing that the internist cared for him beyond their professional connection. That hug encouraged Dr. Brook like nothing else could. It made him feel that he was in the company of someone who genuinely recognized his anguish and distress, who felt his personal tragedy. And at that moment, that meant more to him than a thousand words of support or detailed explanations.

It was the potency of a concerned, human touch. Dr. Brook now knew that he was not alone in his battle to overcome his illness. His doctor would fight it with him.

It was the first time that Dr. Brook had ever been hugged by a medical caregiver. In fact, never had Dr. Brook himself hugged any of his own patients, believing instead in maintaining a professional distance. At that moment, however, he realized that there are times in the medical field when the power of an embrace is so much more powerful than anything else a doctor or professional can provide.

In order to have his cancer removed, Dr. Brooks underwent a total laryngectomy, in which his entire larynx was removed.

The ensuing period was draining, physically and emotionally. Dr. Brook had great difficulty speaking and contended with myriad medical complications.

But he always remembered that hug.

Months of seemingly impossible challenges were made tolerable by the knowledge that his doctor would care for him and help him in any way he could. That emotional support, thoughtfulness, and sensitivity assisted Dr. Brook in surmounting many of the hurdles he faced as a laryngectomee (one who has undergone a laryngectomy). In fact, they played a crucial role in his ultimate recovery.

> *Dr. Brook was dealt a most daunting test that rendered speaking arduous and laborious. But he discovered a different manner of expression that, he says, is so much more powerful.*
>
> *He had experienced the unparalleled impact of a heartfelt hug.*

Anyone can give a hug. We just have to be tuned into the reality that we constantly have the ability to perform such "small" *chassadim* for others.

This book shows us how to recalibrate and modify the way we look at chessed — and the way we look at our ability to give.

Reb Beinish Mandel was a *baal chessed* like few others, whose heart overflowed with *ahavas Hashem, ahavas Yisrael,* and a kindness that was extraordinary. Stories abound of Reb Beinish's selflessness and *tzidkus.* He performed *chassadim* that his recipients never found out about, and sought out opportunities for personal growth and to help others.

One particular practice of Reb Beinish stands out in my mind. There's something so touching about it, so considerate, so thoughtful.

Reb Beinish was a Hatzolah volunteer, and an expert one at that. In addition to going on calls and providing the tender loving care for which he was known, he undertook his lifesaving job with the greatest sensitivity. His daughter related that during the cold winter months,

Reb Beinish made sure to bring the IV bags he kept in his car into his home. He would place the IV bags on a radiator in his house, so that if he received an emergency call in middle of the night, the liquid in the IV bags would be room temperature and not icy cold as it went through a patient's veins.

There's chessed and then there's supreme chessed. It takes a special human being to think of the seemingly smaller components of an act of kindness and expend the effort to carry it out with such perfection.

But we can all do it. We can learn to be like Reb Beinish Mandel.

The volume you are holding in your hands is a handbook to a life of endless chessed. After you read just a few chapters, you'll see a marked difference in the way you view the world around you. The lessons are conveyed clearly and succinctly, in language that is easy to understand and apply, and the stories — oh the amazing stories! — are gems, each and every one of them.

Take my word for it. The book you are holding is a life-changer.

Read it. Enjoy it. Digest it. And start living a chessed-filled life like you never thought possible.

Rabbi Yitzchok Hisiger

# Introduction

## Only One Solution

With war, economic disaster and political strife raging all around them, the Jews of Europe in the Chofetz Chaim's times lived in the shadow of ever-looming danger. During one of these many frightening periods, a community sent a *shaliach* to this great *tzaddik* to ask what the people should do to ensure their safety. The Chofetz Chaim informed them that what they were witnessing was nothing other than the onset of *chevlei Mashiach* — the "birth pangs of Mashiach."

"You are wasting your time asking me what to do to be saved. Even if you go all the way back to the *Rishonim* and ask them, they will tell you there is only one answer for being saved from *chevlei Mashiach*," he explained. "In the Gemara (*Sanhedrin* 98b), the students of Rav Elazar ask him what a person should do to save himself from *chevlei Mashiach*. His answer is "*Ya'asok b'Torah ub'gemilus chassadim* — You should toil in Torah and in acts of chessed."

The Chofetz Chaim clarified that the word *osek* (toil) is used in reference to both Torah and chessed. This means that just as it's not enough to learn Torah once in a while, but rather, it must be a constant occupation, likewise, it's not enough to do chessed once in a while if we are to meet the Gemara's definition of *osek,* the requirement for our security.

Hearing this, we might just throw our hands up in defeat. Although it's not easy to be *osek* in Torah, we know how to do it: a person must sit and learn with focus every moment he has available. But who is *osek* in chessed? If we look around our community, we might think of a handful of people who are outstanding in this mitzvah. They lead the organizations everyone turns to for help, or they volunteer for the organizations or support them with substantial donations. For most of us, this level of involvement might seem out of reach. In that case, how can a "regular Jew" protect himself from *chevlei Mashiach*?

This is a question that arises from a mistaken understanding of the mitzvah of chessed. To understand what the Gemara is asking of us, we have to go to the core of the mitzvah and find out exactly what is required. The *Rambam* answers this question in *Hilchos Avel* (Ch. 14), where he states that *gemilus chassadim* is rooted in the mitzvah of "*v'ahavta l'rei'acha kamocha* — you should love your fellow as [you love] yourself." He then adds a perspective that is crucial, and in fact, life-altering: the essence of the mitzvah is action. *This means that you fulfill this mitzvah not by loving your friend in your heart but rather, by performing deeds of chessed for him.*

Which actions qualify as a fulfillment of this mitzvah? The answer is, whatever we would like our friend to do for us. The *Rambam* uses the term "*kol hadevarim* — all the things," whatever they may be. For example, if our car was at the mechanic, we would want someone to offer us a ride. If we needed a cell phone and didn't have one on hand, we would want someone to let us use theirs. If we need a dollar bill for a vending machine, we would want someone to change our $20 bill. Therefore, doing these things for another person is a fulfillment of a mitzvah of the Torah, just like taking the *lulav*, wearing *tzitzis* or putting on tefillin. Knowing this can change our perspective. For example:

> Back in the days when long-distance calls required pre-paid calling cards, a yeshivah boy asked his friend, "Can I borrow your phone?"

*His friend declined, explaining, "I just put $10 on my calling card. You'll use up my minutes."*

*The next day, the same friend went esrog shopping. He compared two good options, one that was nice and one that was a little nicer. The nicer one cost $10 more, but he chose it, feeling it was worth the money.*

If we look at this situation with clear eyes, we see that this boy missed the boat. Providing the $10 on his calling card would have been a complete Torah mitzvah to his credit. Spending $10 extra on an *esrog*, while it served to "beautify the mitzvah," did not comprise a mitzvah on its own. Either of the *esrogim* would have fulfilled his obligation. If he was willing to spend $10 on beautifying a mitzvah, he should have been more than willing to spend the same amount to acquire a complete *mitzvah d'Oraisa*. Only a lack of awareness would lead someone to set his priorities in the opposite order.

Chessed by definition means that the ability to earn the merit of fulfilling a Torah commandment is at our fingertips throughout the day. We need not search far and wide for *zechusim*, because they are readily at hand. The *Pele Yoetz* (os ches, chessed) examines the efforts people undertake to earn extra merit before Rosh Hashanah and Yom Kippur, such as purchasing the honor of *pesichah*, opening the *aron kodesh*, especially for Neilah on Yom Kippur. In his times, people also paid for the honor of serving as a *sandek* at a *bris*.

The *Pele Yoetz* then awakens us to reality: Giving someone change of a dollar is greater than being a *sandek* at a *bris*, because as great a *segulah* as it may be, being *sandek* is not a fulfillment of a Torah mitzvah. But giving someone change, giving someone a ride, lending someone an egg — these are the fulfillment of a Torah mitzvah. As the *Rambam* explains, doing for another person anything we would want someone to do for us credits us with fulfilling the mitzvah of *v'ahavta l'rei'acha kamocha*.

Now the *Rambam* reveals a stunning insight that can change our entire understanding of our own potential to do chessed. In *Hilchos Dei'os* (6:3) he relates that the **ultimate way to fulfill the mitzvah** of chessed is by praising our friend to someone else or complimenting him directly. This is not a second-best effort, but rather, the premier way to fulfill the Torah's mitzvah of *v'ahavta l'rei'acha kamocha.*

That is because what every person wants for himself, more than anything else, is to feel valued. We can endure physical hardships and inconveniences, but when the foundation of our self-worth is wobbly, our optimism and energy for life collapses around it. Therefore, the greatest chessed we can do is to strengthen the heart of a fellow Jew through a compliment or praise. When we think just a bit deeper into this concept, we realize that we are surrounded by opportunities to do chessed. We can be *osek* in chessed because everyone interacts with someone in the course of the day: a spouse, child, student, teacher, employee, coworker, accountant, doctor, bus driver, grocer. Anyone who crosses our path provides us with a premier opportunity to perform the *mitzvah d'Oraisa* of chessed to the maximum by giving them a compliment.

Therefore, if in the morning we tell the *baal korei* that his Torah *leining* was beautiful, and at work we tell an employee that he's doing a good job, and when we come home, we tell our wife that she's a wonderful mother, we've fulfilled the *mitzvah d'Oraisa* of *gemilus chassadim* in the optimal manner, three times. That means we are *osek* in chessed. How doable, and how amazing!

In this volume, through numerous stories, we will show how Jews, from the great to the seemingly ordinary, fulfill the mitzvah of *v'ahavta l'rei'acha kamocha* in hundreds of ways. My hope is that these stories will open readers' eyes to the opportunities that abound in every person's life, and they will grasp the lifeline the Gemara in *Sanhedrin* has offered us. This way we can survive the upheavals of *chevlei Mashiach,* which only become more intense as the *Geulah* approaches. These are not just stories; they are a must-have roadmap for our generation, showing us how to traverse the rough terrain ahead of us and arrive safely at our long-awaited destination of *yemei Mashiach,* may he arrive very soon in our days!

# 1

## *Considering Others: The Minhag of Minhagim*

$A$t a time when advanced secular education, especially in the medical profession, was a rarity for a religious Jew, Rabbi Abraham J. Twerski M.D. stepped into the wasteland of medical school to become a psychiatrist. Despite his unusual goal, he saw himself first and foremost as a grandson of the Chernobyler dynasty, and the customs of his holy ancestors were of paramount importance to him. He maintained his chassidish way of life in every setting and situation. To ensure that he would properly safeguard his *Yiddishkeit* throughout his training and professional career, he sought personal guidelines directly from the Steipler Gaon.

One of Rabbi Twerski's indispensable Chernobyler customs was to bake Erev Pesach matzah. This was so elevated an occasion that the chassidim would recite *Hallel* with a *berachah* as they baked — a practice conveyed in the writings of the *Meiri*. Without fail each year, Rabbi Twerski spent his Erev Pesach in this exalted way.

*But one year, things were different. A grandchild recalls the story: His zeide had donned his Shabbos clothing, including his shtreimel, in preparation for the grand occasion of baking his Erev Pesach matzos. When his friends arrived to pick him up, he got into the car and then, before the driver drove on, Rabbi Twerski suddenly backed out. He got out of the car and returned to his house. Everyone was in shock. What could have stopped him from performing this holy custom of his zeides?*

*Rabbi Twerski later explained his behavior to his grandchild, whose eyes fill with tears as he recounts the moving story: "He told me that my grandmother, the rebbetzin, had been working very hard preparing for Pesach, and she had fallen asleep. 'You know what's going to happen?' he asked me. 'Soon, all the grandchildren are going to be coming over to wish us a gut Yom Tov and there will be continuous knocking on the door. If I'm not home to answer, they will wake her up.'*

*"If you can fathom what the matzah baking meant to my zeide, you can begin to understand what it meant that he considered my grandmother's needs first. In fact, he told me outright, 'Taking care of your wife comes before anything else.'"*

The renowned *gadol* Rav Gamliel Rabinowitz amplifies this thought. He is a Jew who exists on an entirely different plane than most of us, who sits with his special *siddur* praying with *Sheimos Hakedoshim*. Considering his lofty perceptions, many people come to him in times of trouble to learn of a *segulah* that might help. His answer: The best *segulah* is to avoid hurting others' feelings — to yield to others and make them feel good. This, he says, brings *yeshuos*.

This is what the people who reside up in the highest heights of Torah and *avodah* see from their perspective. The *avodah* that Hashem wants most from us is that we do no harm to His beloved children, and then go beyond that to show them our care and concern.

# Nip It in the Bud

*A* *patient is lying in his hospital bed after surgery. He desperately needs medication to dull the terrible pain he is feeling. He presses a button that calls the nurse, but no one comes. The nurse, meanwhile, does notice the light above the patient's door is lit; that's her signal that help is needed. However, she has three other patients ahead of him. He'll just have to wait. "I only have two hands," she tells herself.*

*Feeling that no one is noticing his call for help, the patient begins to panic. His anxiety adds to his pain, making it seem unbearable. It takes a half-hour for the nurse to come, and it's the longest half-hour in the patient's life.*

Looking at this scenario, we can empathize with the patient. We can imagine what it means to be in pain and see no prospect of relief. We can also feel some indignation at the nurse; even if she was too busy to come to the patient, how long would it have taken to offer a little reassurance that relief would come soon? She planned to help him, but as long as he didn't know that, it did him no good. When it comes to physical pain, we all recognize the cruelty of allowing someone to wallow in it for even one extra minute.

If we transfer that sense of urgency to emotional or spiritual pain, we can take our chessed to a new level. Why let a person's needs wait for later if we can help right away?

Often, we intend to help someone, but we schedule it into our day to suit our convenience. We could give someone money to help with his *chasunah* expenses, but we'd feel more secure about parting with the money if we wait for a certain payment to come in. We could *redt* a *shidduch* tonight, but tomorrow we'll have more time to give the details and answer questions. Meanwhile, the man making the *chasunah* will spend an extra 24 hours wondering how he'll meet his expenses, and the single girl will spend an extra 24 hours wondering why the phone never rings. They may sink a little further into their worries; they may even lose hope or *chas v'shalom* lose faith.

For the *gedolim* of chessed, the timing is as magnificent as the deed itself, as this story of Rav Yosef Shalom Elyashiv portrays:

> *Rav Elyashiv was seated at an engagement party among other rabbanim and roshei yeshivos. The chassan rose to deliver a de-var Torah, in which he quoted the words of the Minchas Chinuch. As the young man spoke, a small commotion erupted in the area where the rabbanim were seated. Rav Elyashiv discovered that it was caused by an elderly Rosh Yeshivah's comment that "There is no such Minchas Chinuch." After the brief stir caused by the com-ment, the chassan continued his derashah.*
>
> *That night before going to sleep, Rav Elyashiv made a point of finding out where the kallah's father would be first thing in the morning. The answer was the mikveh of Batei Ungar, where he went each day at 4 a.m. Rav Elyashiv then retired for the night, but instead of rising for his most precious early morning seder that he reserved to immerse in uninterrupted learning — he made his way to the mikveh and waited for the kallah's father to come out.*
>
> *In Rav Elyashiv's hands was a large, wrapped package. When the man emerged, he ran to him and opened the package, which contained a large, old-print Minchas Chinuch that he owned. He*

*opened the sefer and pointed at a certain paragraph. "This is the Minchas Chinuch your son-in-law quoted last night," he said. And he left.*

Why did Rav Elyashiv feel he had to reach the *kallah's* father at the earliest possible moment of the day? It was because he wanted to nip the father's doubts about the *chassan* in the bud. With every passing hour, he knew the father would be thinking and rethinking his impression of the *chassan,* wondering if he was all he was said to be, searching past interactions for similar errors. By that afternoon, he could have soured on the young man completely, and even if the truth would come out and the *shidduch* be revived, it would be marred.

Rav Elyashiv teaches that we don't have the luxury of time while someone else is worrying, simmering, or sitting with his pain. Rather than waiting for the convenient moment to act, we can prevent the problem from coming into full bloom by acting as soon as possible to nip it in the bud.

# Keeping Them Afloat

O ften, people have problems for which we have no practical help to offer. We can't pay their bills or cure their illness or make their son go back on the *derech*. In such a situation, we might feel helpless and clumsy. We might even try not to encounter the person, just to avoid the awkwardness.

However, even when we don't have answers, we do have something to offer. Although it might not seem like much, our emotional support can make a world of difference. Seeking out someone who is burdened with worries lets them know that we have them on our mind. We're not simply going on with our daily routine while they suffer. The more we connect ourselves to others' needs and feelings, the more natural it becomes for us to keep their well-being in mind; their trouble troubles us, so how can we just forget it and move on? True *ohavei Yisrael* cannot.

> *There was a couple who lived in Bnei Brak. They had a close relative who they believed would thrive in the Ponevezh Yeshivah. Fortunately, this couple lived in the same building as the Ponevezh Rosh Yeshivah, Rav Shmuel Rozovsky. The couple lived on the*

*third floor of the building and the Rosh Yeshivah lived on the first floor. They decided to pay him a visit and see if he could put in a good word for their relative with the Ponevezher Rav, who made all the admissions decisions.*

*When they laid out their request to the Rosh Yeshivah, he said he would be happy to speak on their relative's behalf. However, it was bein hazmanim and the Ponevezher Rav was out of town. There was no way to reach him. The woman was so devoted to the cause of getting this young man into the yeshivah that she burst into tears of disappointment. The Rosh Yeshivah assured her that the Rav would surely call him sometime during bein hazmanim and he would be certain to bring up the woman's request at that time.*

*The couple climbed the three flights of stairs to their apartment. Twenty minutes later, there was a knock on their door. When the man opened it, to his great shock he found Rav Shmuel Rozovsky standing there. What could have prompted him to climb three flights of stairs, the man wondered. "Is there some news?" he asked.*

*"No, I have nothing new to report," said the Rosh Yeshivah. "I was just so bothered to see your wife so upset, to see her crying so bitterly. Please tell her to stay calm and im yirtzeh Hashem, things will work out. I'm going to try. Please tell her to just hold on until I can speak to the Ponevezher Rav."*

*The Rosh Yeshivah returned to his apartment, and an hour later, he was back at the couple's door again. This time it was to share good news. "The Ponevezher Rav called me," he reported. "I put in a good word for your relative and he was accepted on the spot!"*

To learn from this story, we have to ask ourselves a question: Why did Rav Shmuel Rozovsky trouble himself to climb three flights of stairs a mere 20 minutes after he saw the couple when he had nothing new to report? Most people would wait until they had news — preferably good news — before seeking out the couple. But the Rosh Yeshivah saw fit to visit them just to reiterate what he had already told them. The sole purpose of the interaction was to enable the woman to remain calm until her answer came.

This story can change our perspective on chessed. We see that providing encouragement and moral support, even when we don't have practical help to give, is a worthy use of our time and effort. If all we offer is a phone call that says, "You're on my mind," or a visit that says, "You're important to me," we are still doing a true chessed. If Rav Rozovsky felt it was worth his precious time, it's certainly worth ours.

# The Segulah That Doesn't Cost a Dime

Rav Michel Barenbaum was the *mashgiach* of Mesivta Tifereth Yerushalayim under Rav Moshe Feinstein. After Rav Michel's passing, many grandchildren and great-grandchildren were born to his family, and it came to someone's attention that oddly, none of these babies were being named for Rav Michel. People began to wonder about this unusual situation, because in general, family members would be proud and delighted to have their baby carry the name of an illustrious grandfather.

At one point, somebody asked one of Rav Michel's children why there were no babies named for his revered father. The answer was an astounding insight into the depths of chessed that can reside in a Jewish heart.

In Rav Michel's will, he noted that while he would of course be honored to have children named after him, he would prefer that the newborn be named for a grandfather whose widow was still alive. As Rav Michel's wife had passed away before him, there was no widow to feel the comfort and joy of knowing her husband's name had been passed to the next generation. Therefore, he desired that preference be given to a grandfather whose wife was still living. Eventually, as time elapsed, he knew he would have offspring named for him, but while widowed grandmothers were still alive, he wanted them to have the comfort of having a baby named for their husband.

What sensitivity and insight this story illustrates! Can we begin to fathom how precious such kindness is in Hashem's eyes? The *Pele Yoetz* (*os ches*) wonders why people fail to see the vast merit of chessed that is there for the taking, and instead, search high and low for *segulos* to help them. He notes that before Rosh Hashanah and Yom Kippur, people are willing to spend large sums of money for the *zechus* of *pesichah* (opening the *aron kodesh*) at Neilah.

They would achieve more for themselves, he says, by simply changing a coin for someone who asks. This is a favor that doesn't even require an expenditure of money; it's a simple matter of giving them two dimes and a nickel for their quarter, and yet it fulfills the *mitzvah d'Oraisa* of *gemilus chassadim*.

Making change — a less common need in our time — is just an illustration of how a small act of kindness that costs the giver nothing can mean a great deal to the recipient. If someone needs exact change for a vending machine, for instance, the change means that the person can quench his thirst or refresh himself with a snack. Giving someone a ride is another example; a drive that takes 10 minutes can save a person a 45 minute walk. The passenger not only saves time, but perhaps arrives at his destination feeling relaxed and comfortable rather than exhausted and sweaty, thereby better able to succeed at the task at hand.

The calculation of what brings more merit is simple. There is no mitzvah in the Torah to open the *aron kodesh*, to be a *sandek* at a *bris*, or to have an *aliyah*. Chessed, however, is one of the 613 commandments Hashem gave us in the Torah — His instructions for us on how to live our lives. That is why Rav Michel knew where to place his focus when it came to naming children after him; he knew he would have far greater merit by considering the feelings of the widows in his family than by spreading his name far and wide. Every kindness we do is a fulfillment of the *mitzvah d'Oraisa* of *v'ahavta l'rei'acha kamocha*, just as sitting in a succah or putting on tefillin is a *mitzvah d'Oraisa*. Kindness is an act treasured by Hashem and rewarded with merit that no *segulah* can match.

# You Can Open the Gates of Shamayim

I
f we knew that the answer to all our needs and desires was waiting behind a locked door, what wouldn't we do to find the key? The following story of the Tzemach Tzedek teaches that if we know where to look, we will find that the key is in easy reach:

> The Tzemach Tzedek, orphaned at a young age, was the grandchild of the Baal HaTanya, Rav Shneur Zalman of Liadi. He was raised by his renowned Zeide, with whom he had an especially close bond. After the Baal HaTanya passed away, his grandson assumed the role of Rebbe. However, he did not have to carry the burdens of leadership alone, because for many years, his holy Zeide came to the Tzemach Tzedek in his dreams. The grandson would ask him his questions and the Zeide would answer.
>
> Then one day, the dreams stopped. Months went by without the Baal HaTanya's appearance, and the Tzemach Tzedek prayed fervently that he would merit his return. However, the months became years and the dreams faded into an old memory.

*One day, the Tzemach Tzedek was rushing to Shacharis in his town of Lubavitch. Since it was market day, people from throughout the region were gathered in the marketplace preparing for a day of business. As the Tzemach Tzedek passed, a Jewish merchant stopped him and asked, "Rebbe, could you maybe lend me a little money? You see, to do business here, you have to buy a small item. Then you go to another part of the marketplace and sell it at a small profit. With that, you buy another item and sell that in another area. That's how I do business, but I don't have any money to make the first purchase and get started."*

*"Of course I will lend a Jew some money!" the Rebbe replied warmly. "It's a mitzvah d'Oraisa — kesef talveh." He put his hand in his pocket and discovered that it was empty. "But don't worry," he said, "I have to go daven Shacharis right now to be on time for minyan. Then when I'm done, I'll go home and get the money and bring it to you."*

*The merchant was disappointed. He knew that if he didn't get started when the market opened, most of his opportunities would be lost. However, out of respect for the Rebbe, he gratefully agreed to the plan.*

*The Tzemach Tzedek continued on to shul. He put on his tallis, made a berachah and started davening. Suddenly, his mind began churning. "Wait a second," he thought. "A Jew needs money. That takes priority over my davening with a minyan."*

*Without another thought, he removed his tallis, ran home, got the money and returned to the marketplace. Just as he had suspected, the empty-handed merchant was standing idly while the hustle and bustle of commerce swirled around him. The Tzemach Tzedek ran over to the merchant.*

*"Here's the loan I agreed to give you," he said. The other man's face lit up with hope and happiness. He could now do business.*

*With his top priority attended to, the Rebbe returned to shul and donned his tallis for the second time that morning. At that moment, the Baal HaTanya appeared to him. Later, when telling*

*the story, the Tzemach Tzedek said that this was an unusual ap-*
*pearance, because until then, his zeide had always come to him in*
*a dream. Now he had come in broad daylight, while the grandson*
*was wide awake.*

*"I want you to know," said the Baal HaTanya, "that when all*
*the gates of Shamayim are closed, and a Jew does a favor for an-*
*other Jew with his whole heart, he opens the gates. And now, here*
*I am. Ask me whatever you wish."*

The Baal HaTanya did not divulge why the gates had been closed. However, he opened our eyes, through this story, to the means by which we can open the gates. Just by doing a good deed, a favor, or a kindness for another Jew — and putting our hearts into it — we can access the *berachah* that awaits us in *Shamayim*.

# 6

# You Can Always Think of a Way

There was an accomplished talmid chacham whose heart moved him to pay an occasional visit to an elderly man who resided alone in Bnei Brak. The man had no wife or children. He was so sunken into his pit of depression that despite his still-sharp mind, he had no desire to learn, even for a short period. He couldn't bring himself to attend a shiur or mingle with others at a simchah. He just sat alone and wallowed in his despair, living from one interminable moment to the next.

When the talmid chacham would come to bring the man some human warmth, he would often hear a statement that pierced his heart: "There's no point in being alive," the elderly man would declare.

Wanting to do something to alleviate this man's black depression, the talmid chacham sought advice from his rebbi, Rav Avraham Genachovsky, the Tchebiner Rosh Yeshivah. As the rebbi's close talmid, he knew that if there were any way to help this dejected man find some joy in his life, Rav Genachovsky would find it. He had often said, "There is no such thing as being unable to *help someone. You must try, and with siyata d'Shmaya, you will find a solution."*

The talmid chacham described the elderly man's dire circumstances to his rebbi. How, he wondered, could anyone bring this man back to life?

*"I have a very good idea," said Rav Genachovsky. "A person can only feel enthusiasm for life if he has something to give. This gives him a sense of purpose. So if all we do is get more people to go visit this man, we won't accomplish anything. He still won't feel like he's doing anything productive.*

*"What I want you to do is to go to some major chessed organizations, like Bikur Cholim in Bnei Brak. They know many people who need yeshuos — people who are sick, people who have a problem. Tell them in my name that if someone needs a berachah, they should send the person to this elderly Jew, and he'll give them a berachah."*

This talmid chacham, who recorded the story in writing, testified that the plan worked like a miracle cure. It brought about "techiyas hameisim" in the elderly man. People came to him for berachos and he now had an important purpose.

We are still left to wonder if this man actually had a special power to give *berachos* that would have clout in *Shamayim*. The *talmid chacham* writes that he is not sure what was behind his rebbi's thinking. Was the merit of the visitors' chessed in going to see the elderly man that rendered the *berachos* effective? Was the rebbi *davening* that the *berachos* would work? Regardless of the thinking behind the plan, we see that Rav Genachovsky instantly recognized the elderly man's situation as one of life or death. He said he had no reason to live, and the only answer was to give him a reason. He felt he had nothing to give, and the only answer was to find something he would be willing, happy and proud to give.

This story has a hidden message as well. Rav Avraham Genachovsky was able to bring someone from despair to *chiyus* with no physical exertion, no great undertaking, no financial backing. His success in understanding what the man actually needed and finding the answer arose from one vital asset that he had in abundance — his *ahavas chessed*. Someone whose entire being is straining to give, to help and to ease others' suffering will always come up with a way. He quickly realized that those who took part in his rescue plan — who came to this man with their troubles and asked for his *berachah* — were performing the starring role in bringing him back to life. For that, they would surely merit *yeshuos.*

Most people would view a man like the one in our story as a lost cause. He had rejected all the known cures for loneliness and boredom. We learn from this story, however, that if we refuse to say "impossible," we may suddenly find ourselves inspired by an idea that will be effective. The beneficiary could be our own elderly parent, grandparent or neighbor, and ultimately, ourselves.

# Pick Up the Pieces

Nachum* paid a visit to Rav Shlomo Zalman Auerbach, his heart heavy with worry. His daughter had always aspired to marry a budding talmid chacham. At last she was engaged, but to her and her family's great disappointment, the truth emerged that her chassan did not excel in his learning, nor in his dedication to learning. Quite simply, the match was a mistake.

When Nachum finished laying the situation out before Rav Shlomo Zalman, the gadol had no doubt that the shidduch should be broken. That was the Rav's decision, and that was what Nachum would do. Still, he was worried. Breaking a shidduch is never simple. The chassan will surely be hurt and the kallah might find herself beset by doubts and anxiety.

When Nachum returned home, he was surprised to find his household in a state of high excitement. The kallah's face was glowing with happiness. His 12-year-old son ran to him shouting, "Totty! Do you know what happened?"

*"No! What happened?" Nachum asked.*

*"Just a little while ago, the phone rang," recounted the boy. "I answered it and the voice on the other end said, 'This is Shlomo Zalman Auerbach. Can I please speak to the kallah?' My hand was shaking so much that I could barely hand her the phone."*

*Rav Shlomo Zalman, the gadol hador, had personally telephoned this young woman to tell her, "Your father was just here with me. He's on the way home. I want to let you know that I told him to break the shidduch, but I also want to assure you that you have nothing to worry about. Your dreams are going to be fulfilled, I guarantee you. Everything is going to be fine, you will see."*

*Indeed, the situation worked out. The kallah was redt a more suitable chassan and created the household she dreamed of building.*

This touching story that reveals a *tzaddik's* sensitivity has something powerful to teach regular people too. How often do we make a decision — the right decision — that has a detrimental impact on another person? For instance, a business owner sees that a certain employee is not cut out for his job and he rightfully decides to fire him. The owner might even seek *daas Torah* before making the decision. He knows he is doing the right thing, but there are bound to be negative repercussions for the employee. Does he have enough money to keep his family afloat while he seeks a new job? Will his *shalom bayis* become strained? Will his children suffer? Will he become tense and depressed, causing his troubles to multiply?

A person might think, "I don't know the answer to these questions. I'm doing what I have to do. I feel bad that he might suffer, but what can I do?"

With Rav Shlomo Zalman's example before us, we see that we must go one step further in this line of thought. "What can I do?" should not be an expression that means throwing up our hands in surrender, but rather, it should be a call to arms. "What *can* I do? Can I keep him on for an extra month to give him a chance to find a new job? Can I help him find a job that better suits him? Can I find a different position in my company for him? Can I help arrange a loan to carry him over until he starts working again?"

At times people have to make hard decisions and someone comes out on the losing end of the situation. But a Jew has to feel for that person's suffering. A person with a heart of chessed is stirred by others' needs and doesn't feel satisfied until he has done all he can to fulfill those needs. This is especially so if the needs were created by an action or decision we have made. When we must engage in an act of constructive destruction — disrupting the status quo to improve a situation — we cannot just "let the pieces fall where they may." We must do our best to pick up the pieces and set things right again for everyone involved.

# Giving What You Don't Owe

Rav Shlomo Zalman Auerbach was instrumental in another incident, that spread far and wide and inspired many yeshuos. It began with a childless woman who came to him for advice. The woman was bitter. How could Hashem have denied her a child? Why did millions of women have houses filled with children, while she was so persecuted?

Although Rav Shlomo Zalman was known for the soothing manner in which he addressed the troubled people who came to him, to this woman he spoke bluntly. "Hashem does not owe you anything," he told her. "You have grievances against Hashem? You're alive, you're healthy, you have nothing to complain about!"

The woman was taken aback by his sharp words. However, they opened her heart to the advice Rav Shlomo Zalman wanted to give. "It's true that Hashem doesn't owe you anything, but you can still ask Him to give you something He does not owe you. The Gemara (Sanhedrin 90a) says that Hashem treats us middah k'neged middah — measure for measure. The way we act toward others, He acts toward us. So, if you want Him to give you a *kindness even though He doesn't owe it to you, you need to extend kindness to someone to whom you owe nothing — someone who hasn't done you a favor or loaned you money. Help someone for the sake of doing a chessed, and Hashem will do the same for you."*

*The woman took the Rav's advice and began volunteering in a large hospital in Yerushalayim. She visited the sick patients, people to whom she owed nothing. At the end of the year, she gave birth to a child. When word spread of Rav Shlomo Zalman's advice and the beautiful outcome, more people began performing their own "acts of random kindness" and additional yeshuos came about.*

What is the special value of a chessed we don't owe? The Vilna Gaon explains based on an episode (*Yehoshua* 2:12-14) when the *Bnei Yisrael* prepared to invade Yericho. At that time, Yehoshua sent spies into the city and they were hidden by a woman named Rachav. In exchange for her help, she asked the spies to do chessed and *emes* by saving her and her family when the invading forces arrived. The Gaon says that returning Rachav's kindness by saving her was *emes*. It was a favor returned, the right thing to do. Saving her family was chessed, because it was more than what the spies had promised her. When a person gives that which he is *not* obligated to give, this is the purest form of chessed, and it is the type of chessed through which, *middah k'neged middah,* Hashem brings us more blessing than we deserve.

The Gemara (*Shabbos* 151b) says, "Anyone who has compassion (*rachmanus*) on Hashem's creations, for him there is compassion from *Shamayim.*" The *Mesillas Yesharim* (Ch. 19) further explains that this Gemara leads to the obvious conclusion that the greater the compassion we show others, the greater the compassion Hashem will bestow on us.

This has immediate, practical value to each of us. For example, someone asks you for a ride on a hot summer day when you're in a rush. You can take him half-way home without going out of your way — a small *rachmanus* — or you can go out of your way to take him to his doorstep — a greater *rachmanus.* You can call a sick person and ask how she is — a small *rachmanus,* or cook dinner for her family — a greater *rachmanus.*

Rav Shlomo Zalman teaches that we should never despair about our situation because right in our hands, each and every day, we have the power to do that something extra that can bring us the *yeshuah* we've been waiting for — even if we don't deserve it.

# Your Precious Time

*A* *man came to me with questions about the Torah in relation to science. He wondered how to reconcile contradictions he perceived and I, with little background in science, did not feel qualified to answer him. Instead, I gave him the phone number of Rav Yisroel Belsky, who was in Camp Agudah at the time.*

*The man was hesitant. "Rav Belsky doesn't know who I am," he said. I reassured him that Rav Belsky did not have to know him to give him the time he needed. The man called the Rav and a long discussion ensued, flowing over many hours for several weeks. Whenever Rav Belsky had to tend to another obligation, he excused himself politely and urged the man to call back later or the next day. The man never felt for a moment that he was imposing on the Rav's time, even though Rav Belsky was busy answering numerous shailos, handling dinei Torah and giving shiurim.*

How often do we think, "I don't have time for this (or him or her)." But one mark of a *gadol b'Yisrael* is that he has time for everyone who needs him. Did Rav Belsky really have more time on his hands than say, a salesman at a clothing shop? The Rav was productively occupied every waking moment of his day, and yet he gave his time to those who sought him out. Giving your time is giving your heart.

In contrast, let's look at an impatient clothing salesman on a busy afternoon a week before Pesach. One man walks in and asks to see the suits. He's looking at the most expensive imported suits in the store and the salesman hovers around him helpfully. Another customer, who wants to get the salesman's opinion on which of two ties is better quality, keeps trying to get his attention and being told, "I'm busy with a customer." Is he busier than Rav Belsky? Are his minutes more precious?

We all need others' time! Whether we're speaking to customer service or asking about an item on a restaurant menu or consulting a doctor about a medical issue, we want focus, patience, and thoughtful answers. We want to feel that the person to whom we are speaking — someone who can perhaps help us out of a dilemma — cares about us. When people give us their time, we feel their care. They were so helpful! So nice! So patient! When they ignore us or try to dispense with the interaction as quickly as possible, we feel a little bit more alone in the world.

Even people who charge for their time — lawyers, therapists, doctors — can do a great chessed by giving some of their time. We saw this when Reb Sholom Mordechai Rubashkin was in prison. Even non-Jewish attorneys, shocked at the situation, gave time and incurred travel and other expenses without charge to help free him and reverse an injustice.

One doctor I know — a true *tzaddik* — is always going above and beyond the call of duty. When I complimented him on his kindness, he told me an eye-opening story. "I have a daughter who had cancer," he said. "Since I'm not a cancer doctor, I was at the mercy of another doctor, who had *rachmanus* on me. He gave so much time to me, my wife, and my daughter. I learned from him how much this means to the patient. If that's how another doctor acted toward me, that's how I have to act toward my patients."

When someone gives his time with his heart, he remains with the other person until he has done all he can to help. He doesn't keep a meter running. Another instance in Rav Belsky's life is a perfect illustration. Once, a distant relative called him with *shailos* about *kashering* appliances in the kitchen of the house into which he had just moved. Rav Belsky gave him extensive instructions on the phone. A short while later, the man heard a knock on his door. Rav Belsky had detected in the man's voice that he still wasn't quite confident about what to do, and so the Rav came personally to reassure him and give him an on-site demonstration of the correct procedure.

There is a saying that, "If you want something done, ask a busy person." This is borne out by the way in which *gedolim*, who are busy night and day with the needs of Klal Yisrael, always find time for one more Jew. A rebbi recently told me that he was having difficulties with a *bachur* and wanted to find someone to give the boy some encouragement. He was unable to get through to anyone until he called Rav Shmuel Kamenetsky, who answered his own phone and proceeded to look through his schedule and find a time when he would be in Lakewood, where the boy lived. He found a night when he would be attending a wedding there and told the rebbi that he would be happy to meet the boy at the wedding. For Rav Shmuel, there's always time for a Jew in need.

This is a lesson everyone can put into action. As the Baal Shem Tov teaches, the words (*Tehillim* 121:5), "Hashem is your shadow," mean that exactly as we act, Hashem acts toward us, like our shadow which moves exactly as we move. We all want to be seen and heard. We all want people to give us time, to respond to us when we need them. There's one way for us to guarantee that this will happen, and that is to be there for others when they need us. Then, when Hashem shadows our actions, He is there for us, making sure that we are seen and heard by those whose help we seek.

# A Golden Nugget of Recognition

*My son was sitting and learning on a Friday night at his yeshivah when he overheard a conversation. An older man who was visiting the yeshivah was approached by a younger man. "Rebbi, do you remember me?" the younger man asked. "You were my rebbi 20 years ago. You were the best rebbi I ever had!"*

*My son went back to his learning until about 15 minutes later when another man approached this same visitor. One particular sentence floated up from their conversation and struck my son's ear. "You know," said the rebbi, "there may be people who didn't think I was a good rebbi. But someone just came over and told me that I was the best rebbi he ever had!"*

There was such pleasure and satisfaction in this man's voice — an older, experienced rebbi who most likely had been in *chinuch* for decades. Even so, it was obvious that his former student's kind words lifted his heart. Just a few words made such an impact.

This incident is living proof of the magnificent *Rambam* in *Hilchos Dei'os* (6:3) that says that the greatest way to fulfill the Torah mitzvah of *gemilus chassadim* is to give someone a compliment. He is telling us what we already know: that a person's deepest desire and greatest happiness comes from others thinking well of him.

This gives every one of us constant opportunities to become the greatest *baalei* chessed in the world. It's so easy that it's almost a tragedy to overlook these occasions:

1. Tell your wife, "Supper was delicious. Thanks!"
2. Tell your husband, "I really appreciate the way you learn with our son," or "I know how hard you work for our *parnassah*. Thank you."
3. Tell your child who's helped you out, "You add so much to the family."
4. Tell your parents, who help you through a challenge, "Thanks for being there for me."
5. Tell your worker, who contributed to your business, "You're doing a great job."

This is so much more than an "extra touch" that makes life better. The Steipler writes that a wife who feels unappreciated by her husband or a husband who feels unappreciated by his wife are actually experiencing *pikuach nefesh* — a life-and-death situation. When doing this chessed is so easy, so available and doable for everyone, *not* doing it is even a more serious oversight. Hashem may understand why, if you're short of cash, you have trouble parting with money for *tzedakah*, or if you're exhausted, you find it difficult to run out and visit someone in the hospital. But what stops us from saying a kind word to another person who is right there in front of us? Nothing!

A good word is a golden nugget of chessed laying there, waiting for us to pick it up. May we have eyes to see it and wisdom to understand its value. Then, *middah k'neged middah*, Hashem will make sure that we too receive the encouragement we need to carry us through the challenges of our lives.

# Everyone Counts

Imagine the beginning of the *zman* in the Mir Yeshivah in Yerushalayim back in the days when Rav Chaim Shmulevitz was the Rosh Yeshivah. All the *talmidim* were consumed with one issue: making sure they had the best possible *chavrusa* for the coming *zman*. This would set the tone of their learning, and set the bar for the goals they would strive to reach.

We might think that the great Rosh Yeshivah himself would also be consumed with this issue. Wouldn't he be elated by the vision of hundreds of students' passionate efforts to find the perfect learning partner? Wouldn't it be testimony to their love of learning, and to the success of his yeshivah?

Yet this was not the thought foremost on Rav Chaim's mind. Instead, at the start of each *zman*, he would deliver a *shmuess* that awakened the *talmidim* of the yeshivah to the most important priority in their pursuit of a *chavrusa*. "I cannot understand how *bachurim* could sit down and learn with their *chavrusos* if there are other *bachurim* walking around who don't have *chavrusos*," he would say. "There are *bachurim* walking around feeling worthless. If anyone is left without a *chavrusa* at the beginning of the *zman,* I personally will learn with him."

To Rav Chaim Shmulevitz, who presided over hundreds of *bachurim* steeped in learning, those few who were left out clouded the entire picture. He couldn't look at his *beis medrash* and feel satisfied with its booming *kol Torah* knowing that a few boys felt excluded.

This is a trait of greatness, but it's the kind of greatness we can all emulate. Who is left out? Who is left behind? What can we do to give that *bachur* or girl a boost?

Rav Yisroel Belsky headed a highly popular *masmidim* program in Camp Agudah. He believed that the boys could benefit extraordinarily from the intense learning schedule within the camp atmosphere, and they did. One year, a boy could not be accommodated because the program was full; there wasn't space for one more bed. Rav Belsky asked the camp director to take a walk with him on the grounds. "We're going to find a place to put one more bed," Rav Belsky told him. And they found a space.

The camp director didn't understand why the Rav went to such trouble for one boy whom he didn't even know, when he ran a massive program that ignited the hearts of so many boys with excitement for learning. Rav Belsky's answer was simple. "There's so much for each *bachur* to gain. We learn that whoever saves one life in Klal Yisrael saves a whole world. This means exactly what it says!"

In our communities, we too, see the amazing sight of thousands of children setting out every day to learn in yeshivah or Bais Yaakov, and thousands of *bachurim* heading to *beis medrash.* But our *gedolim* are teaching us that we can never be self-satisfied if there are children without a school to attend.

"Imagine their pain," said Rav Belsky. 'Why am I different from all my friends?' They are young children. They don't understand... pardon my expression...they don't yet understand the worthless *meshugas* called *protektzia,* that you can get protection with money. They want to be like everyone else with their knapsacks ready to go to school."

Most people are not in the position to set policy for their schools or their communities, but we learn from these masters of *ahavas Yisrael* that we have to care about those who are left out. If Rav Shmulevitz refused to rest until everyone had a *chavrusa* and Rav Belsky refused to rest until every boy who wanted to be in the *masmidim* program had a place, how can we turn our backs on children who have no school at all?

The answer to these situations is sometimes complicated, but the first step in finding the answer is to see each child as an *olam malei* — an entire world — and to care. This is how the *gedolim* come to such sensitivity. They train themselves to see every Jew as a world, which opens their eyes to each individual's needs and fuels their drive to find a way to help. To strive toward this level of greatness, we do not need any asset other than a warm Jewish heart.

# Minimum Daily Requirement

Speaking on the first *yahrtzeit* of Rav Shach, his close *talmid*, Rav Yosef Heisler, told a story that exemplified the *gadol's* understanding of his purpose in the world.

*Everyone knew that Rav Shach never took a vacation. While numerous gedolim spend the summer months in a serene setting, he never budged from his apartment in Bnei Brak.*

*During one summer bein hazmanim, Rav Shach underwent major surgery. While he was recovering at home, Rav Heisler paid him a visit. Rav Shach was weak; he could barely lift his head. Rarely had Rav Heisler seen him without a Gemara in front of him, but this time, Rav Shach was too weak to learn. He turned down Rav Heisler's offer to bring him a sefer; he had no strength to use it.*

*This unusual situation gave Rav Heisler an idea. He thought that perhaps it was a bit audacious, so he apologized before he shared his thought. "If the reason you don't go on vacation is because you want to be able to learn without interruption," said Rav Heisler, "and right now you have no strength to learn, perhaps this would be a good time for the Rosh Yeshivah to go on vacation and get a real rest."*

*"You're mistaken," Rav Shach told Rav Heisler. "The reason I don't go on vacation isn't only because it would interrupt my learning. Ten minutes before you came, a girl was here to see me. This girl is carrying a huge peckel, a big load of troubles, and she thought I could help her. I couldn't help her, but she poured out her heart and I listened to her and gave her a berachah. That gave her a boost of chizuk and she left feeling much better.*

*"This is why I don't go on vacation. People have to know 'Rav Shach is in his house.' Any broken soul that's out there, that needs to pour out his heart, has to know I'm here to listen."*

We might wonder, why did Rav Shach feel that he had to be there for others every single day? Rav Heisler's story takes on a new dimension when we learn an insight from the *Zohar* (*Parashas Emor*) about ensuring that chessed is a daily occurrence in our lives.

We know that Hashem deals with us according to the principle of *middah k'neged middah* — measure for measure. This is the basis of the Gemara (*Shabbos* 151b), "Whoever has compassion on others receives Hashem's compassion from Heaven."

The *Zohar* sheds a brilliant new light on this concept, that we can grasp by exploring a similar idea: A person cannot fulfill his obligation to *daven* three times a day by *davening* five times on Day 1, three times on Day 2, not at all on Day 3 and four times on Day 4. It's true that he has *davened* 12 times in four days — an average of three times a day — but on Day 3, when he doesn't *daven* at all, he has neglected his obligation and forfeited all the benefits *tefillah* would bring into that day. We know this because *Chazal*, with their power of prophecy and *ruach hakodesh*, informed us that we need three *tefillos* a day.

If we want to bask in the Heavenly compassion every day and enjoy the abundance we bring upon ourselves when we do chessed, says the *Zohar*, we must do chessed every day. There are no "two-for-the-price-of-one" deals.

The *Zohar* further explains that *Shamayim* has the same concept of a "day" that we have in this world. If a person does chessed on a particular day, he creates a *malach* on that day. This *malach* is permanent. It is there to advocate for the person in the future, when he may need to account for how he spent each day of his life. On the opposite side, if one day we show cruelty, *chas v'shalom,* we create a *malach* that will represent our "accomplishments" of that day.

We now understand how Rav Shach viewed his position. He could not say, "I did chessed yesterday and the day before. I spend hours and hours doing chessed. My quota is more than filled." The day he would take himself out of Bnei Brak, the day there would be no one to answer his door when a person in need came knocking, would be a day missing chessed, and that, Rav Shach was not willing to endure.

The Chofetz Chaim in *Ahavas Chessed* writes a great deal about this idea, to counter the misconception that yesterday's chessed counts for today. When we view the situation in the light of *middah k'neged middah,* it makes perfect sense. We do not want Hashem to say, "I gave this person health and *parnassah* last week. That's enough." If we want health today, *parnassah* today, *shalom bayis* today, then doing a chessed today will bring Hashem's kindness down from Heaven and into our lives.

We continually need Hashem's chessed to do this. Only through the blessings that He gives us do we have anything to give. May we be *zocheh* to these blessings in abundance!

# The Life You Save

How do we measure an act of chessed? How much time are we supposed to devote to others? How much kindness are we supposed to offer? How do we know if a certain need is ours to fill? Chessed is difficult to define. It's not like Shabbos, with its set times and detailed laws. For this reason, we can easily make the mistake of thinking that chessed is a voluntary mitzvah, nice if you do it but no great *aveirah* if you don't.

The Chofetz Chaim tells a story in his *sefer Shem Olam* (*Perek 8*), that turns this idea on its head. We see that despite the sometimes-amorphous nature of an act of chessed, carrying it out can make all the difference in our lives.

This story is one in which the Chofetz Chaim was personally involved and which he witnessed, as he says, "with my own eyes."

> *A man came to a "certain chacham" (many believe this was the Chofetz Chaim himself) with a heart-breaking tale. His wife had borne several children over the years, and each had died as an infant. He begged the chacham to suggest some segulah he could undertake as a merit for children who would survive.*

The chacham told the man that the greatest segulah for any kind of blessing is to perform acts of chessed. Since the town in which they lived did not have a gemach to provide free loans to those in need, he suggested that this would be the best chessed to institute.

The man rolled up his sleeves and went to work. First, he laid out his plans in a notebook. There, he delineated all the rules of the gemach — the amounts to be loaned, the schedule for repayment and other important details. Also, he wrote that every three years, all those involved in the gemach would hold a siyum to acknowledge the group's efforts and promote the organization's work. He even set down the exact date of the first siyum, three years down the road.

The gemach thrived. The Chofetz Chaim reports that three years after its inception, a baby boy was born to the man, and as if to show the world the power of chessed, Hashem arranged that this baby's bris would be on the day designated three years earlier for the gemach's first seudah.

The townspeople were astounded by the clear miracle, the unmistakable connection between the man's gemach and the blessing he ultimately received. Everyone came to the bris of this special little boy.

In the years that followed, the man's family grew and so did the gemach. However, this is not the end of the story. The Chofetz Chaim reports that eventually, the man began to feel that the gemach was becoming too great a burden for him to run. He wanted to pass the directorship to someone else. The chacham urged him not to do it, but the man insisted that he had done enough. Finally, the chacham agreed to find a replacement.

The day after he decided to resign from the gemach, he came running back to the chacham in desperation. He had arrived home from his meeting with the chacham after nightfall, and that very night, one of his children choked on a piece of food and died.

"I have many healthy children still," he said. "I'm taking back the gemach."

Drawing a lesson from this story, the Chofetz Chaim explains that life is like a bridge that traverses a massive, churning ocean. Our acts of chessed are the pillars that support the bridge and keep us above the dangers that would submerge us. These dangers are the *aveiros* we all have — the prosecuting *melachim* that wait for their opportunity to bring us to justice. If the supporting pillars of a bridge were removed, those trying to cross it would not be helped by the fact that the pillars were there yesterday. Likewise, without today's chessed, there is nothing to prevent us from plunging into the water.

We may think we've done enough. It's someone else's turn. We don't have time. But when we awaken to the powerful protection our chessed affords us and our families, we don't want to spend even one day without it.

## 14

# *Worth the Effort*

O ne day, a man accompanied by a few bachurim brought a question of halachah to Rav Avraham Genachovsky. Rav Avraham, an expert in every facet of Gemara, provided the answer, explaining that it was plainly stated in the Tosafos on a Gemara.

After the man and the bachurim left, someone informed Rav Avraham that the man who had just come to ask him for an answer was the maggid shiur in a local yeshivah, and the bachurim were his students. Rav Avraham immediately regretted giving such a simple answer that quickly. Perhaps the students now thought less of their rebbi, since he felt the need to consult a gadol hador on what was ultimately a simple question.

Others might have thought, "Oh, well, the damage is done. I can't undo it." However, that was not Rav Avraham's approach. He believed there was always something a person could do to uplift a fellow Jew if he was willing to exert the effort.

*Rav Avraham was willing — not only willing, but so very wise and creative in his approach! He went to the beis medrash of the maggid shiur. As soon has he walked in, students gathered around him — what was a gadol hador doing there?*

*They soon discovered that he had come with several shailos on which he wanted the maggid shiur's opinion. He asked his questions to the maggid shiur and praised the brilliance of his answers. With that, any negative impression the earlier interaction might have left on the maggid shiur's talmidim instantly dissipated. Rav Avraham Genachovsky had come to him for advice and left the beis medrash satisfied with the maggid shiur's answer. What greater accolade could there be?*

Several aspects of Rav Avraham's strategy were remarkable. The first was that he even thought about the impression his interaction with the *maggid shiur* might have left on the *talmidim*. He felt the *maggid shiur's* humiliation, even though he did nothing more than answer a simple question and explain where the answer was stated. Even so, as soon as he understood the context of the *maggid shiur's* visit and the message the entire scenario might have delivered, he was stricken with regret.

Secondly, he didn't just feel regret. He looked for a way to rectify the situation. He felt responsible to comfort and uplift the person he believed he had unintentionally humiliated. How often do we say something insensitive and think, "Oh well, I wish I hadn't said that. Next time I'll be more careful." Rav Avraham, instead said to himself, "I broke it and I'm the one who has to fix it."

Thirdly, he willingly lowered himself to make amends. It meant nothing to him that the *maggid shiur* and his *talmidim* might think less of him because he, a *gadol hador,* couldn't find the answers on his own.

Finally, he did exactly what was necessary to undo the harm he had caused. He had lessened the *maggid shiur's* esteem in the eyes of his *talmidim* and now, he lessened his own esteem and elevated that of the *maggid shiur.*

Rav Avraham was an exemplar of the idea that we have to be willing to work for a mitzvah. We know that we cannot acquire Torah learning without work. We also know that in the material world, we cannot acquire *parnassah* without work. In contrast, we often think that chessed just comes naturally. But to excel at it, to be awarded the title of *baal chessed,* we need to put our minds, hearts and hands to the job.

# Be Enterprising

G ood-hearted people are often willing to open their wallet to answer someone's need. However, a real expert in chessed thinks about the problem and tries to find the optimal solution. We see this idea expressed by the *Rambam*, who tells us that the best kind of *tzedakah* is to find someone a job so he can support himself. Giving him money will help for a short while until he needs more, but with a job, he has a steady income and the dignity of supporting himself. Here is a true story, heard directly from someone involved, of a person who set his enterprising mind to the task of helping a friend in need:

> *Nachman\* met his former classmate Daniel\*, who he hadn't seen in several years. Nachman noticed that Daniel had a drained, tired look about him. As the two men caught up on each other's lives, Daniel disclosed that his wife was having a hard time taking care of their large family. In particular, cooking dinner every night at the end of a long day had become a difficult burden.*
>
> *Nachman suggested that if Daniel's wife didn't object, he should get take-out a few nights a week. However, Daniel admitted that*

there simply wasn't enough money for that luxury. "Baruch Hashem," he said, "a big family has its challenges."

Wanting to help out his old friend, Nachman spoke to another friend, Zev*, who had money available for tzedakah. Zev, however, pointed out that if he gave $360 or even $500, the solution would be short-lived. Right then and there, Nachman conceived of an idea.

He returned to Daniel and told him that he knew of a well-endowed Jewish foundation that was in the "business" of connecting with take-out stores and restaurants to feed struggling families like Daniel's. "They're literally looking for people to help," he said. "They are obligated to use the money for its purpose. I'm going to contact them and give them your name."

Daniel was more than willing to "help out" the organization by accepting the take-out food. The next step was to tell Zev about the "foundation," which was nothing more than the product of Nachman's creative mind. Zev assembled a group of friends who agreed to supply Nachman's family with a few take-out meals a week. Then, he contacted stores in the neighborhood and asked them to participate in the chessed by giving him a 20 percent discount. They agreed, and for the next 10 years, while Daniel's family life was at its most hectic and financially stressful, take-out food saved the day.

Daniel thanked Nachman many, many times throughout those years. That small change — his wife's relief a few nights a week that she did not have the pressure of cooking — made a world of change in his wife and in turn, his entire household. And Daniel was relieved as well, because he no longer had to watch his wife struggling while knowing that he was unable to afford the help she needed. The gloom lifted and the family thrived.

What gives a person the chochmah to come up with an idea like this? What inspires a person to not only give, but to assume the responsibility of others' troubles and carry through all the way to a solution? The answer is *ahavas chessed*. Someone who loves chessed, who lives to help others fulfill their potential and takes his biggest pleasure from alleviating others' burdens, has the motivation to make it happen. No doubt, that motivation opens the way for Hashem to inspire us with just the right idea!

# 16

# Are You Really That Busy?

Everyone has his limits. Sometimes, the opportunity for a chessed comes up and we make the judgment that we don't have enough time, energy, or money to grab the opportunity. Sometimes that's the right decision, but very often, like a ketchup bottle that seems empty, if we squeeze a little harder, we'll find that we do, in fact, have something more to give. The most brilliantly shining examples of this idea are those whose schedules seem packed from sunrise until the wee hours of the morning, and yet they have time for everyone who needs them. Rav Aharon Leib Shteinman was such a person.

Besides being the leader of the generation who handled every difficult question besetting Klal Yisrael, acting as the guiding light for every Torah institution, yeshivah and Bais Yaakov around the world, as well as every kiruv organization, serving as the Rosh Yeshivah to hundreds of *talmidim* and giving *shiurim* all day, he came home each afternoon and gave many *shiurim* there each week. Those who wanted to speak to him knew that the best opportunity was to grab him between these *shiurim*. The room would often be filled with roshei yeshivos and other respected members of Klal Yisrael, hoping to seize their moment. Against that backdrop, the following story becomes all the more awe-inspiring:

*A young man attended one of Rav Aharon Leib's shiurim in his home each week. One day, this man's father-in-law passed away. The following week after the shiur, Rav Aharon Leib went directly to this young man and asked him, "How is your mother-in-law doing? Does she have everything she needs?"*

*The young man thought the questions were kind and thought-ful, and perfectly normal just a week after his mother-in-law had become a widow. However, each week the questions continued. They were not just general, "How is she doing?" type questions but rather, specific inquiries into her health, financial state, emotional state and so forth. The young man began to wonder if perhaps Rav Aharon Leib had some connection with his in-laws.*

*When he disclosed to his mother-in-law that she was the subject of the gadol's concern and asked if there was some connection, she answered that she had never met Rav Aharon Leib. Nevertheless, the questions persisted week after week, month after month. Fi-nally, when his father-in-law had been gone for about six months, the young man asked Rav Aharon Leib if he knew his in-laws.*

*"I don't know them at all," he answered. "But do you want to know why I ask about your mother-in-law's welfare every week, even though there are many other people waiting to speak to me? I'll tell you.*

*"One reason is that a woman is accustomed to have her husband looking out for her. As long as she's married, she has someone who cares about her. Now that she doesn't have a husband anymore, I want it to get back to her that Rav Aharon Leib Shteinman is always inquiring about her well-being. Someone out there is look-ing after her. I want her to feel that.*

*"Secondly, you are a young man with a family. Your wife is a busy young mother. She could forget to call her mother. But if Rav*

*Aharon Leib keeps asking you how your mother-in-law is doing, you will have to make sure you can answer me. You'll make sure that your wife calls her mother and asks specifically how she is doing. Not only that, but her siblings will do so as well."*

With the well-being of millions of Jews resting on his shoulders, Rav Aharon Leib found time to care about the well-being of one widow whom he did not even know. He not only cared, but also made sure she would be aware of it. He did not lose his focus on her, and made sure her family did not lose focus either.

We all know someone who needs the reassurance that others think about him or her. It could be an elderly neighbor, a grandparent, aunt or uncle, or even a sibling or friend going through a hard time. Our call could be the highlight of their day. Rav Aharon Leib teaches us that if we think, "I'll call when I have the time," we may never have that extra time. But if we squeeze that "empty ketchup bottle" just a little harder, we discover that there's more inside us than we knew.

# 17

# Fill Their Tank for the Long Haul

In a million ways, we pick up a sense of what people think of us. How do they greet us? What tone of voice do they use in speaking to us? How much attention do they pay to what we have to say? Sometimes we might feel that someone doesn't like us at all; not because of anything he has done or said directly, but because of the subtle factors we've just mentioned.

We may not realize that in exactly the same way, people read our feelings about them. The day a person is tired and greets his friend with a limp smile and a nod, that friend might think, "He's not happy to see me." The day we're in a rush and give someone an impatient answer, he might feel, "I asked a foolish question." The other side of this dynamic is the incredible, long-lasting good we can do when we honor another person, as illustrated by this story heard from Rav Yaakov Meir Shechter:

> Many years ago in Tel Aviv, nearly every home experienced one or more children leaving the fold. However, Tuvia* was one exception. Every one of his children was a sincere Torah Jew. It was as if his house was untouched by the plague that beset the rest of the city.

*When a friend asked him to what he attributed his family's devotion to Torah, Tuvia knew the answer. It went back to when he was 13 years old, learning at Rav Elchonon Wasserman's yeshivah in Baranovich. One day, the yeshivah was host to a revered guest, Rav Moshe Blau, the head of Agudas Yisrael in Eretz Yisrael. He had come to Europe on important matters of concern to Klal Yisrael.*

*Rav Blau needed a bachur to escort him on his travels from one European city to another. Tuvia, who was familiar with the area and its train schedule, was chosen for the task. At one point in their travels, Rav Blau asked Tuvia to come with him into a quiet shul so they could discuss something. The Rav then laid out his dilemma to the 13-year-old boy. He had to make a decision, and whichever way he decided, one group in Klal Yisrael would be insulted. He asked Tuvia for his opinion.*

*"I was taken aback," Tuvia recalls. "What did this talmid chacham, who was sought out by the gedolim of the generation for his sage advice, need with the advice of a boy? But do you know what he said to me? He said, 'I've been spending time with you over the last few days. You're an impressive bachur. You have intelligence and insight. I trust your advice. Now please tell me what you think I should do.'"*

*Tuvia concluded, "My whole life, I've remained a religious, sincere Jew with a true Jewish home, all because Rav Moshe Blau thought I was praiseworthy. I had to live up to his impression of me. That gave me a standard to uphold."*

The Torah itself teaches us this lesson. When Yosef HaTzaddik faced his overwhelming *nisayon* with Eishes Potifar, he saw before his eyes the image of his father. He thought, "My father cherished me. He thought the world of me. How can I let him down?" This gave him the strength to conquer the *yetzer hara*. Tuvia's story has a different plot with the same theme.

All of us have the opportunity to be the Yaakov Avinu or the Rav

Moshe Blau in someone's life. Our children, relatives, friends and students all perceive, by the way we interact with them, what we think of them. If we instill in ourselves that they are all precious Jews worthy of our respect, we can give them the fuel to last a lifetime.

## 18

# He Caused a Spiritual U-Turn

Feeling valued, feeling that others consider us good, worthy Jews, gives us strength to keep going when our motivation flags. But what is powerful enough to turn someone around when he's already left the path of Torah and is heading in the opposite direction?

Rav Leib Mintzberg, the Rosh Yeshivah of Yeshivas Masmidim in Yerushalayim, had the answer to this delicate dilemma. He was a renowned *talmid chacham,* and a noted educator of our generation. He built up his students, turning them into true *bnei Torah* with the refined *middos* suited to that title. In this story, told by his nephew, Rav Mendel Porush, we learn the secret to Rav Leib's vast positive influence.

> *The scene was the shivah for Rav Leib Mintzberg. A man walked into the house and told the mourners, "I want you to know that I am only shomer Torah u'mitzvos today because of Rav Leib." He went on to relate the unforgettable conversation that changed his life.*
>
> *"I was learning in yeshivah, but I didn't get along with the*

administration. I'm not saying I was innocent, but they were always down my back, always giving me mussar. One day, I decided I had enough. I decided to quit yeshivah and leave the derech altogether. There are plenty of places to go if you want to head miles away from kedushah, so I picked one and got on a bus to set off to my new life.

"Rav Leib Mintzberg boarded the bus. I didn't know him personally, but I recognized him because he was a big name in Eretz Yisrael. He walked by me and must have seen something on my face, even though I was still dressed like a yeshivah bachur.

"'Can I take this seat next to you?' he asked me. I said sure. He sat down and made small talk with me. Then, after a while, he said, 'You know, you make a very nice impression.' He asked me where I learn and when I told him, he said, 'Really! I didn't know they put out such a good product! I see so much potential in you. You really have a promising future. You have what it takes to be someone very special — a true talmid chacham.'

"No one had ever spoken to me like this. I started rethinking my move. Maybe I was worth something after all. Instead of going where I had planned, I got off the bus and headed back to my yeshivah. I'm telling you that until that moment, I was done. Only because of Rav Leib Mintzberg did I change my direction."

The fact that this story first emerged at the *shivah* means that Rav Leib had no idea he saved this boy. He simply did what he saw needed to be done; he built up a boy whose face showed the despair he was feeling. But to do that, Rav Leib had to notice and he had to care.

Having such an outlook on other Jews is not a one-time event. It's a way of life. Rav Dovid Cynamon tells yet another story that illustrates what this means:

A well-known talmid chacham gave classes in a girls' high school. A few years later, he met one of the girls he had taught. He greeted her and then said, "You must be in shidduchim now. What kind of shidduch are you looking for?"

*The girl replied, "I'm not the same girl I was in class a few years ago. I don't even know if I'm going to cover my hair, except maybe when I go to my parents' house."*

*The talmid chacham's instant response was, "I didn't know you were so elevated! Even though you're not planning to cover your hair, because of your kibbud av v'eim you're willing to cover it in your parents' house. That's truly a high level!"*

Rav Cynamon found out the next day, from someone who knew this young lady, that she could not sleep that night because her entire view of herself had been upended by this conversation. Maybe she really was something special. Maybe she really was "the type" to cover her hair. That was the power of those few encouraging words.

# You're My Brother

*A*havas Yisrael is a mitzvah that in theory nearly every Jew wholeheartedly wishes to fulfill. However, when it is called for in practice, the passion sometimes fizzles. This is especially true when the other Jew we are being called upon to love stands staunchly on the other side of a principle that we consider inviolable. The mark of true giants in *ahavas Yisrael* is that they see past these disagreements, straight to the Jewish soul flickering inside the other person. These true stories provide us with a model of how to love a fellow Jew even when we do not love what he believes in:

> *Many years ago, a man who had settled in Eretz Yisrael after World War II suffered a heartbreaking event. His wife gave birth to a little girl who was afflicted with a life-threatening illness. The baby's doctor told the parents that one doctor, who practiced in America, had a treatment that might save their baby's life.*
>
> *Holding on to hope, the parents took their baby to America and met with this doctor. "Yes, I think I can help her," the doctor said.*

However, he also let them know that the bill would be in the tens of thousands of dollars.

The father, who had gravitated to the Mizrachi movement when he emigrated to Eretz Yisrael, knew someone from his hometown who had settled in America, He contacted his friend — a chassid — and told him about his dilemma.

"You have to go to the Satmar Rebbe," his friend told him. "He'll help you."

"The Satmar Rebbe! Are you joking?" the man exclaimed. "I'm Mizrachi. I'm a Zionist. I live on a kibbutz. The Satmar Rebbe will pick me up and throw me out of his house! I'm not setting foot in there."

Although it was well known that the Satmar Rebbe was staunchly anti-Zionist, the chassidish friend denied that any such thing would happen. "You don't know him," he told the father. "You don't know the ahavas Yisrael he has. He'll help you because you're a Jew."

It took convincing, and the chassid had to agree to accompany his Mizrachi friend to the Rebbe's house, but eventually they made the trip. The desperate father laid out his plight and the Rebbe responded instantly. Due to the many kvitlach sent to him, the Rebbe had immediate access to cash, and he instantly instructed his gabbai to bring the father the money he needed for his daughter's treatment.

The man was unwilling to accept help under false pretenses and told the Rebbe, "I just want the Rebbe to know that I belong to Mizrachi. I live on a kibbutz."

"I very, very strongly disagree with Zionism and the Mizrachi movement," the Rebbe responded. "But you… I love you. You're my brother and I love you."

There are hundreds of similar stories of the Satmar Rebbe. He stood his ground when it came to his vision of a proper Torah life, but he stood his ground equally as firmly when it came to doing chessed for a fellow Jew.

The following story of unadulterated *ahavas Yisrael* relates to another passionate personality, Rav Amram Blau, the founder of Neturei Karta. Known mostly for their strident anti-Zionism nowadays, in the early days of the State of Israel, the group was a prominent voice for maintaining *kedushah* and *shmiras Shabbos* throughout the land.

> *Rav Amram Blau burned with such love for Torah and mitzvos that when permission was granted for buses to be driven on Shabbos, he would lay himself down in front of them. He was arrested numerous times and spent time in jail. When he would lead his demonstrations, the police would converge on Meah Shearim to fend off the demonstrators. If it was a cold day, Rav Blau would bring the policemen cups of hot coffee. He would say, "I disagree with your philosophies, but I love you. You're my brothers."*

When we think about these stories, we have to realize the depth and passion with which people like the Satmar Rebbe and Rav Amram Blau held their positions. These were principles of *kavod haTorah* and *kavod* Hashem, not *kavod* themselves. In our own lives, how many of our disagreements are devoid of any trace of personal motive? It's possible to say, "none." Nevertheless, we feel that we have grounds for dislike, *machlokes,* cutting people out of our lives, even cutting off family members.

We can learn from the Satmar Rebbe and Rav Amram Blau that even if we disagree down to our bones with what someone else thinks, if they are Jews, they are our brothers. Our hearts have to be open to their plight and our hands ready to answer their needs.

# An Ounce of Prevention

What occupies our mind when we can't sleep? What pours forth in our prayers? Most often, it's the twists and turns of our own and our loved one's lives. We sincerely pray for health, *parnassah, shidduchim,* children, spiritual clarity, mental health, happiness and every other blessing needed to live a life of *menuchas hanefesh.* If any of these elements are lacking, we become preoccupied with worries for the future and prayers for Hashem's *yeshuah.* What would we not do to prevent troubles in these essential areas of life?

Rav Aharon Leib Shteinman, whose advice and blessings were sought by thousands of Jews facing dire situations, discerned a clear pattern in Hashem's dispensation of *tzaros* and *yeshuos.* Here is one among dozens of stories that illustrate the point:

> *A man came to Rav Aharon Leib for help. He had been married for many years and was still childless. He was aware of a wrong he committed as a yeshivah bachur and felt it might be the cause of his troubles. He wanted Rav Aharon Leib to advise him on how to rectify it.*

*The situation unfolded when the boy was a teenager. Another bachur in the class was the target of a great deal of taunting and bullying, and this young man had been the ringleader of the aggression. The victimized boy finally transferred to another yeshivah, but by that time, his mental state was so weakened that he suffered a nervous breakdown. He was placed in a psychiatric institution.*

*Rav Aharon Leib became increasingly disturbed as the man told his story, finally bursting into tears.*

*"He's now in an institution?" he asked when the story was finished. "And you want to know how you can get mechilah from someone who is in an institution? I don't know of a solution. If a person has his faculties, he can forgive you. Even if someone has died, there's a halachah in Shulchan Aruch that tells you to bring a minyan to his kever and ask mechilah there.*

*"But if someone is alive, and doesn't have his mental faculties, I don't know how to advise you. Go to Rav Elyashiv and see if he has any advice for you."*

*The man was stunned that he might have caused harm for which there was no remedy. He went to Rav Elyashiv hoping for some lifeline he could grasp.*

*Rav Elyashiv told him that he should go to the institution and make it his business to look after the welfare of the young man he had taunted and try to bring him back to his right state of mind, because only by bringing the patient back to a healthy mental state could a valid mechilah be obtained.*

As this young man discovered, the best way to ensure that our basket of blessing is as full as it's meant to be is to think before we act or speak. Rav Shteinman often commented that so much of the suffering people brought to his doorstep could have been prevented with this one simple step. Rather than having to scour their memories to discover who they hurt and how to obtain *mechilah*, they could have tried not to hurt anyone in the first place. "Why do they have to bring the *tzarah* upon themselves in the first place?" he would ask, pained for those who were learning this difficult lesson.

Indeed, the clear cause-and-effect between hurting others and experiencing *tzaros* seems to defy our understanding of how Hashem rewards and punishes. Under the usual system, the reckoning for mitzvos and *aveiros* is reserved for the Next World. However, the Gemara (*Kiddushin* 40a) says that mitzvos of *bein adam la'chaveiro* are an exception to this rule. The *Rishonim* explain that only mitzvos *bein adam la'chaveiro* are rewarded in this world because Hashem deals with us *middah k'neged middah*. When we benefit someone in this physical world, Hashem benefits us in the physical world. Meanwhile, the "principal" — the main reward — remains for us in full in the Next World.

The same system applies to detrimental behavior. When we harm someone in this world, we experience some of the consequences of our actions in this world. The Chofetz Chaim used to say that most of the *tzaros* people experience in this world come to them because they have hurt another person. Rav Aharon Leib strove to awaken people to this fact, for he witnessed and shared the torrents of tears of those who discovered the truth only through their own suffering.

How can we not heed the pleas of two *gedolim* renowned for the mighty *ahavas Yisrael* that surged through their hearts? But an equally important question is, how *can* we heed their plea? How can we— normal, fallible people — prevent our *yetzer hara* from leading us to say or do hurtful things? The only way is to cultivate our own *ahavas Yisrael* — loving and doing for our fellow Jew so that in a very real way, his happiness becomes ours.

# Sharpen Your Vision

The amount of chessed we do in our lifetime doesn't depend on the amount of money we have in the bank, nor on the amount of time we have on our hands. More than anything else, it depends on our vision. Do we see the people around us? Do we see what they need? Are we paying attention? Do we see what we can do to make life better for them?

Many people think of themselves as good and helpful, and they may sincerely want to live up to that image. However, they are nearsighted; they don't notice anything beyond their own small circle of family and close friends.

People who excel at chessed are those whose vision somehow notices those in need. They are the ones who find out who is sick and needs a visit, who is broke and needs a loan, who is lonely and needs a Shabbos invitation. Others may look at those same people and notice nothing, but the *baal chessed* sees with both his eyes and his heart.

Rabbi Shmuel Blech, a long-time Lakewood Rav, tells the following story of Rav Aharon Kotler that illustrates the power of such keen vision:

*In the early days of Beth Medrash Govoha, the yeshivah Rav*
*Aharon established in Lakewood, the Rosh Yeshivah lived in*
*New York and stayed in Lakewood from Thursday until Monday*
*morning. He delivered one shiur on Shabbos or Motza'ei Shabbos*
*and the other on Monday morning before returning to New York.*

*An older bachur, who was an orphan, learned at the yeshivah*
*for several years and then went to work. Although he lived in New*
*York, he preferred to be with Rav Aharon and the yeshivah for*
*Shabbos. He would stay and learn in the beis medrash on Sunday*
*and head home for a new workweek on Sunday night.*

*One day, Rav Aharon called this young man to come speak*
*with him. "I see how much it means to you to be at every shiur,"*
*said Rav Aharon, "and I know that you cannot attend the second*
*shiur on Monday morning because you have to go to work. There-*
*fore, I'm changing the schedule. I will be saying the second shiur on*
*Sunday because I want you to be able to attend."*

Rabbi Blech puts the magnitude of Rav Aharon's deed in perspective. He was someone who had a purpose and calculation for every
moment of his day. If he was delivering his *shiur* on Monday, it was
not a random decision; but the time he deemed best. Furthermore,
the entire yeshivah schedule was affected by the change. Nevertheless, when he saw this older *bachur,* this orphaned young man, he saw
that this was what he needed to do. He saw a working man who trav-
eled every Friday from New York to Lakewood just to imbibe the yeshivah atmosphere and hear Torah from his rebbi, and he understood
how difficult it must have been for him to pick up and leave the night
before the second *shiur.*

Such sensitivity to the needs of one individual is nearly miraculous
when we consider what else was being carried on Rav Aharon's shoulders. He was establishing the yeshivah that was to become the corner-
stone of Torah learning in America. He was involved in every aspect
of building Torah life in the United States and Eretz Yisrael from the
ground up. Furthermore, he himself was commuting each week from
New York to Lakewood. But none of this clouded his vision; Rav

Aharon saw a young man who needed to know he counted, and he moved worlds to answer that need.

This story teaches us how to transform ourselves from people who want to be good and giving into people who truly are good and giving — who have an uncanny knack for perceiving and fulfilling the needs of others. The first step is to sharpen our vision so that we, too, can see the needs that are often hidden in plain sight, right in front of our eyes. Then, with goodness and *ahavas Yisrael* in our hearts, we can find many ways to truly make a difference in people's lives every day.

# The Importance of Importance

"He doesn't need my compliment."

"She knows I love her cooking. I don't have to say so."

"If I'm not criticizing, he should know I'm pleased with his work."

"He's at the top of his field. He doesn't need my endorsement."

People often fool themselves into thinking that others are above and beyond needing approval. By believing this fallacy, however, they are cheating themselves out of a powerful opportunity for chessed, because approval is the fuel for the human drive to work and strive. No one is impervious to its energizing effects, as this story often told by Rav Shlomo Zalman Auerbach attests:

> The Baal HaLeshem, grandfather of Rav Elyashiv, is widely considered the greatest Litvish mekubal in the past century. He wrote a Kabbalah sefer and sent a copy to Bagdad, to the Ben Ish Chai, the most illustrious of the Sephardic mekubalim.
>
> A number of years passed, during which the Ben Ish Chai had pored through the Leshem's sefer, enthralled by its brilliance. He sent a message to several Sephardic mekubalim in Eretz Yisrael

*that they should don their Shabbos clothes, go to the Leshem and tell him, in the name of the Ben Ish Chai, how much he benefited from the sefer.*

*When the mekubalim transmitted this message, the Leshem responded, "If I would have known years ago how much enjoyment the Ben Ish Chai got from my sefer, I would have written another one by now. I didn't realize! I thought, there are so many mekubalim, what am I really adding?"*

Rav Shlomo Zalman would conclude this story with the lesson that everyone needs encouragement. Everyone needs to know that others value what he is doing — even the greatest *mekubal* of the century. That approval, the Leshem said, would have energized him to write another *sefer*. He was not beyond the power of praise, and he's not alone.

*Rav Isser Zalman Meltzer once explained his unusual method of dealing with "klutz kashas" — questions that indicate a lack of understanding of the Gemara. Instead of pointing out the obvious, he would help the talmid rethink and rephrase the question until he came to the correct understanding, and then he would praise the bachur for asking such a great question. The basis of this method was Rav Isser Zalman's own experience as a young bachur at the Volozhin Yeshivah.*

*He was a poor boy, lonely, homesick and struggling to find meals. His roommate was Rav Zelig Reuven Bengis, who became the Rosh Av Beis Din of the Eidah HaChareidis in Yerushalayim.*

*One day, Rav Isser Zalman was feeling low, wondering if he should leave the yeshivah. Rav Zelig Reuven told him that he shouldn't despair, because "the Rosh Yeshivah repeated a kasha in your name." Being so honored, said Rav Isser Zalman, "infused me with a whole new feeling for life." He stayed on and became one of Volozhin's most illustrious talmidim.*

The Leshem had already achieved greatness. Rav Isser Zalman had just started on the road to greatness. Nevertheless, each one needed to hear that what he had done was noticed and valued. How much more so do we — ordinary people with ordinary struggles — need to hear these words? The Chazon Ish used to say that every *bachur* needs a spoonful of honor every day. In our generation, the prescription might be two liters a day.

Recently, a *talmid chacham* who published a *sefer* received a phone call from a well-known *talmid chacham* in Eretz Yisrael. He had searched for the author's phone number and called to tell him how much he derived from learning the *sefer*, which he was learning with a *chavrusa*. But more importantly, he was calling to urge the author to write more. "I can tell you that your *sefer* is doing something. People in Eretz Yisrael are learning it," the *talmid chacham* said, and with that encouragement, the author was inspired to strive further.

The Gemara tells us that Rabbi Akiva's 24,000 *talmidim* perished because they did not show each other sufficient honor on the level that was expected of them. That's the opposite of the power of encouragement. It's life and death. It's oxygen. Fortunately, we all have the power to invest each other with life using just a few words: "I like what you did. I admire what you accomplished." No one is immune to the power of praise.

# 23

## Reward Here and Now

In the *Midbar,* after Bilaam attempted to curse the Jews and failed, the Moabites together with the Midianites chose a new path to defeat them. Their women lured the Jewish men into illicit relations causing the Jews to bring upon themselves the destruction Bilaam couldn't inflict. A deadly plague broke out among *Bnei Yisrael* and in the midst of this, a leader of the tribe of Shimon had the audacity to publicly bring a Midianite woman into the encampment.

One person rose to the occasion and ended this *chillul Hashem.* Pinchas killed the man and the woman and with that, the plague stopped. At this point, Hashem told Moshe Rabbeinu that as a reward for quelling Hashem's anger and thus stopping the plague, Pinchas would receive "My covenant of peace," which meant that he would be elevated to the status of Kohen.

In analyzing this episode, the Steipler (*Birkas Peretz, Parashas Pinchas*) points out that Pinchas's zealous act accomplished two things. First, the *chillul Hashem* was halted in its tracks. Secondly, Hashem brought the plague that had killed 24,000 people to an end. He points out that the *pasuk* specifically states that his reward in this world, the *bris shalom,* was granted because of the second accomplishment; he saved Klal Yisrael from the plague.

The Steipler asks why the reward was linked to this act rather than to the seemingly more exalted act of avenging Hashem's honor. To answer, he refers to the Gemara (*Kiddushin* 39b and 40a), which teaches that the reward for a mitzvah does not come to a person in this world, but rather, awaits him in *Olam Haba.* Any reward we receive in this world is merely a "dividend," as we learn from the Mishnah we recite in the Morning Blessings every day: "These are the things for which a person enjoys the dividends in this world and the principal in *Olam Haba*: Honoring parents, doing acts of kindness…" and several other mitzvos, most of them acts of chessed.

The concept this Mishnah teaches us is that our reward in *Shamayim* is like money in the bank. The bank deposit is the principal, which earns interest. The principal remains intact even when we use the interest it earns. Likewise, the rewards for the mitzvos listed in this Mishnah are "deposited" in *Olam Haba,* but Hashem may grant us the interest payments in this world. We can enjoy these benefits in our lifetime without diminishing the reward that awaits us.

This opens another question. What determines whether a person will receive the interest payments in this world? The Gemara (*Kiddushin* 40a) provides an incredible answer: We only receive interest payments (*peiros*) in this world for mitzvos *bein adam la'chaveiro.* As we discussed in Lesson 20, the *Rishonim* explain that this is based on the concept of *middah k'neged middah.* Because we benefited someone in this world, Hashem allows us to enjoy the "fruits" of our efforts in this world.

This is why, said the Steipler, Pinchas received the *bris shalom* for stopping the plague. Although he also stopped the *chillul Hashem,* that was a mitzvah done for the benefit of *Shamayim.* The reward for that awaited him in *Shamayim,* but the good deed he did by saving the lives of the *Bnei Yisrael* brought him dividends in this world, namely, the elevation to the status of Kohen.

Everyone wants to build a beautiful *Olam Haba* in the course of his years on earth, but we also want to live a good life right here and now. As the Steipler teaches us, the key to earning a generous taste of Hashem's goodness in this world is to take the opportunities that come before us to do the favor, extend the kindness, and show the caring that makes other people's lives better.

# Handle With Care

When we mail something fragile, the box bears many cautionary warnings on all sides so that no matter from which angle we view the box, we will know to handle it gently. Those who load it onto the mail truck and those who deliver it to its destination know not to shake it, toss it roughly or throw something heavy on top of it.

But what warns us when the inside of a person is fragile? He or she doesn't walk around with a stamp that says, "Handle with Care," and yet within that person might be a heart that is easily breakable.

In *Parashas Mishpatim* (22:21-23) we are given a mitzvah that serves as this "stamp." It tells us, "You shall not oppress any widow or orphan. If you oppress him [beware], for if he cries out to Me, I will surely hear his cry. My wrath will be kindled…" and then the verse pronounces a frightening curse upon those who are guilty of this oppression.

However, the Torah (*Vayikra* 25:17) warns us against *onaas devarim*, hurting someone's feelings with one's words. It instructs us, "A person shall not aggrieve his fellow Jew." Here, however, curses are not threatened for those who violate the commandment. It seems that the Torah is setting one overall standard of care for a fellow Jew's feelings, and then a separate standard for the most vulnerable among us — widows and orphans, who have no one to protect them.

However, the Chofetz Chaim, in his introduction to *Sefer Chofetz Chaim*, points out that *Rashi* (*Shemos* 22:21) says that this stricter standard is not reserved for widows and orphans. Rather, it applies to any broken, vulnerable person. "Kicking someone when he's down" is so repulsive an act in Hashem's eyes that He warns us in no uncertain terms of the horrific curses He will bring on those who do so. To protect these people and to protect ourselves, we must Handle with Care," as Rav Shlomo Zalman Auerbach illustrates in this story, told by someone who worked closely with him:

> In all the years I worked with Rav Shlomo Zalman on his various tzedakos, there was only one time when I saw him become angry, and that was at me.
>
> One morning after davening, a man came to Rav Shlomo Zalman's house in a drunken state. He was demanding that the Rav sign a letter for him, but the Rav did not want to do so. The man became agitated and started approaching the Rav as if to attack him, so I picked the man up and took him out of the house.
>
> When I came back, Rav Shlomo Zalman raised his voice and said, "How dare you take a broken neshamah and throw him out of my house!" I told the Rav that I was worried that the man was going to hurt him.
>
> "I'll take care of myself," he told me. "We don't start up with a person who's broken. There's a special prohibition about hurting a broken person!"

This same point came across clearly in a different instance involving Rav Shmuel Feivelson. In this case, there was a dispute between two parties, one of whom had a particularly difficult life. Someone who was attempting to mediate the dispute approached Rav Feivelson for advice. "What is the right thing to do?" he asked. After hearing the details of the situation, Rav Feivelson answered, "The man is *tzebrochen,* broken. It doesn't make a difference if he's right or wrong in this case. You have to give in to him. Remember this rule," he said. "You don't give pain to a *tzebrochener* person."

The final aspect of this concept is that we do not know "what's inside the box" when we look at another person. He could be fragile in ways we do not perceive. The Gemara (*Berachos* 7b) says that if a family has a child who leaves the Torah path, the pain to the parents could be greater than that of the war of Gog and Magog. We don't know what is going on in the lives of the people we meet — even those we see every day. Sometimes, we are in the dark about troubles besetting people who live under our own roof.

The Chofetz Chaim tells us that in the Torah's eyes, these troubled people are like widows and orphans. When wounded, they cry out. Their cry is heard in Heaven and their cause is taken up by Hashem Himself. The only way to avoid hurting those who are vulnerable is to avoid hurting any Jew, which is exactly what the Torah commands us to do.

# The Heart of the Matter

An idealistic group of yungeleit in Yerushalayim formed a chevrah to encourage each other's growth in ahavas Yisrael. They agreed among themselves to undertake whatever self-sacrifice was necessary to help anyone in the group who was in need.

A member of this group became seriously ill and required an operation, but he was unable to pay for it. The group set to work. Although they themselves were yungeleit living on tight budgets, they gave all they could to the cause. One even gave most of his wedding money, which was his major means of support. Ultimately, the group was able to raise enough money to pay for the operation, which saved the young man's life.

Rav Benzion Yadler, who was a famous maggid in Yerushalayim, was so impressed with this story that he approached the great gaon, Rav Yehoshua Leib Diskin, and asked if he should join the group. He told Rav Yehoshua Leib that he, too, wanted to reach this zenith of chessed, to fulfill the mitzvah of 'v'ahavta l'rei'acha kamocha."

"If you want to fulfill this mitzvah, then absolutely do not join this group," Rav Yehoshua Leib answered. Rav Yadler didn't *understand the answer; how could there be a greater demonstration of ahavas Yisrael than what this group did for their friend?*

*"Do you know how this group works?" he asked Rav Yadler. "Each member makes a pact that I'll do for you, and you'll do for me. That is not the way of ahavas Yisrael. The Gemara (Bava Basra 10b) says that this is the way other nations do chessed, but it is not how a Jew defines chessed. This is because they are really doing for themselves, for what they will get in return."*

Rav Yehoshua Leib was a *gadol* of such stature that the Beis HaLevi would make the *berachah* on seeing a *gadol baTorah* whenever he encountered him. This *gadol* recognized that when a person hopes to receive a favor in return for his chessed, the mitzvah is missing its heart.

In fact, the destruction of the second *Beis HaMikdash* proves that an act of chessed is not necessarily an act of *ahavas Yisrael*. The Gemara *(Yoma 9b)* states that Hashem allowed the destruction even though the generation was occupied with Torah, mitzvos and *gemilus chassadim*. Many people are not aware that this was a generation of chessed; it seems to contradict *Chazal's* explanation that *sinas chinam* (baseless hatred) brought about the destruction. Can people hate each other and at the same time, do chessed for each other? The answer is "yes," because the chessed they did was limited to deeds from which the doer could benefit. Whatever was not convenient, did not have a potential pay-back of honor, power or money, or was not for someone to whom they felt obligated, they would not do. Theirs was chessed without *ahavas Yisrael*.

Our acts of kindness are only alive if they have a heart of *ahavas Yisrael*. When this is what motivates our words and actions, we are eager to help people who cannot do anything for us in return, people we don't know and even people from whom we feel distant. All they need to do is be a brother — a fellow Jew. This is the key to undoing the *sinas chinam* that drove us into *galus,* and the merit that, *iy"H,* will return us to Yerushalayim and the third *Beis HaMikdash,* may it be very soon in our days.

# Kavod: We Can't Live Without It

I t was a heart-wrenching conversation. The *navi* Shmuel (*I Shmuel* 15:23-26) had just told Shaul HaMelech that he lost his kingship. Not only has he been dethroned, but Hashem Himself toppled him. He lost not only his personal status, but the entire line that would descend from him. Shaul lost everything. Worst of all, he knew that he disobeyed Hashem's commandment and warranted his fate.

In this light, his immediate response seems puzzling. He had never before sinned, and the weight of it was crushing. He begged Shmuel to accompany him to bow down before Hashem. Shaul dreaded the prospect of walking before the elders of the nation all alone. Please, he urged Shmuel, give me the honor of walking with me.

We have to wonder: What was Shaul thinking? How could this minute gesture of walking with him to preserve a shred of his honor have any meaning to him amid this massive personal and spiritual disaster?

Not only did it have meaning to him, but it was his burning desire and top priority. Why?

Rav Chaim Shmulevitz would pose this question and answer it with fiery passion. Pounding on his *shtender*, he would exclaim: "When Shaul HaMelech lost his honor, he lost everything. A person who has lost his self-respect has nothing left. He cannot survive."

Shaul understood that Hashem had not taken his life; he was still alive and therefore, still obligated to serve Hashem. There was more for him to do, but he could not do it when he felt as if he were nothing. Therefore, he told Shmuel, "For me to go on existing, I need you to show me a little *kavod*." He did not speak from the haughtiness of a king who needs people to escort him as a show of his power. Rather, he spoke as if he were a starving person asking for a bite of food to eat. Finally, Shmuel consented.

The Gemara (*Taanis* 23a) says, "*Amar Rava ha'inu d'amarei inshi oh chavrusa oh misusa* — Either a friend or death." *Rashi* expounds that Rava is saying that if he cannot have a friend who treats him with respect, he would rather not live. We learn from this that when we feel there is no one who respects us, we lose our desire to carry on.

The mirror image of this statement is that when we show a person respect and honor, we give him a powerful dose of vitality. We bolster his belief in himself and his value in the world. There are many opportunities to do this chessed every day. Simply offering a proper thank you, recognizing the good someone has done for us and telling that person how it was helpful, can help them feel, "I matter."

There is one day when this mitzvah is most available to us, and that is on Purim. The sole intent of *mishloach manos* is to build warmth and friendship among Jews. While we can accomplish this by giving *mishloach manos* to friends and family with whom we already have a warm connection, we can accomplish so much more by reaching out to someone who feels sidelined. A person sitting home alone while all of Klal Yisrael is going from house to house or greeting guests at their door is someone who feels as if the world is passing him by. The sound of a knock at the door and the sight of a friendly face can revive his heart. He doesn't just get a basket of food. He gets a message that says, "You do have friends. People do think of you."

This is the main point of *mishloach manos,* and it's unbelievable that Hashem has provided us with such an easy, pleasant way to do so great a chessed. We might feel, "I wish I could be one of those people who make others feel good," but perhaps we don't find the right opportunities, or we feel awkward reaching out to someone with whom we are not close. Purim is the ideal time to break through that boundary and give someone a lift — maybe even a new lease on life.

A person who took just such an initiative tells this true story about the surprising impact of his gesture:

> One Purim, Boruch* decided to bring mishloach manos to a family who had moved into the neighborhood several weeks earlier. The family didn't know anyone on the block and had not yet made any connections. Everyone was busy with their own lives, and maybe even assumed that others had already knocked on the door to welcome the newcomers.
>
> Boruch decided that Purim would be an appropriate time to introduce himself, with a mishloach manos in hand. He knocked on the neighbor's door and was greeted with an expression of pleasant surprise.
>
> "I want you to know," said the new neighbor, "that you aren't just doing the mitzvah of mishloach manos. You're also doing the mitzvah of being kind to a ger (stranger), because that's what I feel like — a stranger in a strange land. You're making me feel that I'm part of the neighborhood."

We can learn from Boruch, and we can teach our children to be the "Boruch" to the people in their lives, as we learn first-hand from this wise father:

> The father realized that his daughter was blessed with a charismatic personality. She was popular, confident and surrounded by friends. On Purim, she was busy all day giving and receiving mishloach manos. One year, her father told her, "You know, normally, I'm not available to drive you around on Purim night. But if you think of one girl who doesn't have friends, who's not going to be getting

*mishloach manos, I will drive you to her house. It's not the right time for mishloach manos, but it's still a good time for chessed."*

*The girl was thrilled. The prospect of her father driving her around town at night motivated her to draw up a list of recipients. Because of her father's significant insight into his daughter's chinuch, she learned how happy she could make a classmate.*

On Purim or any day of the year, we should look around at the people in our neighborhood, shul, office, *beis medrash*, classroom — wherever we may be — and ask ourselves, "Is there someone here who needs a little recognition, a little *kavod?*" It doesn't take much to provide that person with what he needs. It doesn't take much to show someone, "I notice you. You matter to me." When the Gemara says, "either a friend or death," it teaches us that a show of friendship is comparable to *techiyas hameisim.* Giving honor costs nothing, but the rewards are great; *middah k'neged middah,* Hashem will return our lovingkindness and ensure that we will never be without the love and respect of caring friends.

# Chessed in Business:
# The Real Bottom Line

Business is business. But sometimes, it takes astute Torah wisdom to know what that means, as illustrated by this true story, heard first-hand from the people involved:

*Gedalia's small business was coasting along the road to success. He had 10 employees, sales were growing and all his hard work seemed to be paying off. However, the company was still fairly new. It didn't yet have the capability to weather much adversity.*

*That's why Levi, an employee who had been there right from the beginning, felt obligated to discuss with Gedalia a problem that was threatening to become a serious drain on the business. The problem's name was Sol, a well-meaning young man who had recently joined the company.*

*"You can see that he's just not working out, can't you?" Levi asked the boss.*

*"I know, I know. I was just hoping maybe he'd pick up steam," Gedalia answered. "But I really have given him plenty of time and*

*plenty of feedback and it seems that this just isn't the best job for him. I'm going to let him go."*

*Two days later, Levi noticed that Sol was still occupying his usual place, wearing his usual pleasant expression and acting as if nothing was happening. Levi soon found out why.*

*"I want to tell you something," Gedalia told Levi a while later. "I changed my mind about Sol. I'm not firing him."*

*Levi knew Gedalia wasn't afraid to fire someone if necessary. He had once fired the daughter-in-law of someone whose prestigious name was known everywhere. Despite the storm of protest he stirred up, he stuck with his decision because he felt it was best for the company. Why, then, had he changed his mind about Sol?*

*"Before I fire someone," explained Gedalia, "I look into his situation. He's going to lose his job and I need to know what the impact of that will be. I found out that there could be some serious personal repercussions from him losing this job, and I couldn't allow myself to be responsible for that."*

At last report, Sol is still working for Gedalia. The business is still doing well, but the general assumption is that the business could be doing better if someone more focused on the bottom line were in Sol's position. In a company where every dollar and every employee counts, Gedalia's decision to retain Sol is real *mesiras nefesh*.

It is also a brilliant illustration of a point Rav Shmuel Auerbach once made about the Torah way of life. He mentioned a non-Jewish philosopher who had been considered a person of great wisdom. However, the philosopher was also known to indulge in the lowliest behaviors. When questioned about the schism between his lofty thoughts and base actions, the philosopher saw no problem. "When I do those lowly things," he explained, "I am not that wise man. I am two people. Sometimes I act like an animal and sometimes like a wise man."

We know this approach very well. People can be extremely cultured and superbly educated, yet engage in the cruelest brutality.

They can write books filled with idealism and then ruin the lives of those around them. Their beautiful thoughts do not become part of their character.

Torah wisdom is different. It reaches into the fiber of a person and influences him in every way. A person cannot be an *eved Hashem* when he *davens* in the morning and learns at his night *seder,* and then steps on other people as he engages in business during the rest of the day. The *davening* and Torah, if they are real, make him a sincere *eved Hashem* who approaches his business with the same ethics he applies to the "religious" parts of his life.

A Jew cannot say "I'm done *davening* for now. It's time to do business. It's time to make my dollar." Someone who sees a divide between his business life and his spiritual life is like the non-Jewish philosopher who discards his philosophy when it suits him to do so. Our learning and *davening* are meant to penetrate our business life. Like Gedalia in our story, we have to say, "Before I take action, I want to make sure I won't be doing another Jew undue harm."

Especially in the area of *parnassah,* the Torah not only teaches us how to avoid harming others, but also, how to earn fabulous merit for helping others. The *Rambam,* in describing the 10 levels of *tzedakah,* identifies the highest level as enabling someone to honorably earn a living. By this measure, Gedalia earned a glowing, incomparable reward for letting Sol keep the job that maintained the stability in his life. In the middle of the day, outside shul, outside the *beis medrash,* right there in his office, Gedalia was a true *eved* Hashem. May we all be *zocheh* to follow his example.

# 28

## The Chessed of Not Doing

An idealistic man wants to use his money to help Klal Yisrael, and opens a gemach. He offers loans up to $5,000 to help people who have been hit by an unexpected expense or perhaps need some help climbing out of debt.

There is only one drawback to his gemach; many people who come to seek his help walk away feeling hurt and insulted. The man seems to look down upon them. He asks intrusive questions and belittles them by implying that if they were just a little smarter or a little more energetic, they wouldn't be in the position of needing a loan.

What is the balance between the good this man does and the harm he causes? Are his loans still considered a chessed if he wounds the recipient's feelings as he dispenses the money? The Chazon Ish helps us weigh this question.

Someone once asked the Chazon Ish the kind of all-encompassing question that only a *gadol* of his caliber could answer: "What should be the ultimate goal that I aspire to achieve in my lifetime?" The Chazon Ish's answer was simple: "A person's ultimate goal should be that he lives out his 70 years in this world without hurting the feelings of another Jew."

He explains that the mitzvah of *v'ahavta l'rei'acha kamocha* is comprised of two parts. The first is to do for others that which you would wish them to do for you. This is called chessed. But there is another component, and that is to refrain from doing to another Jew anything you do not want done to you. This too is chessed.

But the surprising fact is that this second part is the most important part. The Chazon Ish refers to the oft-quoted Gemara (*Shabbos* 31a) that recounts the conversation between Hillel and a man who came to him wishing to become Jewish. The man said he would convert on the condition that Hillel could teach him the entire Torah on one foot. Hillel fulfilled the man's condition by telling him, "Do not do to anyone that which you would not want done to you."

The Chazon Ish addresses the *Maharsha's* question on this exchange. Why did Hillel only tell the man one part of the mitzvah? Why didn't he tell him about the positive requirement to help other people? The Chazon Ish answers that the Gemara is teaching us that the primary aspect of the mitzvah is to refrain from hurting others. This is more important than doing acts of kindness.

The greatest chessed is to control ourselves and avoid saying something that will make another person feel devalued, humiliated, uncomfortable or worried. Chessed is noticing someone's new purchase without mentioning that you know where he could have gotten a better deal. Chessed is allowing someone to share their opinion with you on some matter without disparaging or mocking them. Chessed is refraining from a critique of the overcooked dinner. This restraint is Hashem's top priority in our *ahavas Yisrael,* so much so that, as Hillel states, it is the foundation of the entire Torah.

On the other side of the equation is our man with the *gemach.* He may consider himself a great *baal chessed,* but he is in fact missing the most important part of the mitzvah. In fact, according to the Chazon Ish's interpretation of the Gemara, he's missing the entire foundation of the Torah the way Hillel described it.

As the Chazon Ish tells us, hurting others while we help them completely misses the mark. True chessed is a desire to uplift our fellow Jew; when that is the motivation driving our deeds, we can be sure that our chessed will be complete.

# Order of Priorities

Abaal teshuvah relates: At his first Pesach seder as a newly minted Orthodox Jew, he was served a bowl of chicken soup. Following the custom of his own family, he proceeded to crumble a piece of matzah into the soup. Before his spoon hit the broth, one of the daughters of his host swooped the bowl out from under him, disappeared into the kitchen and came back with a fresh bowl of soup.

Once again, he crumbled some matzah into the bowl and once again, the alert young lady removed it and replaced it with yet a third bowl. By now, the guest was becoming uncomfortable. Everyone was looking at him. What was going on? Why was his soup the subject of such concern?

Before he had the chance to crumble another piece of matzah into his soup, his host cleared his throat and said, "Seth, did you ever hear of gebrochts?" The host then explained the custom. For the rest of the evening, Seth fought to ignore the feeling that he had made a fool of himself.

As we learned from the Chazon Ish, the foundation of the Torah is "That which you do not want done to you, do not do to others." Not hurting other people is the most important chessed we can do, standing above any positive act we might perform to help someone. However, this idea seems to send us into a head-on collision with the mitzvah to rebuke people who are committing a sin or disregarding a positive mitzvah. Hashem wants us to rise to the occasion and set our fellow Jews on the right path rather than allowing them to lose out on the merit they could earn or, *chas v'shalom*, making themselves liable for punishment.

The dilemma that arises is that very few people welcome rebuke. It almost always arouses detrimental emotions, embarrassing the recipient and making him feel ignorant or misunderstood. Only a person with great insight into human nature can give rebuke in just the right way. In fact, the same *pasuk* that the Torah commands us to rebuke adds, "so that you will not bear a sin because of him [the person you are rebuking]." This is a warning to us that we must be very sure that the person warrants the rebuke and calculate the right time, the right words and the right place to speak, because otherwise, we bring guilt upon ourselves for embarrassing him as *Rashi* states regarding that very *pasuk*.

The previous Skverer Rebbe taught one other very important factor to consider when deciding whether to point out a flaw or error to a fellow Jew:

> The Rebbe was known to be extremely protective of the Skverer minhagim. He did not tolerate any changes in the dress, davening or other customs of his chassidim. Among those customs was to omit the pizmon "Kah Keli" in davening. While most shuls sing this melody before Mussaf on Yamim Tovim, in Skver it was not sung.
>
> One Yom Tov, a guest came to the Skver community and was invited to daven Mussaf for the shul. Unaware of the minhag to omit "Kah Keli," the guest baal tefillah began singing it. The chassidim sitting near him were about to jump up and stop him, but

*they noticed that the Rebbe was not budging. Following the Rebbe's lead, they kept their peace while the man sang the pizmon.*

*When the davening was over, they approached the Rebbe and asked him why, when he so strongly defended the Skver customs among his chassidim, he let this breach go unaddressed.*

*"It's also a minhag in Skver not to embarrass another Jew," he said.*

The Rebbe's answer brought the situation into perspective. Often people feel that in the name of *tochachah,* they can abandon their concerns about another Jew's feelings; whether the recipient likes it or not, they need to tell him the truth so that he can improve himself. However, the mitzvah of *tochachah* is not an unlimited license to rebuke others for their wrongdoing; it does not override Hillel's statement that the foundation of the Torah is to avoid hurting others. He does not say that the Torah rests on whether we refrain from eating *gebrochts,* whether we say *Kah Keli,* whether we recite *Krias Shema* at 50 minutes or 72 minutes after *shekiah.*

The Skverer Rebbe loved and protected every *minhag* of his *chassidus.* However, when he had to choose between violating a *minhag* and violating the foundation of the Torah, he knew where the priority lay. As treasured and important as our *minhagim* are, the Torah is built on our compassion for our fellow Jew. Therefore, that comes first. May we always have the wisdom to keep our priorities straight!

# The Well-Chosen Gift

**D**ovid thought his elderly father would benefit from being more active. Dovid's father, on the other hand, knew that anything more than a casual stroll around the block was too much for his arthritic knees and weak heart. When Dovid gave his father a year's membership to the local gym as a birthday present, his father had to wonder, "What is he thinking?" Dovid, of course, was thinking, "This is just what my father needs."

When we look at this scenario, we see clearly that Dovid made one big mistake in his effort to do a kindness for his father: He didn't step into his father's shoes and try to understand what would be helpful.

*Chana thought her husband would benefit from expanding his taste in food and trying things a bit more exotic than chicken and potatoes. He insisted that exotic spices and unfamiliar dishes gave him indigestion. "Once he tries it, he'll see how good it is," Chana thought as she prepared her husband a lamb dish favored by the Jews of Libya. When he walked into the house that evening, the aroma of the cooking food turned his stomach.*

Here, we see another way in which a chessed can go wrong. Instead of uplifting the recipient, it makes him sick. From both these scenarios, we see that a chessed, however well-meaning it may be, only does good if we tailor it to the other person's needs. If we force something upon him that he doesn't want, it is not helpful. In fact, it often harms.

This is especially true with words meant to comfort a person in a difficult situation. When someone is suffering, other people's words can sting like a friendly slap on a sunburned shoulder. The person offering the friendly slap means to show affection, but instead, his action causes pain. Words that are meant to be sympathetic, but hit a sore spot, can be exactly this kind of slap. The following story, witnessed first-hand, illustrates the point:

> An older single bachur became engaged. The vort was an especially joyous occasion as it was clearly the answer to many years of prayers by many people. This young man had a few friends who were still unmarried, and one of them — a neighbor — came to join in the simchah despite the strong, mixed emotions he knew it would arouse.
>
> Another neighbor, a married man with a family, saw the friend and struck up a conversation that touched on a few neutral topics of interest.
>
> "Well, great to see you," the man told the chassan's friend as they parted ways.
>
> "Wait," said the friend. "I want to tell you something. You're the first person tonight who shmoozed with me and didn't stab me in the back with an 'im yirtzeh Hashem by you.' I just want to come and participate in my friend's simchah, but nobody can let me. They have to keep stabbing me with 'im yirtzeh Hashem by you.'"

Everyone has unfulfilled goals and challenges in their lives, but some issues, like difficulty finding a shidduch or having a child, are public knowledge. People dealing with these challenges may be rising to the occasion beautifully or they may be struggling, but when they feel that everyone who sees them only sees "the older single" or "the childless couple," that can evince a pain they cannot bear. Therefore, they end up denying themselves the pleasure of sharing their friends' and relatives' *simchos,* just to avoid the constant "stabbing."

If we know of someone's challenge and want to invoke Hashem's help, the best way is to *daven* for him in private. Giving him a blessing as he comes to say hello at a wedding or eats his bagel at a *bris* may be giving him a gift he does not want, one that hurts rather than helps. Step One in chessed is to step think, "Is this what I would want?" With that one short moment of forethought, our encouraging words and small acts of kindness can do so much good.

# Brief Letters, Long-Held Treasures

W hen Raizel* passed away at a ripe old age, her eldest daughter, Tzippora*, began the task of sorting through her mother's belongings. She found an unlocked steel box that contained important papers. Among the papers was just one letter. It was the grateful letter of gratitude Tzippora had written to her parents 30 years earlier when they gave her and her husband a down-payment for a house. She wrote that she knew their gift represented decades of hard work, and that she hoped they would have a long lifetime of nachas from Tzippora's family.

"I can't believe they kept this letter all these years!" Tzippora thought. She remembered being unsure of whether to write it, thinking it was perhaps a bit too much for her reserved, down-to-earth parents. Only now did she realize how much her two brief, loving and appreciative paragraphs meant to them.

Sometimes we think about giving someone a call or dropping them a note, but we wonder if it really matters. As Tzippora in the above story learned, it might matter far more than we can imagine. And once we discover how much these small gestures matter, we regret the opportunities we've missed; we feel like investors who decided against buying a certain stock at a dollar a share, only to find out that it's now worth $100 a share.

A famous story about Rav Pam illustrates that even this *gadol*, renowned for his chessed, was surprised at the impact of a few kind words. The episode occurred when someone who *davened* at his *minyan* at Yeshivah Torah Vodaath was admitted to the hospital. Rav Pam wanted to visit but could not enter the hospital because he was a Kohen. Instead of a personal visit, he wrote the man a quick note and put it in the mail.

When this man passed away, Rav Pam went to be *menachem avel*. At the *shivah*, the man's children took out the note and showed it to Rav Pam. He wondered why they had this note in their possession. "Our father kept it under his pillow," they told him. "He would show it to everyone who came to visit him. He'd say, 'Look! I got a letter from Rav Pam!'"

Rav Pam used to tell this story, saying that from it, he learned on a whole new level that small gestures, the things we do almost without thinking, can give another person exceptional comfort and encouragement. He had no idea when he jotted down his good wishes and blessings that the letter would be so treasured by this man.

Sometimes, a quick shot of encouragement bears incredible fruit, as shown in the following story.

> There was a talmid chacham who was about to marry off a daughter. The invitations had gone out, and one day, the chassan came to his father-in-law to share one specific return card with him. It was from a relative of the chassan who didn't know the talmid chacham. The chassan's relative wrote that he was learning a sefer this man had written and found it to be the best on its topic. He wanted to express his excitement that the chassan was marrying the daughter of such a person.
>
> Knowing that his sefer was being learned in a kollel in another

*city gave the man a boost of energy and confidence to write more. Therefore, the writer's merit extends not only to the kindness he did in uplifting the talmid chacham, but in the future sefarim he will write and the Torah learning those sefarim will engender.*

In the same way, small gestures bear fruit. A boss tells his employee, "That was a great idea." The employee feels valued and accomplished. He comes home in an expansive mood and puts more positive energy into helping his son review his *Chumash*. The boy goes into yeshivah the next day with more confidence and does well on his test. All the good that blossomed from the boss's five words of praise are a merit for him.

A little recognition means so much to people. Not only do they treasure these words, notes and gestures, but the benefits ripple out into the world, touching people we don't even know in ways we may never imagine.

# For Them, Not for You

After the passing of Rabbi Dr. Yaakov Greenwald, his son Itcha Meyer spoke about his father's legendary chessed and what he learned from him:

*Living in Monsey in the years before Tomchei Shabbos became active there, Itcha Meyer worked with an informal group that delivered food boxes to needy families. He was a teen at the time, and he helped by making the deliveries. One evening, he came to the home of a widow, and she refused the box. He then brought the box to the garage and placed it inside. He was pleased that he had found a way to give the woman the food, even though her pride would not allow her to receive it at the front door.*

*When he got home, he told his father what had happened. Rather than being proud of his son's persistence, he was pained. "Chessed isn't what you want to do for the other person," he said. "It's what the other person wants you to do for him." The widow didn't want to accept the food box because doing so offended her pride. Therefore, in her case, the true act of chessed would have been to refrain from giving it, because that's what she wanted.*

The *pasuk* (*Tehillim* 41:1) states, "Fortunate is the one who considers the poor." The word used for "considers" is *maskil,* from the word *seichel,* intelligence, which teaches that it's not enough to keep the poor in mind. Rather, we have to use our *sechel* in caring for their needs. Just as a person learning Gemara has to engage his mind and get to the core of the issue, someone doing chessed or giving *tzedakah* also has to apply his mind to the matter. He may discover that he must find a more subtle way to give the person what he needs, or he may discover that there is no way to give without embarrassing the person. In that case, he has to realize that the mitzvah is to hold back.

Rabbi Dr. Greenwald's care for the widows in his community was a perfect illustration of *"maskil el dal"* — wisely considering the poor. Each Purim, accompanied by his son, he would bring *mishloach manos* to a long list of widows. Included in each *mishloach manos* was a personal note. His son sometimes wondered why his father wrote these notes. Many years later, Itcha Meyer learned that enclosed in each note was a generous gift of cash. Rabbi Greenwald knew that Purim was a day of giving and receiving; there could be no shame in receiving a food basket on that day, and the *tzedakah* that was tucked into the notes quietly, but effectively, helped these struggling women.

The need to deal insightfully with those we help can seem like an obstacle that deters us from doing chessed. We might worry that we'll do the wrong thing, and inadvertently hurt someone we are trying to help. It is indeed a balance that requires a certain amount of intuition, because sometimes people make a show of refusing help when underneath their protest, they hope we will persist.

But we're not required to be mind-readers. We only have to do the mitzvah of *v'ahavta l'rei'acha kamocha,* as Rabbi Greenwald described it: Don't do what you would like for the other person, but rather, do what the other person wants you to do. With these words as our guide, we can put our minds in gear, find the way to help our friends, relatives and neighbors in need, and leave them feeling good about it.

# More Than Words

Rav Kehas Borek was the mashgiach of Beis Yosef-Novardok, in Boro Park. He lived in a two-family house on the ground floor. Above him lived his younger brother-in-law, Rav Moshe Lipschitz. The two rebbetzins were sisters.

Despite the fact that Rav Borek, who learned in Bialystock, was imbued with pure Novardok ideals, and Rav Lipschitz was a Gerrer chassid through and through, the two couples lived in complete harmony. In fact, every Shabbos, Rabbi and Rebbetzin Lipschitz, who were childless, would join the Boreks for their seudos. The two men would engage in deep discussions and relate stories from their own traditions, listening to each other's words with interest and respect. Rav Borek sat at one end of the table and Rav Lipschitz at the other, creating two "heads" of the table. The Borek children and grandchildren who visited the home knew they were witnessing a rare life lesson in how to value another Jew, despite differences in his path of avodas Hashem.

One time, Rav Lipschitz was visiting Rav Borek on a Motza'ei

*Shabbos. The tablecloth had been removed and the dining room table was uncovered. Rav Lipschitz had poured himself a hot drink in a teacup, and he put it down on the table. Seeing this, Rav Borek responded a bit sharply, telling his brother-in-law that what he had done showed a lack of derech eretz.*

*Nothing more was said about the matter, but a short while later, Rav Lipschitz returned to his apartment upstairs. Twenty minutes later, the elderly Rav Borek slowly made his way up the staircase — an effort he very rarely undertook.*

*Normally, his Motza'ei Shabbos was spent immersed in uninterrupted learning. In fact, he always took great care not to lose any time from learning. However, on this Motza'ei Shabbos, he went to visit his brother-in-law in his home. Rav Lipschitz was known for his vast repertoire of stories about chassidus and the various Rebbes, especially those of Ger and Kotzk, and Rav Borek wanted to hear all about it. He asked questions about various personalities and events, listening intently and responding with sincere interest. For well over an hour, he shined the spotlight on his brother-in-law and gave him the stage.*

Often, when we say thoughtless words that hurt another person, we feel a pang of remorse even before we're finished speaking. Sometimes we jump to correct the error right then and there. More often, we rationalize: "She didn't seem hurt." "He knows I didn't mean anything by it." "That's just my sense of humor." "What I said wasn't really insulting." "He's forgotten all about it by now. Why should I bring it up?"

After all this, we might come to the conclusion that indeed, an apology is in order; better to clear the air than risk having another person carry around a grudge against us. At that point, we bring up the matter. "I hope I didn't insult you when I said…. And if I did, please be *mochel* me."

How does the other person respond? Unless the harm done was truly egregious, he'll say, "Of course I'm *mochel*. Don't even think about it." Sometimes, he will claim that he didn't even feel the sting of the words: "I wasn't insulted. There's nothing to apologize for." Nobody likes to show their vulnerability. Nobody wants to appear pathetic.

At this point, the wrongdoer feels he's taken care of business. He's admitted his wrong, apologized and received *mechilah*. But that *mechilah* does not come with the necessary component of appeasement. Asking for forgiveness requires an effort to appease the person we've harmed. We can understand this easily in financial matters. If we break our neighbor's power-drill, we realize that "I'm sorry" will not be enough. We need to replace the drill or give him its equivalent in money.

But what happens when we break someone's spirit? What happens when we make him feel diminished in importance? Rabbi Borek realized that this is what his sharp words had done to his dear friend and brother-in-law, and he had to appease him. The only way to do that was to show him how much he valued him — to fix what he had broken.

Therefore, this elderly man climbed the long staircase, which said, "Seeking you out is worth my effort." He opened a conversation that would focus on Rav Lipschitz's special area of expertise, which said, "Your knowledge is valuable. I want to learn from you." He spent one and a half hours of focused time engaging in this conversation, which said, "Nothing I have to do this evening is more important than spending time with you." To Rav Borek, who would not give up a moment of learning unless absolutely necessary, repairing the hurt he had inflicted was absolutely necessary.

As we've learned in other lessons, not hurting another Jew is the foundation of *ahavas Yisrael*. We see from this story that if we stumble in this, there's so much more we can do than mumble, "I'm sorry." We can find a way to fully restore the other person's spirit, showing him, "You're important to me!"

# There's Something You Can Do

Rav Mordechai Hager, the Vizhnitzer Rebbe of Monsey, called a trusted chassid to his home one Motza'ei Shabbos. When the chassid arrived, he found his Rebbe sitting at a table in front of a large pile of $20 bills, amounting to hundreds of dollars in cash.

"Do you see this pile of money?" the Rebbe asked. "I want you to call 10 people you really trust and tell them this: There is a new shul that opened here in Monsey, and it's having a hard time getting off the ground. Tonight, the Rav is making a Melaveh Malkah.

"Tell these 10 men to each take some of this money and go participate in the Melaveh Malkah. They should give it to the Rav for his new kehillah. They should stay for a while — 45 minutes to an hour — to encourage the new rabbanus. With their presence and with the money, they should strengthen him."

Often, beginnings are difficult. Everything needs extra care and support at its beginning stage. A plant that's just beginning to grow needs extra watering and fertilizing. A baby needs to be fed, carried from place to place, dressed properly for the weather and rocked to sleep. New things have not yet built strength and resilience, and so, any challenge can knock them down.

The Rebbe realized that this new *kehillah,* which had not yet firmly rooted itself in the community, needed an influx of support — both financial and personal — to make it through this first stage. It needed to be nursed along until it could stand on its own, and then it would become an asset to Klal Yisrael, the merit of which would belong in part to those who helped it get on its feet.

We can learn from this how to recognize many opportunities for chessed. Life is filled with new beginnings, even in the later years. With a small fraction of the Rebbe's wisdom and foresight, we can find ways to fortify people going through new beginnings such as those listed below.

Newlyweds: Once they're set up in their new home with their shiny new dishes, appliances and furniture, we might think they have all they need. But how is the new wife adapting to balancing her job with housework? Could she use a few meals prepared for her? Could she use a little cleaning help? We might think, "It's just the two of them. How hard can it be?" but the feeling of others caring and being there for her can make the transition easier.

Opening a new business: He's done his research, made his plans and now he's opened his doors. Can we send him customers? Can we use his services? Can we connect him with helpful resources?

Entering a new profession: When people start out in a field, their lack of experience and connections can be a high hurdle to surmount. Do we have expertise to offer? Can we connect the person with someone who could serve as an adviser?

New in the neighborhood: Busy families may barely notice when someone moves into the neighborhood, but those newcomers are hoping for that knock on the door. Can we advise them about shuls, shopping, traffic patterns, playgrounds? Can we just visit to say welcome?

By being on the lookout for the "tender shoots" that are just breaking through into the sunlight, we can find many ways to provide a little extra strength and support. May we have the merit to help all these worthy beginnings flourish to full bloom.

# Don't Go Public

"If you see something, say something." This motto of our time is also a mitzvah in the Torah (*Vayikra* 19:17). When we see someone doing something wrong, *"Hochei'ach tochiach es amisecha* — You shall surely rebuke your neighbor." But sometimes, in our zeal to "say something," we forget the end of the same *pasuk,* which warns us not to embarrass a person when we rebuke him.

This story, witnessed first-hand, illustrates the point:

> One morning, at a busy Lakewood shul with multiple minyanim throughout the day, a man from out of town stepped forward to serve as the baal Shacharis. He was apparently in the year of mourning for a parent, and thus was obligated to lead the davening.
>
> When the man finished Shemoneh Esrei, instead of saying Tachanun, he immediately began reciting Kaddish. While there are times when Tachanun is not said, there did not seem to be any such occasion that morning. People assumed that perhaps there was a chassan present, in which case Tachanun would be skipped.

*When the davening was over, a sincere, learned member of the minyan went to the baal tefillah and asked why he hadn't said Tachanun. A cluster of men were in the vicinity of the conversation, and they all heard the baal tefillah's weak answer: "It was late, so I figured we could just skip it."*

*The man who had asked the question rebuked the baal tefillah, not in anger, but simply in an effort to make him aware that he hadn't acted properly. "When you come into a shul, you have to follow its minhagim (customs)," he said. "Here we say Tachanun. We don't just skip it. You have to ask before you do something like that."*

*The man then walked out of the shul. The baal tefillah then said to the men around him, who were wrapping their tefillin and preparing to leave the shul. "There was no reason for him to have embarrassed me in public. He could have told me privately."*

*An onlooker, realizing that the man had inadvertently stepped on a landmine by embarrassing a fellow Jew in public, went out to find him. He found him in another beis medrash in the building and told him, "The person you just spoke to said you embarrassed him in public."*

*"Oy! Really? I didn't mean to do that!" the man exclaimed.*

*He went back into the shul and in front of everyone who was there, asked the baal tefillah for mechilah. "I said it in public and it wasn't right," he confessed.*

*The baal tefillah, who moments ago was smarting from the comment, broke into a wide smile. "Don't worry," he assured the man. "It's fine. I'm mochel."*

The way this man shuddered at realizing he had embarrassed the *baal tefillah* and rushed to undo the harm is evidence of the gravity of the situation. *Chazal* warn us that someone who embarrasses his friend in public, "has no portion in *Olam Haba*."

We need to keep in mind that "public" doesn't mean that the words are spoken from a microphone in the presence of an audience. According to the *Pri Megadim* (in his *Matan Secharan Shel Mitzvos* §5), it means speaking in front of three people, one of whom is the speaker. Reuven, Levi, Shimon and Yehudah are standing together when Shimon says something that embarrasses Yehudah. That's "public."

As we've mentioned, the second part of the mitzvah of *tochachah* alludes to the horrendous troubles we cause ourselves when our words shame the other person. It says, *"velo sisa alav cheit* — and you should not bring sin upon yourself." This is no contradiction to the need to rebuke because rebuke is almost always more effective when it's given in private. The person feels the sincerity in words spoken with care for his dignity.

In cases where something must be said in public, for instance, to uphold the honor of the Torah or of a *talmid chacham,* Rav Chaim Brisker would say that a person should not speak up unless he is 100 percent sure that he understands the *halachah* and whether it applies to his situation. When in doubt, *daas Torah* is essential. In our effort to right wrongs and awaken others to their mistakes, we have to tread carefully, doing our best to protect the honor of a fellow Jew.

# Don't Stop Now!

O n Sunday, Shimon drove for an hour to visit his grandmother in a nursing home. He stayed with her for an hour and then drove home, taking up his entire afternoon. On Monday, Shimon met a friend who was collecting money to help a different friend marry off his daughter. Shimon dug a little deeper than usual and gave a substantial contribution. On Tuesday, Shimon learned with a public-school teen through a kiruv program. On Wednesday, Shimon's friend called and asked him to give an elderly man a ride to the supermarket.

"I'd love to help out," said Shimon. "But what I really need to do today is catch up on my work. Sorry. If no one else is available, let me know and I'll see what I can do."

Looking at Shimon's week thus far, we would think he is on safe ground turning down this one chessed. After all, he's done a chessed every day this week. The merit he has accrued would seem enough to "cover" him for one day on which he has chosen to focus exclusively on his own needs.

But is that so?

In *Tanach* (*Daniel* Ch. 4), we learn that Nevuchadnezzar, king of Bavel, has a terrifying dream. In it, he sees a massive tree beneath which all the animals of the world take shelter. All the birds of the world occupy its branches, and all these creatures take nourishment from its fruit. Suddenly, a *malach* appears and demands that the tree be cut down. The tree comes down and all the life that it had sustained scatters in every direction.

When none of Nevuchadnezzar's wise men are able to interpret the dream satisfactorily, he calls upon his trusted advisor, Daniel HaNavi. Daniel explains that the dream is a sign that the king will lose his empire, and instead of generously sustaining his subjects, he will develop the heart of an animal, thinking and behaving like a brutish beast.

In shock, Nevuchadnezzar begs Daniel to tell him how to avert this decree. Daniel cannot provide him with a way to overturn it. However, he does advise him on how to postpone it. The only way, he says, is for the king to redeem his sins and stop forcing his subjects to bow to idols. In addition, he should give *tzedakah* to the poor people of Klal Yisrael, and should have mercy on them. As long as the king follows this advice, says Daniel, his reign will be prolonged.

Following Daniel's instructions, Nevuchadnezzar opens his storehouse to all the poor Jews every day. For 12 months, they come to the palace and are given money to sustain themselves, and during that entire time, the king governs his empire. At the end of that period, however, he rescinds his orders, loses his mind and begins behaving like an animal. He remains in this state for 11 years, at which time Hashem alters the situation again and he returns to his senses.

This opens a question: What happened after 12 months? Why didn't Daniel's advice continue working? *Rashi* citing *Midrash Tanchuma*, explains that after 12 months, Nevuchadnezzar became annoyed by the tumult in his palace. He asked his servants what was going on and they reminded him that he had opened his doors to the poor of Klal Yisrael. He responded that he needed the money for other purposes and the charity would have to stop.

At that moment, his animal heart found the strength to dominate him. And at that moment, Hashem said, "The decree starts now."

From this episode, we learn two powerful truths. First, we learn that even a person who commits the worst sin — idol worship — can postpone the consequences of his deeds by sustaining the poor and giving them *tzedakah*. Secondly, we realize that the day the chessed stops, the consequences are set in motion. Yesterday's merits do not protect him.

We do ourselves the greatest kindness when we see every day as a new day that awaits a new act of chessed. If we make this our way of life and do not stop, Hashem's protection and kindness toward us will not stop either.

# 37

## You've Got to Love It

"You should do justice and love chessed." That is what the *navi* Michah instructs Klal Yisrael. From this *pasuk,* the Chofetz Chaim derives the title for his *sefer, Ahavas Chessed.*

In this *sefer,* he explores the deeper meaning of this verse, asking why it doesn't simply instruct us to "do justice and chessed." Indeed, although we do strive to love the mitzvos, very few of them actually make that a requirement. "You shall love Hashem your G-d" is one, and "You shall love your neighbor as yourself" is the other." Hashem does not command us to love shaking the *lulav,* putting on tefillin, eating matzah or any other positive commandment.

Why does Hashem tell us, through Michah, that He wants us to love chessed? Why is it not enough to simply do chessed? There are two inspiring answers to this question. Let's look now at the first.

> At the age of 17, a girl is told by her mother: In a few years, you are going to be having children. This means you will spend about 25 years of your life being awakened from your sleep by crying infants or frightened toddlers or young adults coming home from yeshivah or school events or shidduch dates. You will be doing

*about four loads of laundry a day. You will be cleaning up sticky spills from the floor and wiping fingerprints off your walls and appliances, only to see it all reappear in short order. You'll be cooking and cleaning up from meals three times a day every day.*

The poor girl might think to herself, "Help! I can't! It's too much for me!" But a wise mother never offers her daughter this heads-up. Instead, she trusts that when her daughter marries and children come along, her love for her family will keep her going. Not only will she do what is necessary, but her love will inspire her to keep seeking new ways to make their lives happier, easier, more productive and more successful.

Chessed is a non-stop obligation in our life, and it often entails toil. Unlike shaking a *lulav*, chessed isn't performed at its set time and finished. The only way we can find the strength to fully rise to the continuous demands of this mitzvah is by loving it. When we love our fellow Jews and love helping them, we are like a mother caring for her family; we know we will never be done, but we're not looking to be done. We're looking for new ways to make a positive impact.

This is why Hashem tells us to love chessed. He knows that only if we love it will we do it continuously. But why does He want us to do it continuously? This question touches on the most profound understanding of the world in which we live. The Chofetz Chaim reminds us that Hashem created the world in order to bestow chessed on us. The way in which He designed it, *Chazal* say, makes the chessed we receive from Heaven dependent on the chessed we do here in this world — *middah k'neged middah.*

Therefore, says the Chofetz Chaim, Hashem is beseeching us, "Please love chessed so that you will do it continuously, and I will be able to continuously shower you with My chessed." Hashem knows how he designed the world, and He is letting us in on His operating system so that we can use it wisely. He wants nothing more than to fill our lives with blessing, and when we develop a love for chessed, we open our lives to receive it.

# Shalom Is a Shield

What caused the destruction of the second *Beis HaMikdash*? Everyone knows the answer; the Gemara (*Yoma* 9b) tells us that *sinas chinam* was the cause. But in a seemingly contradictory statement, the same Gemara also describes the generation of the destruction as people who "toiled in Torah, mitzvos and *gemilus chassadim*." How could people who were so involved in chessed as to be described as *osek* — working hard at it — be guilty of baseless hatred?

This tells us that even while they were soliciting *tzedakah* money marrying off poor brides and tending to the sick, there was a lack of *shalom* among them. Jews were divided among each other, each clinging to their own group of like-minded people and finding fault with the other Jews. How could this be?

We need not look too far to understand it. How many families — people who grew up under the same roof as siblings — have difficulty speaking to each other in a peaceful way? How many communities have difficulty accepting people that come from a different tradition or follow a different Rav, Rebbe, or Rosh Yeshivah?

The Gemara (*Gittin* 56a) offers us a glimpse of the upshot of this mentality with the story of Kamtza and Bar Kamtza. The well-known incident details the fate of Bar Kamtza, who was mistakenly invited to a feast at the home of his enemy. The unnamed host insisted repeatedly that Bar Kamtza leave his home. Even when Bar Kamtza offered to pay for the entire feast, the host banished him, and he left in shame. The Gemara then "connects the dots" between the humiliation of a fellow Jew and the onset of *galus.*

When we read this story, we wonder, who would do something as cruel as what this host did to Bar Kamtza? This is an even greater question in light of the fact that the host was a respected and established person; no doubt, he was involved in many good causes. We might think no one would do such a thing in our times, but if there are people who we wouldn't invite to our *simchah,* or people whose *simchah* we wouldn't attend out of dislike or revenge, we are reenacting the plot of this story. We're feeding the fire of *machlokes,* the same fire that brought down the *Beis HaMikdash.*

The repercussions of these seemingly petty divisions among people are frightening. The Torah portrays them for us in vivid detail through the story of Korach, who rebelled against Moshe Rabbeinu. *Rashi* tells us that when the ground opened to swallow Korach and his followers, even the innocent babies of these families — children who had never sinned — went down into the abyss. *Machlokes* sets in motion destructive forces that can carry away the innocent with the guilty. It brings nothing but trouble upon us.

On the other side of the balance, we can create a protective shield for our families by doing our best to build *shalom.* With so many troubles striking so many families, it would seem foolish not to take the high road, pulling ourselves out of the mud of *machlokes.* Why not reconcile? Why not apologize? Why not be *mochel?* Why not make the first move? Why not get to know someone better before judging him to be "not my type?"

Sometimes, the reason people do not take this path is because they feel that someone has wronged them, and that dropping their personal animosity is like admitting defeat. When the damage is financial or practical, however, the cost of *machlokes* has to be figured into the calculation. Often, the fight to achieve our due costs far, far more than we stand to win; the cost is the grief *machlokes* brings into our life.

> *Rav Nissim Karelitz was the head of a beis din known for its expertise in monetary issues. One day, someone was walking with Rav Karelitz when a neighbor approached. The neighbor told the Rav that a leak emanating from the Rav's house had damaged his house. The Rav asked him how much the damage cost to repair and the man replied "450 shekel." The Rav reached into his pocket, withdrew the cash and gave it to the man. "Thank you!" the man said gratefully, and walked away.*
>
> *The Rav then turned to his companion. "You should know that according to halachah, I didn't owe that man a shekel. I paid the money for peace. Otherwise, he will be walking around feeling that I wronged him, and he might have a bit of hatred against me. For the sake of peace, I paid the money."*

Often, being willing to "pay for peace" prevents small issues from becoming big ones. For instance, siblings join together to make a *sheva berachos,* and some want to make it a bit more upscale while others want to keep it simple. The extra money the "simple" camp agrees to spend for the event is not a waste, but an investment in *shalom*. It will pay dividends in this world and the next. And, it's a statement that says in action, not just words, that "I'm doing my part to bring the *Geulah*."

## 39

# A Perfect Setting for a Perfect Gem

*A jeweler acquires a rare, costly diamond. He knows that if he designs an exquisite setting for it, the finished jewel will be worth hundreds of thousands of dollars. As he sits down to work on the design, he focuses on bringing out the stone's natural beauty. The setting must be just right — light and airy so that the diamond's fire will not be obscured, graceful and elegant, and yet strong enough to secure the precious stone. The perfect setting will bring out the full potential of the diamond's beauty and value.*

This scenario portrays an expert who knows the value of what he has acquired. If he were someone with less discernment, he might craft a setting too plain or too elaborate. The stone would still be beautiful, but its full potential would not shine through.

Chessed can be like this diamond. Someone who is a true connoisseur of chessed thinks about the setting; he wants to make sure that he doesn't waste this priceless gem's potential. How can he best maximize the value of his chessed? His finely developed instincts for *ahavas Yisrael* guide him as he chooses the perfect way to design his kind deed so that it generates every last bit of potential merit. Rav Yaakov Kamenetsky depicted what it means to be a chessed expert:

*Many years ago, a young man became a chassan. Although the custom is for a chassan to ask his Rosh Yeshivah to serve as the mesader kiddushin at the wedding, this chassan's family had close ties to Rav Moshe Feinstein, and therefore chose to ask him to fill this role. Rav Moshe agreed, but as the wedding day approached, he was not feeling well. His rebbetzin told the chassan that she would not permit Rav Moshe to wear himself out by attending the wedding.*

*The chassan was disappointed, but he understood. Anyway, he still had the perfectly acceptable alternative of asking his Rosh Yeshivah to be his mesader kiddushin. Unfortunately, the Rosh Yeshivah had a prior commitment and could not do it. Now the chassan was stuck. He went to Rav Moshe and related his dilemma.*

*"I'll tell you what I think will work out for you," said Rav Moshe. "Please call Rav Yaakov Kamenetsky and see if he is available. Tell him what happened and I'm sure he'll come and be the mesader kiddushin for you. But if he can't make it, I will come."*

*The chassan was hesitant. Neither he nor his family had any connection to Rav Yaakov. It seemed strange and audacious to call him up from out of nowhere an ask him to serve in this capacity. However, Rav Moshe assured the chassan that Rav Yaakov would be happy to help out the young man.*

*The chassan did as Rav Moshe suggested. He called Rav Yaakov, explained what had happened and added that Rav Moshe had told him to call.*

*"Sure, of course, it will be my pleasure to come and be mesader kiddushin," he assured the young man. "Tell me, what's your name and where is your wedding? I'll be there."*

*Two days later, the wedding day arrived. The chassan and kallah and their families came to the hall hours before the reception to take pictures. Much to the chassan's surprise, Rav Yaakov was already there.*

*"I wanted to get here early," Rav Yaakov explained to him.*

*Rav Yaakov knew, without a word being spoken, that the chassan would be worried that he would forget to come. He would be looking around anxiously until the moment he saw Rav Yaakov enter the hall. He would think, "Rav Yaakov doesn't know me. I'm not a student, I'm not a relative — I'm someone he never even met in person!"*

*This, in Rav Yaakov's estimation, was no way for a chassan to spend the first hours of the most important day of his life. The nagging worry was not conducive to the elated feelings that should prevail. Therefore, Rav Yaakov came early — very early, before even the first guest had arrived.*

*The chassan later related that not only did Rav Yaakov come early and serve as mesader kiddushin, but he stayed to the end of the wedding. He did not want the chassan to feel a sense of loss because Rav Moshe couldn't come and his Rosh Yeshivah couldn't come. Rather, he should have the security of knowing that his mesader kiddushin was there for him from the first moment to the last.*

Rav Yaakov's chessed was not just a precious gem, but more than that, it was a precious gem in a perfect setting. Someone else would have thought he was doing a big enough favor by serving as *mesader kiddushin* at the last minute for a person he didn't even know. But Rav Yaakov didn't just accept a role under the *chuppah*. He knew that he could do so much more; he could be there to instill the *chassan* with confidence and calm as he moved into this new stage of life. He shows us how to become a chessed connoisseur, and like so many other great Torah figures, he shows us that when it comes to helping a fellow Jew, there's always enough time to do it right.

# Disturbing the Peace

The Tchebiner Rav, considered the undisputed *gadol hador* of his time, gave a *shiur* in his home every night for a group of close *talmidim*. A man, who worked during the day, asked the Rav for permission to join the *shiur*, which the Rav gladly granted.

The next night, when the man took his place among the students, the Rav's fine-tuned senses picked up a foul odor emanating from the man's work clothing. Because the Rav was sensitive to odor and anything that exuded uncleanliness, he began to feel physically ill. However, he knew that if he broached the subject with the man, he would certainly shame him.

The Rav felt that he had no choice other than to put up with this disturbing odor wafting up from his new students' clothing. The situation persisted night after night. Realizing that the Rav was suffering, a few people offered to speak to the man and ask that he change his clothing before coming to the *shiur*, but the Rav forbade them to risk hurting the man's feelings.

*A few days later, the Rav thought perhaps he could hint at the issue without singling the man out. He mentioned in his shiur that there is a concept of putting on clean clothing before coming to learn. The next night, however, the man showed up in his malodorous work clothes again; he hadn't picked up the hint.*

*Finally, the Rav realized that he could not continue to endure the situation. Every night he was forced to power through the shiur while his stomach churned and his head ached. There seemed no good solution; speaking to the man was out of the question and continuing in this way was also impossible. He decided to cancel the shiur.*

Could it be that when balancing the value of a brilliant nightly *shiur* against the possibility of hurting the feelings of someone who carried around an offensive odor, the correct solution was to abandon the *shiur*? The Tchebiner Rav, the *posek* of his generation, ruled that this was the proper solution.

Obviously, this is not a decision that each person can make for himself. It takes someone of the Rav's stature to step out on a limb in this manner. However, the story provides a powerful lesson for us; the other person's feelings must always be placed on the scale, even when our own interests seem as holy and righteous as can be.

We have to think about this when someone is making noise that disturbs us. If for instance, someone is learning in a loud voice that distracts us from our own learning, or *davening* out loud, one line behind where we are in the *tefillah*, we might think, "I need to say something. This is important!" And it is. But how can we be sure that it's as important as the feelings of a fellow Jew? The only way to know is to ask a *shailah*.

We often think that we know what Hashem wants in a certain situation. For instance, if someone is disturbing our learning, we can easily tell ourselves that our *avodas Hashem* is to learn with all our capacity. If this person is forcing us to learn at 85 percent instead of 100 percent, then surely Hashem wants us to stand up for His Torah and ask the person to quiet down. However, it could be that, at this moment, Hashem wants us to learn Gemara at 85 percent capacity and use the other 15 percent to learn *ahavas Yisrael,* patience and restraint.

When we recognize just how serious a matter it is to hurt another Jew, we are far less likely to be prodded by our inconvenience to jump up and deliver a rebuke. Like the Tchebiner Rav, we will weigh the matter very carefully, and if we are not sure of the right approach, we will seek *daas Torah.* Our Torah and *tefillah* are precious beyond words and we rightfully go to great lengths to protect their integrity, but hurting someone in the process may very well do far more damage than good. The best way to avoid this is to be aware that the equation is not as simple as it seems.

# To Give Life

The Steipler once penned a letter regarding a respected *talmid chacham* who, despite the fact that he had a beautiful family, had fallen into depression. In the letter, he ascribed the man's malaise to a lack of respect from others. He wrote that the *talmid chacham* himself may not realize that this is the cause of his melancholy, but "I'm telling you that the real reason is that subconsciously, he feels he is not getting enough respect."

The Steipler's observation awakens us to the surprising fact that even a person who is receiving a decent amount of respect in his life is vulnerable to feelings of despair if he is not being acknowledged to the degree that he feels he deserves. The letter ended with a request that the recipient help to establish a *shiur* the *talmid chacham* could give. Being able to disseminate Torah to students would restore his self-respect and with it, his vitality.

Because we see ourselves through others' eyes, they have an extraordinary power to give us vitality or drain it from us. Obviously, this means that we hold that power as well in our interactions with the people in our lives. The message we communicate to others about their lovability, intelligence, goodness and importance can literally mean the world to them.

This perhaps explains an eye-opening *Rambam*. We have learned already that he defines the mitzvah of *v'ahavta l'rei'acha kamocha* as a mitzvah of action, not one of feelings. His surprising observation is that the most powerful action we can take to fulfill this mitzvah is to compliment another person (*Hilchos Dei'os 6:3*).

When we consider what this means, it seems astounding. More than starting a chessed organization, more than lending money, more than collecting clothes for the needy or visiting the sick, the greatest deed we can do is to notice another person's effort, his belongings, his family, the speech he made or the cake she baked, and praise it. "Therefore," says the *Rambam*, "you are required to compliment your friend."

We can understand why this fulfills the mitzvah of *v'ahavta l'rei'acha kamocha*; the mitzvah calls upon us to treat others in the way in which we would like to be treated, and everyone loves a compliment! However, why is this the premier way of fulfilling the mitzvah? Aren't actions more powerful than words? Can a mere, "Nice job!" rate so highly on the scale of chessed that the *Rambam* calls it the best way to fulfill the mitzvah?

Rav Moshe Shapiro once related a thought he heard from Rav Yechezkel Sarna, who cited the Alter of Slabodka's words: "If a person feels that he has no worth, if he feels no respect or honor for himself, such a person cannot stay alive. His *neshamah* cannot remain inside his body." This may sound extreme, but it is the truth. Even someone who has a family, a job, a nice house and plenty of money in the bank needs acknowledgment.

We can conclude that words of praise are not just one among many forms of chessed but rather, are a life-giving medicine for the human heart. Living without praise is more debilitating than living without enough food. Someone who is hungry can survive and go on to thrive if he has a will to live and faith in Hashem's guiding "hand." Someone who is sitting with a full, satisfied stomach, however, cannot survive for long if he feels cast aside and worthless.

Since our greatest need and greatest desire is to have someone think well of us, this is the greatest way to fulfill the mitzvah of *v'ahavta l'rei'acha kamocha*. When we notice someone's "good things" and praise them, we are giving the other person exactly what we would like most to have. We are not just easing his troubles in life; we are giving him life.

The most encouraging aspect of this *Rambam* is that it gives each one of us multiple opportunities every day to do chessed at its highest level. Give a compliment and give life!

# 42

# A Thousand Chances a Day

As we learned in our previous lesson, the *Rambam* tells us the amazing fact that praising someone is considered chessed on the highest level. This means that the Torah mitzvah of *v'ahavta l'rei'acha kamocha* is doable by every single Jew every single day. Whenever we are with another Jew, we have the opportunity to fulfill it. All it takes is an extra dose of awareness: "What can I say right now that will make this person feel acknowledged?"

The *Zohar* tells us that a person needs to do a chessed every day in order to maintain the daily flow of chessed from *Shamayim* into his life. This makes the *Rambam's* insight even more valuable, because many people may believe that there is no time for a daily chessed in their busy lives. They don't have time to join Hatzolah or make deliveries for Tomchei Shabbos. They don't have the network of contacts to raise funds for a worthy cause. They are just trying to get through a day; to find time for *davening* and learning with focus, taking care of their job or business, spending time with their spouse and children — there are only so many hours in the day!

But when we look at the schedule we've just described in the light of the *Rambam's* words, we see that it doesn't preclude our acts of kindness. Instead, it presents us with dozens of opportunities. Let's consider some possibilities.

A boy in yeshivah or a girl in school: You can light up someone's day just by saying that you're happy to see him or her. You can compliment a new article of clothing, a trait you notice about the person (You're always such good company.…You were so calm when the bus was stuck in traffic.…You told that story so well.…You always have interesting questions to ask the rebbi/teacher.)

An employee: The employee-boss relationship is an especially fertile field for planting compliments, because a boss's approval means the world to an employee. Some bosses fear that their praise will make their workers complacent or inspire them to ask for more money, and therefore, they give it sparingly or not at all. This is a great loss of an opportunity to do chessed. (I see how hard you work.… That was a great idea.… I can always count on you.… You have a real talent for this.… I really appreciate your help.)

Parents to their children: This is where we have the opportunity to make all the difference in the world, because for children, a parent's praise is the nourishment of their heart and soul. Their home is where they build a sense of themselves and their place in the world, and parental praise is the material from which they build it. However, we're often so busy getting children to do what they need to do that we overlook the opportunities to praise them. A little extra focus is all it takes to "catch them being good" or just acknowledge our pleasure in their presence. (Thanks for hanging up your coat. It keeps the house looking clean and neat.… I love how you share with your sister.… You got up for school so nicely today.… I see you've really improved in your *kriah*. Keep up the good work.… Welcome home! I missed you!)

Rebbi/teacher to a student: Like a parent, an educator plays a vital role in building a child's sense of who he or she is. A child feeling smart or slow, capable or inept, hopeful about the future or hopeless, can spring from that child's experiences and interactions in the classroom. (Good question…. You're really making progress…. We missed you when you were absent…. You're a real leader…. You add so much to the class…. I appreciate how serious you are about you studies.)

You might wonder, "How can I think to say these things?" The answer is to internalize the *Rambam's* words that every single positive comment is a *mitzvah d'Oraisa!* When we ingrain this fact in our mind, we naturally want to grab every opportunity to compliment someone. As we see in the examples above, one chessed a day is within our easy reach. Not only do we earn the great flow of Hashem's protection that a chessed-a-day brings us, but we uplift ourselves as we learn to look for the positive in everyone we encounter.

# Reach Out

I n his book *Touched by a Story,* Rabbi Yechiel Spero relates:
*A young couple got married in 1989. In those days, before
digital photos were common, wedding photographers would
send the couple prints of the photos, from which they would choose
the ones they wanted in their album. The excited kallah chose her
pictures and after several weeks, the photographer called to tell
her that the album was ready. The cost was $1,500.*

*This couple were not the recipients of any financial assistance
from either family and they couldn't afford the $1,500 expendi-
ture. The kallah offered to pay for it with a payment plan. "That's
fine," the photographer's secretary told her. "Only we do not re-
lease the album until the bill is paid in full." With no other choice,
the kallah agreed to the terms.*

*Eleven years later, in 2001, a wealthy young chassan went to
the office of this same photographer to choose a photo album for
his wedding pictures. The secretary showed him various styles.
"Why are there so many albums lying around here?" the chassan
asked. "Don't people want them?" The secretary explained that*

*many of the albums had not yet been paid for in full. At that point, the young man opened one such album, noting the 1989 date on the cover. He saw the smiling couple and his heart ached for them; it was eleven years since their wedding and they still didn't have their pictures!*

*"How much is still owed on this one?" he asked the secretary.*

*"Oh, this one belongs to such a sweet couple," the secretary said, smiling at the memory of their long-ago visit to see the album. "The kallah was so thrilled with the album. She's been sending in $100 a year for the past 11 years and I think she's just as excited about it as she was when she first saw it," she answered. "They still owe $400."*

*The young man opened his checkbook, wrote a check and paid the outstanding debt.*

This story shines a light on several points. We are moved by the young man's generous gesture. We also admire the idealism of the young wife, who faithfully paid the $100 a year — all she could afford — waiting for the day she would have her wedding album in hand.

But a pressing question hovers over the entire episode; why was this young man — a complete stranger — the only one to step in and help the couple cover this expense that was beyond their budget? The answer to the question is most likely that the couple did not ask anyone for help. People are proud; they do not like to ask for handouts. They do not want others to see them as a charity case. They would rather incur a debt or do without, than tell someone, "I can't afford to pay for my pictures. Could you help me out?"

This factor sometimes veils an opportunity for chessed that might be right at our fingertips. In the story above, we can be reasonably sure that there must have been some sibling, aunt, uncle, or close friend in a financial position to easily pay the photographer's bill. What was missing was the "chessed sixth sense" that enables some people to sense that help is needed. This is a sense we can all work to develop.

Here are some true-life examples of how it expresses itself:

1. *A couple is marrying off their daughter just three months after marrying off their son. Although the couple is all smiles, a friend realizes that they need financial help to make a wedding and still have resources to support the couple. Knowing the parents of the kallah would be embarrassed to accept money from him, the friend works through the shul's gemach to raise the money, which the Rav then gives them. People might also give money to the kallah's grandparents to pass along to the parents, since accepting financial contributions from parents is normal in most circles.*

2. *A wealthy man in Lakewood, known for his giving heart, sends many thousands of dollars each summer to people who cannot afford to pay for their children's day camp. He lets people know that he offers this help; it's his pleasure to be able to do it. Because he lives in a modest house and presents himself like an ordinary man, people are comfortable coming to him for help. They don't feel intimidated by his status.*

We all know people who seem to be "living on *mahn*." We may marvel at their ability to make multiple weddings, support multiple couples, pay tuitions, send children to Eretz Yisrael. Indeed, so many people appear to be managing, although we cannot imagine how. What we may not know is that some of them are under outlandish pressure. Some cannot sleep at night worrying about how to cover the bills.

It could be a brother. It could be a parent. It could be a friend. Hiding in plain sight, there are people who need our help but will not ask us. This means that we have to ask them. "Can I help you out? How are you doing? What do you need?" If asking them directly might insult or embarrass them, then we can solicit the help of someone with whom they feel comfortable disclosing their situation. If we give before the person falls under the weight of his burdens, then *middah k'neged middah*, Hashem will make sure that we do not fall.

# Be a Matchmaker

A true story heard directly from the school secretary involved in the situation:

*One day, a school secretary received a phone call from a woman who had an unusual request. "I have a relative in your school," she said. "and I know that the family is struggling financially. You wouldn't know it because they pay their tuition every month on time and in full. This is something they're very careful to do. But I know that they have almost no money for their regular household expenses.*

*"I want to give you a credit card," the woman said, "and I would like to pay the next six months of tuition. Just bill me every month. But please do not tell them it is coming from me because I don't want them to feel embarrassed. This way they'll have money for normal expenses and they won't be under so much pressure."*

*The secretary took the credit card information. However, she wondered how she would explain to the student's family why their tuition was covered. She discussed it with the director of the school and they thought of a cover story. The family was relieved of tuition for the rest of the school year, and they were finally able to breathe a little easier.*

This anonymous *tzedakah*, provided by a caring relative who saw exactly what was needed and went about answering the need, is a glowing example of chessed at its best. But it does more than fill a financial gap; very possibly, it restored *shalom bayis* to this home as well. As one prominent *dayan* in Williamsburg observed recently, the majority of *shalom bayis* issues spring from financial stress.

When the wife can't find money to replace worn-out shoes or outgrown clothing, when her house is falling apart around her and she can't afford to repair anything, when her children ask for a treat or a trip and the answer is always, "Now's not a good time," her discontent is bound to grow. Likewise, when the husband works hard every day but doesn't earn enough to satisfy his family's needs — when he's faced with stacks of unpaid bills and the complaints of his wife and children — he, too, is bound to feel frustrated and depressed.

The woman who paid her relative's tuition, therefore, did more than cover that one expense. Very likely, she freed an entire family from the vise-like grip of tight financial straits.

The obstacle to this kind of chessed is that not everyone can afford it. Many people see the struggles of their relatives and neighbors and wish they could help, but they're not in much better shape themselves. However, the woman who paid her friend's tuition does have something to teach us all, something anyone can emulate. That is to be proactive.

When we notice that a family is under strain, especially when we notice tension rising between husband and wife, this should trigger a thought: "Are money problems weighing heavily on them? Do they have some unusual expense? Has someone lost a job or taken a pay cut? Is there a new baby in the house, a new tuition to pay, a big repair to make? Can he pay for camp? Can he continue to support his son-in-law?"

When finances create *shalom bayis* issues, we might think, "They're not getting along. Money can't fix that." But it's surprising to see what money can fix. Money often appeases someone who has previously declared, "I'll never forgive him." Obviously, money doesn't erase the hurt, but it has a way of soothing the heart and igniting a spark of good will. Likewise, injecting money into a household that is under strain might not seem like a long-term solution, but it can remove the pressure, open the channel of good will and let healing happen.

If we cannot provide the necessary money, we can at least be the one who notices that it is needed, and we can seek out a person who is equipped to help. Perhaps the family has a wealthy relative who is not proactively looking to see who needs help but would be happy to contribute. Perhaps there's an organization or *gemach* that can help. Many shuls have a *gabbai tzedakah* who distributes money to needy families, but he may not realize that a certain family is needy. We can be the one to let him know.

The other lesson we can learn from the school secretary's story is the importance of maintaining the recipient's self-respect. This takes thought and insight. Here is one way a community Rav managed the situation:

> *A family opened a grocery store in an area of Brooklyn that was on the outskirts of the major Jewish areas. The clientele proved inadequate to support the business, and within a year, the store closed.*
>
> *One morning in late August, the chairman of the tuition committee of their son's yeshivah called and told the now-unemployed store owner, "Someone donated money for a few scholarships and we chose the recipients by lottery. You won! You only have to pay the registration fees and that's all."*
>
> *Many years later, the family figured it out. There was no big donor. There was no lottery. Their Rav had collected the money and paid the tuition.*

We don't have to be wealthy to take the financial pressure off someone. We only have to be aware and proactive. Hashem gives the challenge, and He also provides the remedy. We can be the matchmaker to put the two together.

# The Difference Between
# Avraham and Iyov

A true story heard from the author's father-in-law, Rav
Moshe Hillel Glazer, *maggid shiur* in Ner Yisrael, Baltimore:

*A wealthy lawyer from Baltimore walks into a makolet — a small,
neighborhood grocery store in Eretz Yisrael — and witnesses a
heart-rending scene. A boy is doing his family's shopping. When
he steps up to the cashier's counter and asks that the order be
put on his family's account, he's told that his family has no more
credit. The boy turns around to return the items to their shelves.
Meanwhile, the lawyer asks the cashier how much the family owes
and writes a check to cover it.*

This is a beautiful chessed. This man saw a need, felt for the boy's
situation, thought to himself, "I can be the one to relieve this family's
strain," and acted on his thought. Here is another story, heard from
the source, that is similar but with a crucial difference:

> *A man who lives in Beit Shemesh makes it his practice to visit various grocery stores in the neighborhood and ask if there are any families with outstanding balances. He finds out how much they owe and pays off their debt.*

This, too, is a beautiful chessed. It seems nearly identical to the first story, but there is one important difference in the details. We can discern what that difference is by learning about the difference between Avraham and Iyov as conveyed in *Avos d'Rabbi Nosson* (Ch. 7) and first heard by the author from Rav Moshe Hillel Glazer:

Avraham and Iyov were both renowned for their *hachnassas orchim* — their hospitality. In fact, like Avraham, Iyov's tent had four open doors, one on each side, so that anyone passing by from any direction would find a welcome. Everyone traveling through the area knew they could find a meal with Iyov. When tragedy struck Iyov, he asked Hashem why his *hachnassas orchim* did not protect him.

While the text doesn't provide a direct answer to that question, *Avos d'Rabbi Nosson* says that Hashem told Iyov that his *hachnassas orchim* did not measure up to even half of that of Avraham. One reason for this was that Iyov would sit in his tent and wait for people to come to him. Then he would graciously feed them. Avraham, however, went out and looked for guests.

This idea teaches us how to do chessed at its highest level. While we certainly earn exceptional merit for answering the needs of the person who comes knocking at the door, we accomplish far more when we look for people we can help. That is the chessed of Avraham Avinu.

It also marks the difference between the lawyer who saw a boy in need of help in front of his eyes and the man who went store-to-store inquiring about who needed help. Any Jew with a heart and the financial ability would be moved to pay the bill for the boy's family. Any Jew with a heart would reach into his pocket for someone who comes to the door and asks for food or a donation. These are wonderful deeds that earn abundant merit. However, they are not equal to the chessed of Avraham.

The man who went from store to store reaches this level. He went out of his way to find people who needed someone to pay their bill. Although we don't understand why Iyov's chessed did not protect him, we do understand that in comparing the two, Hashem is implying that Avraham's form of chessed provides extra protection.

How does this play out in our lives? If we have the ability to pay off people's grocery bills, tuition bills, camp fees, rent or mortgage arrears — whatever we can do — going out and finding those opportunities brings us the very highest level of merit and protection.

It is the optimal expression of *v'ahavta l'rei'acha kamocha* as the *Rambam* describes it: doing for someone else what you would want done for you. Avraham's chessed prevented the needy person from having to beg, just as Avraham would not have wanted to have to beg. When we follow Avraham's exalted example, we can hope that Hashem will make sure to always take care of our needs before we must beseech others for help.

# 46

# A Yom Kippur Avodah

The Torah keeps a Jew busy. Between *davening,* learning, preparing for Shabbos and Yamim Tovim, raising our children and earning the *parnassah* to keep the wheels of our lives turning, there's never a moment to waste. A great part of our ultimate success and reward depends on how we prioritize these many demands. Since *talmud Torah k'neged kulam* — Torah learning is the equivalent of all the other mitzvos, we would assume that only the most pressing needs should cause us to put it aside. Does chessed qualify as such a need? The Chofetz Chaim helps us answer that question:

*In the Chofetz Chaim's yeshivah in Radin, a man named Rav Herschel Kamenitzer sat and learned. He was already 60 years old at the time of this story, and due to medical problems, he had never been able to marry. Rav Herschel related this story to Rav Shach, who repeated it many times.*

*One year, on Yom Kippur night, Rav Herschel sat alone in the empty beis medrash. The davening was over and everyone had* gone home to their families. He was feeling the pain of his loneliness, wondering why this was his lot in life.

Suddenly, he turned and saw the Chofetz Chaim sitting next to him. The tzaddik began confiding in Rav Herschel about some of the hardships he had suffered, having been orphaned early in life.

"You know," he said, "sometimes a person has to realize that Hashem gave him a certain lot in life. There could be aggravation, hardship... and his purpose in life is to serve Hashem in those trying circumstances. We don't know why we are chosen for these challenges, but we know it's what Hashem wants from us."

The Chofetz Chaim sat with Rav Herschel for most of the night — Yom Kippur night. He didn't open a sefer. He didn't speak divrei Torah. He just talked about life, trying to soothe Rav Herschel and help him feel positive about his situation.

To fully understand the impact of this story, let's compare it to another story of the Chofetz Chaim: It happened when the Rosh Yeshivah in Radin, Rav Naftoli Trop, became ill. The students at the yeshivah were asked to dedicate a portion of their learning time as a merit for his recovery. Everyone dedicated at least a few hours. The Chofetz Chaim, however, dedicated only two minutes. When asked how he arrived at that decision, he explained that since a second of Torah learning is the equivalent of all 613 mitzvos, two minutes was a donation of 120 seconds times 613, for a total of more than 73,000 mitzvos. That's what he was giving up for Rav Naftoli's refuah sheleimah.

This episode attests to the value the Chofetz Chaim placed on every moment of learning. But when he saw Rav Herschel sitting in despair, even on Yom Kippur night when every Jew wants to amass all the merit possible, he saw his priority as lifting the downcast man's spirits. And the Chofetz Chaim knew that in doing so, he would not lack any merit before the Heavenly throne. Rather, he would be creating for himself an army of advocates.

We learn from this how to set our priorities. If someone needs a shoulder to cry on or some encouraging words, there's no greater chessed than being the someone he turns to. To say, "I'm in the middle of learning," or "I'm on my way to a *shiur*" when we have the opportunity to lift up another human being and help him feel positive about himself and his life is to miss the opportunity Hashem is placing before us at that moment.

Hashem apportions a certain length of day in each person's life, and we are obligated to use it wisely. As the Chofetz Chaim shows us, encouraging a fellow Jew is indeed the wise person's priority.

# 47

# *Why We've Got to Love It*

A true story: A few decades ago, most kollel couples in Lakewood lived near Beth Medrash Govoha, and only a few owned cars. Most of those cars were borderline jalopies, with dents on the fenders and duct tape holding together various wobbly components.

One young man who lived in an apartment complex near the yeshivah owned a late-model car. He would frequently tell others in the building, "If you need a car, you're welcome to borrow mine. Don't hesitate to ask."

At first, people did hesitate, because a car is an expensive item and accidents can happen. Also, they worried that as they were driving it, the owner would need it and not have it on hand. However, none of this troubled the owner. He told people that he would only lend it when he didn't need it. "Why should it sit in the parking lot doing nothing when people could use it?" he urged. "This is why I have a car!"

If he wasn't doing enough "business" lending his car, he would *walk around reminding his neighbors, "Remember, my car is available." After a while, people no longer hesitated to borrow it. One man had a weekly "reservation" to take the car Shabbos shopping on Thursday nights, since the owner didn't use it then. With this car, one man made life easier for many families.*

We learned earlier that the Chofetz Chaim cites two reasons why we must not only do chessed, but we must love doing it. The *navi* (*Michah* 6:8) tells us that this is what G-d wants of us: "to do justice, love chessed and walk humbly with your G-d." The Chofetz Chaim observes that chessed is the only mitzvah that requires love, aside from "*V'ahavta es Hashem Elokecha* — You shall love Hashem your G-d," and "*v'ahavta l'rei'acha kamocha* — love your neighbor as yourself."

The second reason chessed must be done with love (the first is discussed in Lesson 37) is because if it isn't, we are not really doing for the other person what we would want done for us. We would not want to feel that we are imposing on someone when he does us a favor. We would not like to borrow someone's car or vacuum cleaner if he lends it with a sour expression. We would not want to know all his calculations about what this might cost him in time, money and convenience.

If we detect that the person helping us would rather not do so, we feel embarrassed about asking. If he details all he will have to go through to accommodate us, we feel guilty accepting his help. The favor might be done, but the actual chessed, the physical expression of *v'ahavta l'rei'acha kamocha,* is very much compromised.

On the other hand, someone who is happy to be in the position to give makes those he helps feel that they are doing him the greatest favor.

Here was a man who fulfilled the mitzvah of loving chessed. Nothing made him happier than seeing someone get behind the wheel of his car and go to the supermarket, take a child to the doctor, go to a *simchah* — in the most convenient and comfortable way.

Hashem wants every Jew to have the full merit of the chessed he performs, and that's why He wants us to do it with love. This means making sure the person we help feels good about taking our help. We have to show the person that we are doing it with love, which means we have to work on building this love sincerely in our heart. An *esrog* won't feel hurt if we don't love holding it. Matzah won't feel hurt if we don't love eating it. But a fellow Jew will feel hurt if we don't love helping him, and that's why Hashem requires of us not only chessed, but *ahavas chessed*.

# All Hands on Deck

The following is a true story (some personal details are changed):

*The time was 6:30 p.m. on a Friday in the summer. Shabbos would be starting in an hour and a half, and Levi was telling his neighbor about his problem. That morning, he had undergone an hour-long outpatient surgical procedure. He left the office with a sheet filled with instructions on how to care for himself and what to expect in the days following the procedure. The doctor, a non-religious Jew, told Levi, "If you have any problems, call and leave a message and I will call you back."*

*"Thanks," said Levi, "only please call me back before Shabbos, because otherwise I can't answer the phone." The doctor agreed to keep that in mind.*

*Around 1 p.m., Levi started noticing that the pain was increasing. He took some Advil and tried to rest. By 3, the pain was worse, and he realized he should contact the surgeon. He called the office and left a message, specifying that he would not be able to pick up the phone after Shabbos began. He called again at 4 and again at*

5. No one had yet called back, and Levi was becoming desperate.

He spoke to his neighbor. "Maybe I should go to the emergency room, but I don't want to be stuck there for Shabbos. I don't know if this is a serious situation or not. I wish the doctor would just call me back!"

The neighbor heard the agitation in Levi's voice. "You know, my cousin is a noted urologist. Let me give him a call and see if he can give you some advice."

The cousin was happy to help. "Have him call me right now," he said. "Let me see what I can do for him."

Levi called the cousin — Dr. Randy Makovsky, a highly regarded urologist whose services are widely sought — and explained his situation. Dr. Makovsky listened carefully, calmed him down and told him how to alleviate his symptoms. "You should be fine for Shabbos," he said. "But make sure you call me right after Shabbos to update me."

Levi hung up the phone and exhaled fully for the first time in hours. He followed the instructions he had been given and greeted Shabbos already feeling better. As he ate his meal on Friday night, he heard his own doctor's voice on his answering machine. "I know you can't pick up the phone," the doctor said, "But you may be experiencing a blood clot. You should go to the emergency room." Fortunately, Levi felt well enough to disregard the doctor's too-late advice. By the time Shabbos was over, the pain was gone.

For Dr. Makovsky, it wasn't enough to advise Levi, someone who was not even his patient, on an emergency basis on Erev Shabbos. He kept Levi's situation in mind throughout Shabbos. He cared: Was Levi still in pain? Did matters improve? Would he need further instructions or advice? He didn't just wonder. After Shabbos Dr. Makovsky himself called to inquire about how the patient was feeling!

When we read this story, we can ask ourselves, "Wouldn't we rather be like the top surgeon who felt a fellow Jew's pain and went the extra mile for him?

Klal Yisrael is blessed to have people with many different areas of expertise. We have professionals like doctors, dentists, lawyers and accountants. We have entrepreneurs, educators, experts in finance and investment, retailers, chefs, farmers, therapists, teachers, musicians and artists. Each of these areas of expertise represents a way to do chessed. And to make sure that chessed is done, Hashem created each person with needs. Nobody is a self-sufficient island. All of us, at times, need someone to go the extra mile for us in an area in which they can provide help.

In the story above, Levi needed the help of a prestigious surgeon. But the surgeon also needs help — some business advice from his neighbor the accountant or some car advice from his friend in shul who owns an auto leasing company. In fact, if this surgeon needed surgery, he might need a favor from a doctor; even in his own area of expertise, he needs others.

Hashem made a world built on chessed; everyone has something to give and everyone needs others. As the *Rambam* explained, chessed is a mitzvah of action, requiring us to do for someone else what we would want them to do for us. When people come to us for help or advice because we have the expertise they need, we have to think — what would I want done for me in this situation? The surgeon knew that if he were worried about a potential health crisis an hour and a half before Shabbos, he would want someone knowledgeable to talk to him. Therefore, he made himself available to Levi.

Sometimes, a parent needs help for his child. Perhaps the child did not get into a school and the parent calls to speak to the principal. The principal might think, "This school isn't suitable for this child. There's nothing to discuss." However, if he sees his position from the perspective of chessed, he will think, "This parent needs to do his best for his child. Let me see if I can help him. Let me see if I can connect him to the right school." The principal could use his connections and expertise to give the parent direction and hope. He could do for this parent what he would want done for him if he were in the position of having no school for his child.

We all need other people. If we rise to the occasion, using the skills and talents Hashem has given us to help those who need us, Hashem will do for us as we do for them. As the Baal Shem Tov expounded on the words "*Hashem tzilcha* — Hashem is your shadow": At the moment we reach out to help someone, He reaches out to help us.

# The Mitzvah of the Moment

What is our top priority? As we've seen in many of our stories, our opportunities for chessed sometimes overlap with other pressing obligations. We may not always know which to choose, but we step up to a new level when we simply begin to realize that there's a question to be asked. Like any area of Torah, a person has to know enough to know what he doesn't know.

In this heartwarming story told by Rabbi Yitzchok Hisiger, we see two yeshivah students wrestling with priorities, and in doing so, demonstrating that they know enough to know that chessed is a mitzvah that counts:

> *Two yeshivah students were driving to Boston for their close friend's wedding. Calculating their likely arrival time, they realized that they would arrive past the time to daven Minchah. They had two options: Stop in a city along the route to daven Minchah with a minyan, which would cause them to miss their friend's kabbalas panim and chuppah, or get to the wedding on time and daven on their own.*

In their estimation, stopping for a minyan seemed to make more sense. After all, they would still arrive at the wedding in plenty of time to dance with their friend. However, they were close enough to the chassan to be traveling a long distance to be at his wedding. Perhaps their presence at the chuppah was the more important priority.

They decided to call Rav Chaim Epstein to ask what they should do. The Rav told them to go straight to the wedding and daven Minchah on their own. One of the young men asked a further question. "I just want to explain to the Rosh Yeshivah," he said, "that I'm 21 years old, and since my bar mitzvah, I have never missed a minyan. I want to ask the Rosh Yeshivah if this decision still applies — that even though I haven't missed a minyan in eight years, I should miss one now to make it to the chuppah."

The Rosh Yeshivah replied with a penetrating insight:

"If you miss the chuppah and come for the dancing, you'll give the chassan joy and it will be wonderful. But earlier, at the kabbalas panim and the chuppah, he'll be looking for his two good friends who were coming all the way to Boston for him. And he'll be disappointed because he'll think that maybe they aren't coming. Until you show up, the chasunah won't be the same for him.

"So that he should go the chuppah with a happy heart, it's worthwhile for you to miss davening with a minyan, even though you haven't missed a minyan in eight years.

"You know, in baseball, teams have what they call a winning streak. They take pride in winning as many games in a row as they can. But with mitzvos, we don't look for winning streaks. We look to see what Hashem wants from us right now. For eight years, Hashem's ratzon has been that you should not miss a minyan. But right now, there's an opportunity to do a chessed, and now it's Hashem's will that you end the winning streak. If what He wants now is that you get to the chasunah a little earlier so that your friend can go to the chuppah with a happy heart, then right now, for you, that's Torah."

One point we learn from this story is the importance of acting as soon as possible. The boys could have arrived an hour later and danced with their friend. They could have made him happy an hour later and still *davened* with a *minyan*. But after consulting with a *gadol*, they knew that saving the *chassan* from an hour of tension and disappointment before his *chuppah* is a mitzvah so great that it overrode the obligation to *daven* with a *minyan*.

A second point is that our only concern in any situation is to do the *ratzon* of Hashem, whatever it is at that moment. We might assume that *davening* with a *minyan* is always what Hashem wants of us — that we can't go wrong by making that our top priority. But we see from this story that when the choice is between making another Jew feel good — which we have learned is the highest form of chessed — and some other mitzvah, we have to realize that there's a real question in front of us. Once we have that realization, we will know how to find the answer.

# The Top of the List

Tax time came around and the Reiners brought their bundles of documents to their accountant.

"How much are you claiming in charitable deductions?" he asked.

They named a number.

"But it's really at least twice that," said Mr. Reiner, "because we paid for overnight camp for my sister's three boys and gave my brother-in-law $8,000 toward his daughter's wedding. We also pay for an aide for my mother. Can we get deductions for this stuff?"

"Well, no, the government doesn't count that kind of thing. You have to have a receipt from an official non-profit organization," the accountant explained. "Sorry."

The IRS may not recognize contributions we give to family members, but to Hashem, they are considered *tzedakah* of the highest quality. **The *Shulchan Aruch* (*Yoreh Dei'ah* 251:3) specifies that we are obligated to give to our relatives before anyone else,** including neighbors, the poor of our town, the poor of Eretz Yisrael, community organizations, yeshivos and *kollelim*. Parents in need of support are at the top of the list. After that come married children, and after that, brothers and sisters.

But when people want to give *tzedakah* and feel that they are givers, this is not the direction in which they tend to direct their eyes. Many of us are more motivated to give to the yeshivah building campaign or one of the many excellent chessed organizations in the community. We want the people raising the money to see us as supporters, both for altruistic reasons and for the status it gives us.

Sometimes, we dig into our pockets for a fundraising campaign just because there's a Chinese auction or raffle involved. We're willing to shell out more than we might normally give because we're enticed by the prizes. Succos in Eretz Yisrael! Isn't that worth a $100 chance? We may also favor official charities because, as our opening scenario points out, the donations are tax deductible.

Sadly, our relatives aren't likely to create a non-profit organization, or send us a shiny brochure, or set up an interactive website to solicit our help. They are more likely to suffer in silence, wishing someone would notice but ashamed to disclose their situation. We won't enhance our status in the community when we write them a check. Nor will we purchase for ourselves a chance at a new bedroom set or Pesach in Switzerland. Our relatives won't display a plaque on their living room wall to honor us. They might not even thank us in a way we consider adequate. However, none of this should stand in the way of giving to those whom the Torah deems to be at the top of our list.

There's a well-known story about the Klausenberger Rebbe, which makes this point clearly:

> The Rebbe once made an appointment with one of his chassidim, a wealthy diamond dealer, at the chassid's office in the diamond district in Manhattan. When he arrived, he informed the chassid of the dire situation of one of the families in the kehillah and asked for a donation. The chassid was ready with a $1,000 check. He only needed to know to whom it should be payable. The Rebbe answered, "Make it out to your brother."

The life of a *frum* family has become very expensive; we seem to be living on open miracles as we raise large families and pay for their schooling, dignified clothing, day camps, overnight camps, weekly Shabbos feasts, Yamim Tovim, Chol HaMoed trips, *simchos,* health insurance, car expenses, rent or mortgage for comfortable living quarters — we could go on and on. While it's possible to simplify or do without in some areas, in many areas, it is not a reasonable option. We may not understand why matters have to be this way, but we can clearly see that the situation has opened thousands of opportunities for us to think about our family members, consider what their life might be like, and look for ways to help. Our expensive lifestyle carries with it an ocean of potential *zechus.*

Sometimes, the need is obvious. If a whole family of children are "doing Camp Mommy" for the summer, unless this is something they do on principle, we can assume they're short of camp money. If children are sitting home after the school year has begun, we can assume they haven't paid off last year's tuition. As we mentioned earlier, if we begin seeing signs of friction in an otherwise happy marriage, we can suspect that financial strain might be behind it. If our elderly parents' housekeeping or personal hygiene is beginning to deteriorate, we can assume they need some help.

The next question is who can help and how can they do so without embarrassing the recipient. Obviously, family members who are well-off financially are the ideal source of help. If they don't notice the need, those who do notice can inform them. Newly married couples who are not yet carrying the load of large families might also have *maaser* that could make a big difference. If siblings don't want to be in a position of offering a sister or brother money, they can give the money to their parents and ask them to pass it along in their own name. Most children accept money from their parents or in-laws without embarrassment. There's nothing demeaning about saying, "Zeidy and Bubby want to treat the kids to camp this summer." With a little empathy, a little curiosity and some sensitivity, we can fulfill the halachah that obligates us to give *tzedakah* first to our relatives in need. In doing so, we make life better for the people we love.

# The Answer in His Pocket

When someone's the "real deal," he doesn't have to worry about how he will explain himself. That might be why, on the occasion of his 80th birthday, Rabbi Uri Zohar agreed to be interviewed on national television by one of Israel's most aggressive interviewers. What could she ask that he wouldn't be able to answer?

> *Rabbi Zohar, as is well known, had a long, successful career as an actor and director in Israel's movie industry. In the late 1970s, he became religious, and since then, his fame and charisma were utilized to inspire others to return to Torah. His interviewer obviously took issue with his trajectory in life, and she thought she had just the needle with which to deflate his image of righteousness.*
>
> *"Rabbi Zohar, you were one of the most beloved movie stars in the history of Israel," the woman said. "Then you became religious and left all your friends and fans behind. Just like that, you turned your back on all of them. Decades have passed and you are still religious. But isn't a big part of religion about how you treat your*

neighbor? How can you justify letting so many people down, just walking out of their lives?"

The question seemed like a perfect trap, meant to illustrate that religious Jews don't care about anyone but each other. However, Rabbi Zohar did not need to fumble for an answer. He had one right in his pocket.

"The truth is, I do care — on a very practical level. I do something for my fellow movie actors and old friends that no one else does for them," he said.

"Really? What is that?" asked the woman.

He reached into his pocket and pulled out a small notebook. "Here," he said, "Let me show you something. My actor friends who I used to work with every day did not become religious as I did. Many of them have already passed on to the next world, and they have no religious children. There's no one saying Kaddish for them on their yahrtzeit.

I make it my business to find out their Hebrew names and mark down their yahrtzeit so I can say Kaddish for them."

The camera zoomed in on his book as he showed it to the woman. All of those watching the show saw the names written into it. The moment created a small tremor of amazement across the country among the non-religious Jews.

Rabbi Zohar had no idea what questions he would be asked. He had the book with him because he always carried it to ensure that he would not miss a *yahrtzeit*. The viewers understood immediately that his love for his fellow Jew became stronger, not weaker, with his embrace of Torah. His *bein adam la'chaveiro* rose to the level of chessed *shel emes* — a kind act that is totally pure, because it has no possibility of being reciprocated.

Part II of this story occurred several years later. Rabbi Yosef Karmel, executive director of the *kiruv* organization Lev L'Achim, worked closely with Rabbi Zohar. This is the story Rabbi Zohar told him:

One day, a woman from Tel Aviv called Rabbi Zohar at his home.

*She said that she had nothing to do with religion, but needed to give him a message. The woman was the daughter of an actress who was no longer alive.*

*"My mother came to me in a dream three times in one week. She told me, 'My neshamah is not given any elevation in Olam Haba except for one time a year, on my yahrtzeit, when Uri Zohar says Kaddish for me. But my yahrtzeit passed a few weeks ago and he didn't say Kaddish. He needs to rectify this!'"*

*Rabbi Zohar was confused. He had been saying Kaddish for this actress since she had passed away a few years earlier. But when he checked his notebook, he realized that this year, his wife had lost a relative on that date. The day was taken up with the funeral and burial, and the actress's yahrtzeit slipped his notice.*

These two stories provide an insight on two important aspects of chessed. First, we see that someone who looks for ways to do chessed will find them. How could Rabbi Zohar show his love and caring for the people who had been his friends and colleagues for so many years? His life went in a different direction, so that it no longer intersected with actors and celebrities, but that didn't stop him from caring about them. He found a way to help them that no one else in their lives would have thought of. He brought them elevation in the Next World — an act of caring with eternal ramifications!

Another point is that in this incident we were permitted to see *Chazal's* words come to life: that saying *Kaddish* and learning Mishnayos elevates the souls of those who have passed on. Here, Rabbi Zohar received a "phone-call from Heaven" telling him outright that this woman's soul was waiting for his *Kaddish*. We were privileged to be granted a glimpse of the spiritual reality, which should only serve to remind us that everything *Chazal* tell us reflects the true reality of how Hashem runs the world.

# 52

# For the Price of a Pastry

What could be worse than *avodah zarah*? The Torah answers that nothing can be worse. It's among the three sins a person must refuse to commit even if refusal costs him his life. That makes the following Gemara (*Sanhedrin* 103b) truly remarkable:

It recounts the incident of Michah (*Shoftim* Ch. 17), a person so steeped in *avodah zarah* that he built an entire house of worship for his idol, a distance of a mile and a half from where the *Mishkan* stood in Shiloh. The Gemara recounts that the smoke from Michah's profane sacrifices would ascend into the air, and there it would mingle with the smoke from the *Mishkan's* holy offerings.

The *malachim* were enraged by the tainting of Klal Yisrael's offering and asked Hashem permission to *"dochafo* — push him" (*Michah*), which most commentators interpret as "to kill him." However, *HaKadosh Baruch Hu* refused permission because Michah consistently fed hungry passers-by.

If we imagine these two deeds on a scale, idol worship on one side and feeding the hungry on the other, this Gemara illustrates that the scale tips to the side of feeding the hungry. Michah's chessed protected him from the punishment he well deserved for committing the Torah's worst sin in an especially egregious way, so that he sullied the *korbanos* from the Altar of the *Mishkan*.

While this doesn't mean that Michah was absolved of his sin, it highlights with startling clarity the vast protective power that comes from feeding a hungry Jew. Hashem looked down upon his kindness to the passers-by and said to the *malachim*, "I cannot kill him. I cannot give you permission to kill him."

The Gemara continues (104a) by quoting Rav Yochanan, who explicitly states that the merit of feeding a hungry Jew is so strong that Hashem "turns His eye from evildoers." According to *Rashi*, this tells us that if a *rasha* warrants punishment, but he is involved in feeding the hungry, Hashem looks away from his evil behavior. In fact, earlier the Gemara (103b) lists people who lost their portion in *Olam Haba*. It lists kings and other notables, but absent among them is Michah. The Gemara explains that he retains his portion because he fed the hungry.

Obviously, the Gemara is not telling us that a person can get away with *avodah zarah* as long as he feeds the hungry to balance it out. It's not telling us that *avodah zarah* isn't as wicked as we might think. Rather, it is telling us loudly and clearly that feeding the hungry is so much more powerful a merit than we think. If it can bring Michah Hashem's mercy when he has committed the worst of sins, we can only imagine how much merit and spiritual elevation it brings a well-meaning, Torah observant Jew who occasionally stumbles over the normal obstacles of life.

Best of all, this is a chessed that is right at our fingertips. We can do it by donating to any organization that feeds the hungry, or by putting credit on their grocery store account. We can do it from home, simply by offering the *meshulachim* who come to our door an individually wrapped pastry and a bottle of water to take along.

If our task in this life is to build ourselves a beautiful *Olam Haba*, feeding the hungry is clearly the deal of the century.

# Connected by Caring

Who will be Mashiach? When we consider all the different types of Jews comprising Klal Yisrael, we might wonder how any one person could earn the allegiance of all of them. People tend to imagine Mashiach as someone who wears their style of clothing, speaks their language and follows their customs. Perhaps unity is a prerequisite for Mashiach for the simple, practical reason that otherwise, how will Klal Yisrael fall in line behind one leader?

In 2019, an event occurred that hinted at what might motivate Jews from many different walks of life to identify themselves with one leader. It was the *levayah* and *shivah* of Rav Shlomo Gissinger, the Rav of Kehilas Zichron Yaakov in Lakewood. Anyone who scanned the throngs who came to the *levayah* would be struck by the broad spectrum of Jews in attendance. Although Zichron Yaakov is a mainstream Lakewood shul, the attendees spanned the spectrum. Nonreligious Jews attended. Chassidim attended. Modern Orthodox Jews attended. Out-of-towners drove for hours to be there. Members of other shuls throughout Lakewood were there too, alongside the Zichron Yaakov *kehillah* that had come to mourn their beloved Rav.

But not only did people attend. It was clear from the tears, the words spoken and the bereft expressions on people's faces that their sense of loss was profound.

How did this one Rav connect so closely to the hearts of so many different Jews? The stories told at the podium, and later at the *shivah* house, and still later in *At Any Hour,* a biography of Rabbi Gissinger, provided the answer.

He took every Jew's troubles as his own. Not only did he feel for them, but he applied his brilliant mind to understanding the troubles that afflicted them, whether it was a couple's complicated fertility issue, a teen's collapsing self-esteem, a divorcing couple's intractable disputes, a business issue or any other area. If it required knowledge, he sought knowledge. If it required advocacy, he advocated. He was known for appearing at the principal's office of a school that was refusing a child a seat, and campaigning until the principal gave in. His understanding of fertility issues was so profound that renowned physicians assumed he had a medical degree.

The key to his impact was not his great mind, but rather, his great heart. He knew that he was Hashem's partner in bringing relief to the long lines of petitioners who crowded his office every night. They were his fellow Jews, and he was his Father's *shaliach,* His emissary, entrusted with the resources to help those who came to him. His passion for Torah and love of Hashem expressed themselves in his deep care for his fellow Jew.

He wasn't just the brains and heart behind the operation, but the arms and legs as well. As we've learned throughout this *sefer, ahavas Yisrael* is a mitzvah of action, not emotion. Action is what connected people to Rabbi Gissinger in such a powerful way. Here are just a few of the thousands of stories that illustrate this:

> When Rabbi Gissinger was first developing his expertise in fertility issues, a couple called him for advice. After some time had passed, they were surprised to receive a follow-up phone call from him. He didn't know them; he had only one conversation with them, but he wanted to know, "How are you doing?" The couple testified

*that no other person they called for help ever called them back. "He really cared," they realized. And because they felt that care, they felt close to him.*

*Another episode occurred on Erev Shabbos, a day when Rabbi Gissinger was often busy all day on the phone with the doctors involved with fertility treatments. Since there was no option to speak at night, he plowed through the day taking care of all the outstanding questions, realizing that often, time is of the essence. On one such Friday, he remembered that someone in his kehillah had been hospitalized for a psychiatric episode. He stopped what he was doing and called the patient's family member to find out what food the patient enjoyed. He then went out, bought it and brought it to him. "He should know someone cares about him," he reasoned.*

*Even in his last days, his ahavas Yisrael didn't wane. He was in so much pain that it took his son, Binyamin, 45 minutes to help him find a comfortable position in which to lie down in bed. But only two minutes later, the Rav called his son back. He was sitting up and asking for a phone so that he could call a young woman who had contacted him earlier in a state of turmoil. "I need to calm her down," he explained.*

Rabbi Gissinger was the rare Jew who seemed to draw superhuman resources from *Shamayim*. Most of us cannot imagine living at that level. But we can learn from his example that caring and doing for others is what knits Klal Yisrael together, and if we each take on just our part of this mission, we may someday find the answer to our question, "How will we all unite under Mashiach?" Caring creates connection.

# Everyone's Protektzia

One of the biggest challenges in fulfilling *"v'ahavta l'rei'acha kamocha"* is knowing what another person needs. If the measure of the mitzvah is to do for others what you would want them to do for you in similar circumstances, then clearly, we need to know what the other person's circumstances are. If we don't know someone is hungry, we cannot think, "Well, if I were hungry, I would want someone to offer me food."

The true experts in *ahavas Yisrael* somehow end up being privy to others' hidden needs. Perhaps Hashem shares this information with them because He knows that they will rise to the occasion.

Rabbi Zeev Rothschild was one of those people. He quietly took upon his shoulders burdens that few others even knew about, guided by the words of *Pirkei Avos* (1:15), "Say little and do a lot."

Due to the great chessed organizations of our Jewish communities, there are many places for people to turn for help in times of need. In addition, there are many *askanim* and rabbanim who give their heart and soul to helping their fellow Jew. However, there are people who are on the fringes of the community, who don't feel comfortable knocking on the door of an *askan* or Rav. There are also those with challenges that don't fall within the scope of the regular community organizations.

Who do those people have to help them? Who is able to love them "*kamocha*," understanding their need and knowing how to fulfill it? For many in Lakewood and no doubt, beyond, Rabbi Rothschild was that person. Here is one instance this writer witnessed personally:

> *My wife had a friend who had become extremely anxious about a flurry of legal actions being taken against Lakewood families. Innocent people were being targeted, and she worried that despite having done nothing wrong, her family could be next. She confided in my wife that her anxiety was keeping her awake at night. My wife told me about the situation, and I wished I had some way of allaying the woman's fears.*
>
> *I thought of R' Zeev Rothschild. I knew his name as a major askan who was involved in helping to stop the witch hunt that was going on, and I decided to call him. We had no prior connection whatsoever, but he picked up my call and listened as I explained the situation. He told me that someone he needed to speak to had just walked in, and he would call me back in 10 minutes.*
>
> *Rarely does someone as sought after as Rabbi Rothschild call back. It's almost assumed that the caller will have to keep trying until the askan has a few spare moments to talk. But that wasn't Rabbi Rothschild. Ten minutes later, the phone rang. He told me to relate to my wife's friend that the problem had been solved. There would be no more arrests and she could relax. "If she's still nervous, tell her she can come to my house at 8:00 tonight and I will personally assure her."*
>
> *He was there for every unprotected Jew. He answered their calls and he called them back. If you were a Jew in trouble, he was there. For the person without "protektzia" he was the connection.*

Later, the author was privy to another glimpse of the lengths to which "*kamocha*" can go.

> *I was talking to someone who I knew had no parnassah. I asked him how he managed to care for his large family. He told me the bank had put his house up for auction because he had fallen far behind in his mortgage payments, but Rabbi Rothschild attended the auction and bought the house. "He lets me live there rent-free," the man told me. "He also lets me take $2,000 worth of groceries a month from his store (NPGS in Lakewood) to feed my family."*

An essential point to understand about *baalei* chessed such as Rabbi Rothschild, and Rabbi Gissinger of whom we read earlier, is that their love of chessed is an expression of their love of Torah and mitzvos. They do chessed with love to serve Hashem to the very best of their abilities, just as they learn Torah and keep every other mitzvah with energy and a passion to do so properly, down to the last detail. Rabbi Rothschild was a *talmid chacham,* an expert in many areas of halachah including *shechitah, mikvaos,* matzah and kashrus. The grocery chain he founded never compromised where there was the slightest question of kashrus. In his chessed, he held himself to the same standard.

It is no wonder that our *gedolim* in Torah are *gedolim* in chessed.

# You're Included!

I t is a human need that starts in nursery school and continues until old age. We might think we should outgrow it, but somehow, we never do. What is this persistent desire in the human heart?

It is the need to feel included in whatever social circle we happen to find ourselves in. Shul, a *shiur*, a classroom, a school event, a community *simchah*, a family gathering — no matter where we are, there are the people to whom everyone gravitates. Introvert or extrovert, no one feels good standing on the sidelines watching the popular people and their friends interacting with each other, looking so comfortable, so natural.

A person might be right there in the circle with everyone else, but no one seems interested in what he has to say. No one asks his opinion. He cannot even find an opening in which to say a word or two. He feels invisible, uninteresting, disconnected; if he vanished into thin air, no one would realize he was missing.

Drawing people into the circle, showing them that they count, is a chessed with an unquantifiable potential reward. We learn this from the life of Rav Yaakov Edelstein, the chief rabbi of Ramat Hasharon. In a recently translated biography, we learn of a conversation between Rav Edelstein and the great *posek* Rav Shmuel Wosner, in which Rav Wosner asked him to disclose the secret of his power of *tefillah*. Rav Edelstein was known as someone whose prayers were answered.

At first, Rav Edelstein dismissed the idea that he had any special power, but Rav Wosner persisted. Finally, he suggested that Hashem was treating him *middah k'neged middah*. Any Jew with a burden to share knew he would receive Rav Edelstein's undivided attention for as long as necessary. Since he patiently listened to Hashem's children, he surmised, Hashem patiently listened to him.

One of the remarkable expressions of his care for his fellow Jew was in his extreme sensitivity to anyone in his surroundings who seemed to feel out of place. As a community Rav, he interacted with Jews of all types, from those frum-from-birth and *baalei teshuvah* to those completely non-religious. However, even when he was surrounded by *gedolim*, he made sure everyone felt included. Two stories from Rav Edelstein's biography illustrate what it means to give each Jew a place of honor in our circle:

> A man recalled that, as a newly arrived 12-year-old immigrant from France, his father brought him along to Rav Edelstein's son's wedding. The room was packed with gedolim, as well as the Rav's family and friends. The boy stood against a wall feeling completely out of place.
>
> At that time, the Rav had been injured in a car accident and was walking with crutches. Although it was his own son's wedding and hundreds of people were there to honor him and share the simchah, Rav Edelstein's eyes zeroed in on the boy standing by the wall. On his crutches, he made his way over to his young guest.
>
> "Thank you so much for coming to the chasunah," the Rav told the boy. "I would really appreciate if you could come and sit at my table with me." The boy did the Rav this "favor," and the Rav indeed spent time with him as if he were the most honored guest. The boy later related that he had been having major difficulties

*adjusting to life in Eretz Yisrael and this episode was the turning point that eased his entire transition.*

As great as it is to be expansive and concerned for every guest's comfort at a *simchah,* the achievement rises to a new level when someone exercises that same concern at his time of personal sorrow. Rav Edelstein never lost his focus.

*While sitting shivah for his rebbetzin, Rav Edelstein was surrounded by great rabbanim and roshei yeshivah from across Eretz Yisrael, as well as a wide-ranging swath of Jews from his own community and all over. Those who were at the shivah remarked that he made every person who entered the room feel welcome and comfortable. He gave each one his personal attention even when they were sitting side-by-side with the gedolei hador. No one felt "I don't belong here," no matter who else was in the room at the time.*

Rav Edelstein's life teaches us the value of opening our eyes and noticing who is sitting alone. Who is standing on the sidelines? Who is left out? Who doesn't know anyone at this table? By reaching out with a friendly word or gesture, we can transform the sad feeling of isolation into a happy sense of friendship and belonging.

# You're Included! Part II

Rav Raffi Wolf, who worked closely with Rav Shach for many years, told this story:

*A yeshivah bachur approached Rav Shach with a question. The young man was a talented musician. Since he did not have time to do the vital mitzvah of chessed during his learning hours, he wondered if he might take his instrument to a nearby old-age home and play for the residents once a week.*

*Rav Shach showed him a different perspective. "A bachur thinks that to fulfill the mitzvah of chessed, he has to leave the yeshivah and do chessed somewhere else. But there is so much chessed for a bachur to do right here. How many bachurim feel depressed because they're not part of the clique? How many are struggling because they don't understand the Rebbi's shiur? Yeshivah is a goldmine of opportunities to do chessed!"*

Children who are blessed with popularity among their peers have been gifted with an opportunity to utilize their blessing for its true purpose, and to ensure that it will be theirs for a lifetime. They have the power to bring other children into the group, to draw them close and give them value in others' eyes.

This is much more important than simply enabling quieter, less popular children to enjoy school more. It can actually save their spiritual lives. The author illustrates this by relating this true incident, told to him by his brother-in-law:

> When my brother-in-law was in eighth grade, he encountered another boy in the class as he was walking. This boy had been struggling; yeshivah was not going well for him. On meeting my brother-in-law, he announced, "I'm finished with yeshivah. I'm not going back ever again."
>
> My brother-in-law asked what had caused him to say this.
>
> "Today at recess, I was talking with a few boys about some random topic, and I gave my opinion," the boy related. "One of the boys said, 'Who are you? Your opinion isn't worth anything.' Nobody argued with him. Everyone seemed to agree. So if in my yeshivah, my opinion isn't worth anything to anyone, what am I doing there?"

This boy abandoned Torah and mitzvos for years. *Baruch Hashem* he eventually returned, but the story points out the truth of *Chazal's* statement, "*oh chavrusa oh misusa* — either a friend or death." Each school, each yeshivah, each classroom is, as Rav Shach pointed out, "a goldmine" of opportunity for our children to draw each other in, lift each other up and give each other life.

They need not look elsewhere for a chance to do chessed, because the awareness they will build simply by looking out for each other will train them for a lifetime of *ahavas Yisrael*. If we want them to merit the *berachos* brought by chessed, this is the most direct road to follow.

# The Reset Button

A well-known phenomenon among people at odds with each other is this: Their feud goes on for so long that they forget why they are at war. Sometimes the situation doesn't even rise to the level of a dispute; there's simply a coldness between two people. They think of the other as "not a friend," even though they cannot pinpoint a reason.

A true story that occurred one year at the end of the summer illustrates how easy it can be to repair long, drawn-out antagonism.

*Two men had been enmeshed in a dispute with each other and were no longer on speaking terms. One of the men went away for the summer, and the two men did not see each other for a full two months. When the summer was over, the man returned home. On his first Shabbos back in shul, he saw his "enemy" and without thinking, said "Shalom aleichem." The other man stared at him for a second, wondering if the words were meant for him. Then he responded, "Aleichem shalom. How was your summer?"*

*The two men exchanged a few more words and after davening, continued their conversation.*

What happened here? The first man "forgot to be mad." He had been away for two months and had fallen out of practice. For two months, he hadn't looked away when the man walked by him in shul. He hadn't ignored him when he saw him at a *simchah*. Neither man had rubbed salt in his own or the other man's wound for two whole months.

This leaves us wondering what happened to the affront that caused the falling-out. If it had been so outrageous that two neighbors stopped talking to each other, how could it have lost its sting? The episode proves that very often, we remain in a *machlokes* because it becomes "what we do," like a holy *minhag* we dare not breach. In this case, when circumstances caused the man to curtail his "custom" of snubbing his neighbor, he fell out of the habit and reverted to his previous, more ingrained habit of greeting him. After breaking the ice, the men found that their relationship was not difficult to repair.

This episode took place in Elul, an ideal time for "forgetting to be mad." In fact, there are many times of year that open a door for us to reach out to people with whom we've fallen into a *machlokes,* or to warm up our relationship with someone who, for no particular reason, seems distant. Here are some opportune occasions:

1. Purim, when we can send *mishloach manos* as a gesture of friendship.
2. Rosh Hashanah and Yom Kippur, an appropriate time for asking and giving *mechilah.*
3. A *simchah,* when we can send a gift or food.

The point is that sometimes — often, in fact — it's not the issue that keeps the *machlokes* alive, but rather, it's a rut into which we've fallen. We can climb out of that rut, and when we do, we give ourselves a new lease on life. Our negative emotions are no longer pumping their poison into our system. Furthermore, we protect ourselves and our children from one of the most destructive forces in existence. As the Torah illustrates for us through the episode of Korach, when people instigate *machlokes,* even their innocent children can be swept up in the tragedies they bring upon themselves.

The calendar is replete with occasions to press the reset button and become the friends and brothers we are meant to be. Why not make the most of these golden opportunities?

# Staying Power

Astudent of Rav Shmuel Auerbach was once visiting the home of a widow. On the dining room wall was a large portrait of his rebbi. He wondered why the woman was so prominently displaying the picture, and so he asked her what her connection was to Rav Shmuel.

She explained. "I have been a widow for 17 years. When I first lost my husband, people were concerned about me. I was left with a house full of children and they realized I would need help. However, as time went on, fewer and fewer people called. They forgot about me and went on with their lives, assuming I was managing.

"But Rav Shmuel Auerbach, for the past 17 years, has called me every Erev Shabbos. He doesn't just wish me good Shabbos, but he asks me how my children are doing, if everything is okay, if I need any money, if my kids need any help. He is a steady source of inspiration for me, and he is keeping me alive."

The ongoing concern the Rav had for this widow is a lesson for us. In our times, we have developed a decidedly short attention span. Perhaps it is a result of the relentless flow of information that comes our way. Before we absorb the facts of one situation, another one is on the way. It may be that our compassion for others enters our mind, but not our heart. We know we should do something to help someone, and we do it. Then we check it off as "done." However, we have not let this person's dilemma enter our heart. If it did, we would not be able to forget his or her suffering the minute we write the check or make the phone call or do the favor.

Rav Shmuel felt the widow's void, and as long as she felt it, he felt it. He continued to console and help her because she continued to need consolation and help. Therefore, the chessed wasn't checked off as "done."

By seeing chessed as a person and his needs, rather than as an obligation to fulfill, we are far more likely to make chessed a way of life, as the Chofetz Chaim tells us we must. He quotes the Gemara (*Bava Basra* 9b) on *Mishlei* (21:21), which says that a person who "runs after" *tzedakah* and chessed, "*yimtza chaim* — he will find life."

The Chofetz Chaim asks why the *pasuk* uses the expression "run." He answers that "running after" chessed means that a person is engaged in it constantly. He cannot afford to let up because the prosecutor never lets up. Every day, we commit sins and every day, he stands ready to prosecute. Therefore, our pursuit of chessed must be constant. In this way, we are saved from health crises, accidents and calamities. Every day that we're alive, that we don't suffer a heart attack or a car accident, is a day we are benefiting from Hashem's attribute of *rachamim*. By keeping in our heart the needs of our fellow Jews and running after the opportunities we have to help them, we maintain this plentiful flow of Hashem's compassion. When we run toward chessed, we run away from disaster and instead, we "find life."

# 59

# *Hit the Bull's Eye*

W hen the Satmar Rebbe came to America after World War II, one burning mission he hoped to accomplish was to establish a Satmar school system from the ground up, for every child of every age. That ambitious plan required an abundant flow of money, but the Satmar Rebbe, whose anti-Zionist views rankled many American Jews, was not in a good position to solicit funds. Instead, he appointed executives to undertake the task, and expected them to pour their heart and soul into it.

However, even without actively raising funds, millions of dollars of "kvitlach money" came into the Satmar Rebbe's hands, given by those who sought his berachos and guidance. He transferred this money directly into the hands of the needy. It was never even transferred to a bank account. Someone who needed food, someone who needed to make a wedding, someone whose rent had fallen into arrears — these were the people who received the money.

Had he diverted even some of the kvitlach money to support the

*Torah institutions he was devoted, heart and soul, to building, he would never have had to struggle to achieve his dream. However, the Rebbe's burning passion to build his Torah institutions never overshadowed his concern for the troubles of each individual Jew. He would never allow a Jew to suffer as long as there was money in his possession that could ease their suffering.*

Today, *baruch Hashem,* our communities abound with institutions of Torah education for our children. Although many of them must still work hard to survive financially, most manage to support themselves through tuitions, generous donors, and fundraising events.

However, none of this helps to mitigate the pressure on the individual families that must pay tuition for their children. When the end of August rolls around and parents prepare to send their children back to school, many are faced with the dilemma of unpaid bills from previous years.

For the average family, the situation is almost unavoidable. Let's consider a family with six children in school — four in elementary school, a boy in yeshivah and a girl in high school. Tuition bills for this family, living in Lakewood, are going to be in the range of $30,000. If they are bringing in a combined salary of $100,000 — considered a healthy middle-class income in New Jersey — they are left with $70,000. This must cover everything else — food, gas, rent/mortgage, clothing, medical expenses, insurances, camp, *simchos* and more. For so many families, the math simply doesn't work.

This means pressure. This means unpaid bills, letters from the school, frantic efforts to borrow, forestall, work out a deal — whatever it takes to enable their children to get on the bus with their peers on the first day of school. We might think such scenarios are out of the ordinary, but unless all our friends are millionaires, each of us knows at least one family in this position. As the Satmar Rebbe taught us, when we help alleviate this kind of personal suffering, our *tzedakah* money hits the bull's eye.

As we receive our welcome packets for our children's schools, filled with supply lists, schedules, calendars, rules and school policies, we need to stop and think: What's happening with that family across the street? Does their son avoid the question when asked, "Who's your rebbi this year?" Does the mother ask to borrow your daughter's supply list because hers hasn't come?

Supporting our *mosdos* is a beautiful and important use of our *tzedakah* money. However, *mosdos* can hire fundraisers. They can run parlor meetings and Chinese auctions. The family across the street will not, can not, and does not.

They are suffering, and if we have *tzedakah* to give, we can help to alleviate that suffering and all the shame that comes along with it. All we need to do is call the school in which their children are enrolled and offer to pay as much of their arrears as we are capable of paying. The school can send the parents a receipt, no explanation necessary, and remove a boulder from their hearts.

# Right Number

Rav Elimelech Biderman related this story, which he heard directly from the Rav involved:

*The Rav of a Boro Park shul went to the mountains for a summer vacation. While there, he wanted to call someone who was also staying in the area. Scrolling through the contacts on his phone, he mistakenly selected the wrong number. It belonged to a member of his shul, a divorced man with no children.*

*The Rav's first impulse was to cut off the call, since he had no real reason to contact the man. However, his second impulse was that perhaps Hashem had a reason for him to make this mistake. He let the phone ring, and he noticed that the ring sounded strange — like the ring a caller hears when calling overseas. He wondered where he was calling and what time it was in that location. Maybe he should hang up… but no, he waited for an answer.*

*The man picked up the call. "Sholom aleichem," said the Rav. "How are you? How is your summer going?"*

*"Well, I happen to be in Italy," the man answered. "Why is*

the Rav calling?" The Rav assured him that he was calling just to check up on the man and say hello. They spoke for a few more minutes and then the man asked again, "Why is the Rav calling?" The Rav assured him that his purpose was "just to touch base." They talked a bit about the man's vacation in Italy and before the Rav concluded the conversation, the man asked him yet again if there was any reason for the call. "No special reason. I was just thinking about you," he said. They said goodbye and hung up.

Two months later, when both the Rav and his congregant had returned to the city, the man told the Rav something that explained the true purpose of the accidental call. "You know that I don't have my parents anymore, and I'm divorced with no children," the man said, "I was in Italy all by myself, and I had some very big nisyonos there. When you called me, I was literally standing at the door of Gehinnom.

"All of a sudden you called and I picked up the phone. You just wanted to see how I was doing. I said to myself, 'There's somebody in the world who cares about me. My Rav cares about me.' You should know that you saved my life."

Rav Elimelech Biderman commented that this story illustrates the inestimable value of a phone call. We may never become aware of our impact, as this Rav did when he learned of the outcome of his call. Calling to give someone a little positive attention, to show some concern and offer some encouragement, can change their day. It can change their week. It might save their marriage. As we see in this story, it can save their entire spiritual life. People are so very desperate for a little encouragement; we can never tell ourselves that our bit of input doesn't matter.

The second point the story illustrates, says Rav Biderman, is that however lost we may be spiritually, Hashem will send us a lifeline — something to help us choose the right path. Whenever we are feeling alone and lost, we should look for that help. For this man, it was the Rav's "mistaken" phone call. For Yosef HaTzaddik, it was the image of his father Yaakov that enabled him to turn away from sin. The same help is there for all of us; Hashem will never leave us without something to grab onto, something that says, "I'm here! Just reach out!"

In this case, Hashem's lifeline was the Rav's phone call. We can all merit to serve as Hashem's lifeline to those who need something to grab onto, simply by taking the time to make a call.

# Equal Time

A person walks into a bar mitzvah kiddush after davening. He heads straight to the baal simchah to wish him a mazal tov, but the baal simchah is in the midst of a conversation with a few other men. The person stands on the sidelines until at last, the baal simchah breaks off from his group and looks at him. "Mazal tov!" the guest says. "Thanks for coming!" The baal simchah replies. "Enjoy!" Then he turns back to the conversation.

The person walks away feeling a bit rejected. He understands the host's challenge, having to acknowledge and give a little attention to all his guests, but he is hurt nevertheless.

Let's imagine if instead, the host said, "Great to see you. Let me introduce you to my cousins. We were just talking about the Rav's *devar Torah*. Maybe you know the answer to our question...." The guest's experience would have been completely different.

Here is another scenario:

*Moshe, an elderly man, is sitting shivah for his sister. Tova, the second cousin of Moshe's wife, comes with her husband Avi to be menachem avel. The room is filled with Moshe's many extended family members, most of whom had never met Tova and Avi. Moshe says, "These are our cousins Tova and Avi, for anyone who doesn't know them. It's so nice... everyone in this room is family."*

What could have been an awkward situation in which Tova and Avi felt out of place among a close family group instead became welcoming and comfortable. Being acknowledged, introduced and identified as "family" made all the difference.

We look at these situations as examples of social skills or people skills. Some people seem to know how to draw others in and make them comfortable. However, this is infinitely more than a social skill. It is a mitzvah of chessed that Rav Elyashiv treated with greatest care.

*For many years, Rav Elyashiv spent all of Purim, from the moment he finished hearing megillah and distributing mishloach manos and matanos l'evyonim, secluded in a room in the home of his daughter and son-in-law, Rav Ezriel Auerbach. He would sit and learn with special fire and intensity the entire day.*

*However, it had not always been that way. There had been a time in the past when Rav Elyashiv would remain at home on Purim, receiving mishloach manos and greeting visitors, from the greatest Torah figures to the simplest Jews. Each person would be granted a few moments of his attention. Many brought shailos with them, which, with his quick mind and vast breadth of knowledge, he would answer on the spot.*

*Then one year, this practice stopped, even though receiving visitors and mishloach manos are mitzvos of the day. Years later, his family members explained why.*

He had always stressed to his family that when people came to bring *mishloach manos*, everyone should be extremely careful to make them feel welcome and honored. This was of the utmost importance to him. However, when answering their *shailos* and engaging visitors in discussion, there would sometimes be discrepancies in the amount of time each visitor received. One person's question took 30 seconds to answer, another's took a minute. Many visitors were respected rabbanim themselves, and yet, Rav Elyashiv worried that those who were answered more briefly would feel slighted. They would feel as if they didn't matter as much to the Rav, that they were not as close to him as someone who received more time.

So unacceptable was this to the Rav that he constantly kept track of the time he spent with each person. The process was exhausting and stressful, and ultimately, he could no longer bear the strain. Sitting cloistered with his learning for 18 hours, his heart and mind immersed in the Torah's holy words, was nowhere near as difficult! Rather than handle the explosive possibility of slighting someone, he removed himself from the situation.

We learn from this that it's not enough to just avoid actively excluding or slighting people. It's not enough to just not do wrong. We have to be aware of how we allot our time and attention. Who is standing on the sidelines waiting to be drawn in? Who is getting the message that their presence isn't important? It's our mitzvah to make sure that we don't cause anyone such pain.

If Rav Elyashiv worried that *gedolim* and *talmidei chachamim* might come to feel rejected, we can assume that no one is invulnerable. We're all human. We all need to feel that others are interested in us, in our presence and in what we have to say. Acknowledgment is a commodity so precious that Rav Elyashiv measured it by the second.

# The Golden Years

Choni HaMe'aggel experienced a waking nightmare. The Gemara (*Taanis* 23a) relates that the famous *Tanna* woke up after a 70-year sleep and discovered that there was no living person who believed he was who he claimed to be. His grandson didn't believe him. Those learning in the *beis hamedrash* didn't believe him. Despite the many amazing stories surrounding his earlier life, 70 years later he was unable to prove to anyone that he was this same revered figure.

The Gemara says that because he was not being treated with any respect, the only alternative, in his mind was to leave the world. He *davened* for Hashem to take his life. The Gemara then comments that people say: "*oh chavrusa, oh misusa* — either a friend or death." *Rashi* explains that this means, "Either a friend who shows me respect or death."

We've already discussed many times the concept that a person's will to live is tied to the respect and acknowledgment he receives from those around him. However, Choni HaMe'aggel's story adds another dimension; he was well known, respected, accomplished and venerated in the years before his long sleep. All that seems to dissipate as if it never existed when he wakes up 70 years later.

If we would survey 100 elderly people, we might find that they feel much like Choni HaMe'aggel. Once they slow down physically, and especially if they slow down mentally, all their years as sharp-minded, energetic men and women seem to vanish. People looking at them don't see the veteran first-grade morah or the busy mother and Bubby upon whom dozens of children and grandchildren depended. They don't see the businessman whose hard work supported his family, or the high school rebbi who influenced hundreds of *bachurim.*

People just see "old." They will come and offer a warm hello at a *simchah,* and maybe even converse for a moment or two, but they're looking to move on. They don't expect an interesting conversation to ensue. The family will seat the grandmother in the middle of the *kallah's* dance circle at a wedding, but when the dance is over, she is sitting alone, watching the *simchah* from her empty table.

Even at more intimate family gatherings, the conversation often flows above and around the older members of the family. Sometimes there's a physical reason, such as hearing loss or cognitive issues. Sometimes, when everyone is enjoying their time together, talking about the things that interest them, there's little thought to the grandparents sitting quietly eating their soup.

It's almost as if the past 70 years of their lives have been erased and no one recognizes them anymore. This, as the Gemara implies, can do as much damage to their grasp on life as any ailment.

The revitalizing power of reaching out to older people with sincere interest and respect is immense. Whether they are our own elders or someone else's, we can accomplish so much by engaging them in conversation. They have a long lifetime of experience and knowledge to share. We can ask about life in the times in which they grew up and raised their families. We can ask about their careers, or any pursuits that occupy them in the present. We can talk in learning to men who are still learning. We can discuss recipes with women who still know how to cook and bake, or who have some recipe secrets to share.

Whatever we do and however we do it, the aim of our chessed is to recognize that this is the same person he was many years ago, when he was making his mark on the world. A little recognition goes a long way. Sometimes a visit, a phone call or a conversation can be the highlight of an otherwise empty day.

We've learned throughout this book that Hashem treats us as we treat others, *middah k'neged middah*. This is especially true regarding the way we treat our elders, because we teach our children by example. The more we show our parents, grandparents and great-grandparents sincere interest and respect, bringing out their strengths and valuing their words, the more our children will absorb this value. The respect we give will someday become the respect we receive.

# 63

# A Correct Correction

Rav in Eretz Yisrael once ruled on a question of halachah using a certain leniency. The question was whether a certain melachah could be performed on Yom Tov Sheini shel Galuyos, and this Rav said it was permitted. When Rav Avrohom Genachovsky heard this Rav's decision, he declared it to be mistaken.

Rav Genachovsky was an expert on all aspects of halachah, and an expert on gemilus chassadim as well. He knew the Rav's mistake needed to be corrected, but knew it had to be done deftly, so as not to deflate his self-respect. Rav Genachovsky consulted the Steipler about the issue. "Clearly the melachah is not permitted, and the Rav needs to be corrected," the Steipler told him.

A student who was very close to Rav Genachovsky wondered how he would manage to make the correction without hurting the Rav's feelings. When he saw Rav Genachovsky take out a piece of paper to write the Rav a letter, he supposed that the strategy would be to start out with great accolades for the Rav's Torah knowledge and then point out that he had made one error.

*However, Rav Genachovsky wrote something else entirely. He wrote that he had heard that the Rav had ruled that the melachah in question was not permitted, and he wanted to compliment him on his astute ruling and assure him that he was correct. He included the fact that the Shulchan Aruch confirmed his ruling, and that the Steipler had confirmed it as well.*

What would this Rav's reaction be to Rav Genachovsky's letter? He would have thought that the *gadol* misheard his ruling, believing that he said the opposite of what he said. He would have also absorbed the compliment conveyed in the letter; the great Rav Genachovsky thought well of him and reached out to contact him! But at the same time, he would have learned of his mistake and been grateful that his incorrect ruling could be corrected. His mistake was addressed without him ever having to feel the shame of a great *posek* pointing it out to him, even in the kindest way.

This story awakens us to a stumbling block we may not be careful enough to avoid. That is the way in which we correct people. People sometimes feel that when someone does something wrong, this is the time to let them know what is wrong with them. "You should be more careful." "You should have paid attention." "You need to think before you speak." But there is no need to rub salt in the wound when somebody makes a mistake. This is true with employees, students or children, and especially so when we're speaking to a spouse or a parent. Chessed means handling the situation the way we would want our own mistake to be handled — with the least possible amount of pain and embarrassment and the most possible protection of our dignity.

# 64

# The Gift in Your Passenger Seat

Every day, Aharon makes the long commute from Lakewood to Brooklyn where he works. He listens to shiurim and music to keep his mind occupied, and difficult as the routine is, he enjoys the time to himself. It's a little refuge between his busy household and his hectic office.

Then his neighbor calls him. He is the young father of a large family, and recently began teaching elementary school at a yeshivah in Brooklyn. His pay is barely adequate, and commuting costs take a big bite out of his tight budget. He asks, "Could I get a ride home with you on Mondays and Thursdays? I'd be happy to split the tolls."

Aharon knows he has to say "yes." There's no real reason to say "no," except that he doesn't want company. He soon regrets his decision because this young man loves to talk. Furthermore, he doesn't talk about anything that interests Aharon. Aharon feels as if his mind is taken captive for an hour and a half every time the young man gets into the car.

But he works on developing a different attitude. "I'm saving *this family a lot of money by giving him a ride. Hashem gave me the chance to do a Jew a big favor, and I'm doing it. I might as well do it happily."*

What Aharon doesn't know is that he is doing himself an even bigger favor. The *Zohar* in *Parashas Vayeira* teaches that if, *chas v'shalom,* a person is due some punishment for his sins, Hashem can send that person a "gift" in the form of a poor person in need of *tzedakah* or *chessed.* The gift is an expression of Hashem's love for the person, reflecting His desire to help him save himself from pain.

If the person accepts the gift, his kind deed becomes "imprinted" on his body. When the prosecuting *malach* approaches the person and sees this imprint, he flees, and the person is saved.

Imagine how we would react to that annoying individual who comes to us for a ride or a loan or some other favor, yet again, if we knew that he was a gift from Hashem. If we knew that a danger lay ahead for us, and by helping this person we are able to bypass the danger without ever knowing what awaited us, we would be seeking out difficult *gemilus chassadim* to take on. We'd be calling up the lonely guest who dominates our Shabbos table with long, pointless commentaries and inviting him for a seudah. We'd be offering a ride to the person who takes the opportunity to ask us a barrage of personal questions. We'd be volunteering to babysit for the neighbor's child who needs non-stop attention. If we saw illness, accidents, disputes and other misfortunes looming in the distance, and they dissipated like clouds when we grasped these acts of chessed, how different our perspective would be!

Through the story of Rabbi Akiva's daughter, the Gemara (*Shabbos* 156b) teaches us that chessed has the power to overcome bad *mazal.* Rabbi Akiva was told by astrologers that his daughter would die on her wedding day. Although he worried about the prediction, her *chasunah* took place. That night, she removed a long hair pin and stuck it into a crevice in the wall for safekeeping. In the morning, when she withdrew the pin, she found a dead snake attached to it. The pin had apparently killed the poisonous snake, which was lying in wait for her.

When she showed this to her father, he asked her, "What did you do at your *chasunah*?" She answered that a poor man had come to the wedding and called out, but nobody noticed him. However, she did, and she gave him her portion of food. Hearing this, Rabbi Akiva concluded that *tzedakah* not only saves a person from an unusual death, but from death itself.

The decree on Rabbi Akiva's daughter was so powerful that protection could only come from an equally powerful chessed. A *kallah*, consumed with the joy and excitement of her wedding day, might be the last person we would expect to notice a beggar, and go so far as to feed him her portion of food. Rabbi Akiva's daughter accepted the beggar graciously, not realizing that she was accepting Hashem's wedding gift to her.

This is a perspective that can help us overcome our irritation when people seem to demand a bit too much from us. They might be the best gift we could ever ask for.

# For Shalom Bayis

Rav Naftali Amsterdam was one of Rav Yisrael Salanter's greatest talmidim. At one point in his life, he decided to work on breaking himself completely of any hint of gaavah — arrogance. As part of his self-training in humility, he stopped wearing clothing befitting of his stature as a gadol hador, and instead donned clothing worn by the simplest of Jews.

Rav Naftali's wife was bothered by her husband's new image. She approached his rebbi, Rav Yisrael Salanter, and expressed her dismay. Later that day, Rav Salanter engaged Rav Naftali in a discussion about the mitzvah of chessed. After delving into the meaning of the mitzvah, Rav Salanter said, "So we understand that if the mitzvah of chessed is to make someone else happy, then we don't work on our humility at the expense of hurting our wife's feelings." Rav Naftali Amsterdam immediately stopped wearing his "humble" clothes.

Our desire to grow in *middos* and *avodas Hashem* is one of the most precious traits of a Jew. We're always reaching higher, striving to overcome our *yetzer hara* and feel a closer connection to Hashem.

However, as Rav Yisrael Salanter taught his venerable *talmid* in this story, if we are adopting a *chumrah*, stringency, as our path to growth, we need to take into consideration whether that stringency will come at the cost of our *shalom bayis*. Chessed is not a *chumrah*; it is a Torah obligation. By taking on a *chumrah* that upsets or inconveniences our spouse, we're losing a mitzvah.

*Gedolim* see the situation clearly, as this story illustrates:

> An Israeli policeman became a baal teshuvah and began wearing tzitzis. Since he was Ashkenazi, he followed the custom of the tzitzis being visible on the outside. However, his superiors insisted that while he was in uniform, the tzitzis needed to be tucked in. If he would not conform with the rules, said the officer, then he would lose his job. The policeman consulted with a Sefardi rabbi, who told him that according to the Shulchan Aruch, he was permitted to wear his tzitzis tucked in. This is the Sefardi custom.
>
> However, the policeman wasn't happy with this answer. He felt that since he was Ashkenazi, he should rightfully go according to Ashkenazi custom. He decided to ask an Ashkenazi rabbi, and if he was told to wear his tzitzis on the outside, he would do it, even if it cost him his job. He was ready to sacrifice for the mitzvah, come what may.
>
> However, when he brought his question to Rav Elyashiv, he discovered that there was more to the decision than Sefardi-Ashkenazi. "How will your wife feel if you lose your job?" the Rav asked him. "Not good," the policeman admitted. "She'll be apprehensive about our parnassah."
>
> "Then you can tuck your tzitzis in," he said. "You don't have to do something that is not a Torah obligation. It's a custom, and you can follow the Sefardi custom for the sake of shalom bayis."

Sometimes, we can feel disappointed that our spouse doesn't support our great new effort to grow in *avodas Hashem*. We are excited about taking on a new challenge and pushing ourselves to a new level, and our spouse is holding us back! Aren't we supposed to help each other grow? We are; but it could be that in this case, the growing we need to do is in the area of chessed. Often, a *chumrah* that will diminish our spouse's happiness — even a little — is not worthwhile. We should at least ask a competent Rav if we're not sure what our priority should be in a particular situation.

Besides not adopting a *chumrah* that our spouse objects to outright, we need to also consider if it might cause extra work or inconvenience that our spouse may not even mention. Rav Aharon Leib Shteinman surely had a wife who supported his *avodas Hashem* at the very highest levels. However, he was careful not to adopt practices that would burden her. One example of this surfaced after his wife passed away. As Pesach approached, he called upon his grandchildren to help him collect and store the water he would be using on Yom Tov. This was a *minhag* he had never kept, but now, at age 90, he wanted to begin. When his grandchildren asked him why, he replied that it required gathering great quantities of water in buckets and tubs — an arduous task that he knew would have fallen on his wife. Therefore, during all the years of his marriage, he put aside his desire to follow this custom.

We see from this story that greatness does not always mean adopting every stringency. We have to internalize the idea that when our *chumrah* causes our spouse toil, worry, or any other source of pain, we might very well be getting lost along the road to growth.

# Now Is the Time

Aperson wakes up in the morning with a full agenda in front of him. He pictures himself moving along, getting things accomplished, and he plunges into action. Then someone calls. The caller needs some help, but the help will take time, and this will result in something else on the man's agenda being left undone. He tells the caller, "I've got a full day today, but I'll be happy to help you tomorrow."

When we approach a request for a chessed in this way, we must ask ourselves if we are setting our priorities in the correct order. A story of Rav Shach, told by the *mashgiach* in Beth Medrash Govoha, Rav Matisyahu Salomon, shows us how to weigh the situation.

> *One Erev Shabbos, Rav Shach asked a talmid to accompany him in a taxi from Bnei Brak to Yerushalayim. The Rav explained that a bachur who at one time had learned in Rav Shach's yeshivah — Ponevezh — had left learning and was struggling with his Yiddishkeit. The talmid and Rav Shach made the one-hour trip to*

*Yerushalayim, where the bachur lived. When the bachur answered the door, his bare head signaled that he was indeed falling off the path of Torah.*

*"I will go inside and speak with him alone," Rav Shach told his escort. The young man remained outside waiting for an entire hour while Rav Shach engaged the struggling bachur in discussion. When he emerged, he indicated to his talmid that he had failed to get anywhere.*

*Then Rav Shach told the young man that they should hurry and get a bus back to Bnei Brak, as Shabbos was fast approaching. The young man suggested that, given the time, they should take a taxi home, just as they had come. However, Rav Shach deemed it inappropriate to spend the yeshivah's money on the return trip of a failed mission.*

*"Saving 20 minutes getting here was worthwhile," he said, "because if I had been able to help him, that would have meant that he would be out of pain 20 minutes earlier."*

Rav Mattisyahu drew a lesson from Rav Shach's calculation. Even if the young man had been suffering spiritually for months or years, to this *gadol*, saving him 20 minutes of pain was worth the expense. Rav Shach would not allow someone to wallow in his misery so he could save transportation money. When it came to helping the *bachur* out of his situation, Rav Shach would spend the yeshivah's money, but when it came to his own convenience, he would not.

Another well-known incident involving Rav Shach illustrates this point further, pointing out that even when our plan is to spend our time doing a mitzvah, when someone needs our help, we should do our best not to make him wait.

*The night of bedikas chametz, someone saw Rav Shach walking around an apartment building in Yerushalayim. Why was he not home in Bnei Brak, searching for chametz like everyone else? Why was he waiting around, walking up the steps, down the steps and all around?*

*The person who witnessed this scene later found out that a bachur at Ponevezh needed to see a special psychologist in Yerushalayim. The bachur was embarrassed to go alone to the appointment. Therefore, Rav Shach offered to accompany him and wait outside. "I'll be waiting for you the whole time," he assured the boy. And he did.*

We might feel justified in telling someone on Erev Shabbos or *bedikas chometz* night or even when we're busy with work, "I'll help you later." However, Rav Shach knew that when the giver says "later," the one in need must endure his situation for longer. He is left in doubt and pain. Will the person actually help? Will the help actually solve the problem? If we have the power in our hands to end his long hours or days of suffering, why not do it?

*One summer, a man was going through a difficult time, and he reached out to a few people, hoping someone would help. Because people were out of town, he had difficulty finding anyone with whom to speak. His troubles continued to churn in his mind and keep him on edge. Then, a well-respected Rav from his hometown called him. "I heard you've been trying to reach me," he told the man. "I will be away in the mountains for the next few days, but when I come back, I am going to help you."*

*The man later commented that his Shabbos was of a completely different quality than it would have been without that call. Someone heard his plea for help and was there for him.*

We see from this story that even if we truly cannot help right away, we can call back right away. We can acknowledge the person who is turning to us for help and not leave him wondering if we're thinking, "Oh, him again! I'll ignore him and see if he goes away." Whatever we are able to do, we should do as soon as possible. This alone, apart from the substance of the help we might give, is a significant chessed.

# Don't Keep Them Waiting

The *Mechilta* (*Mishpatim* 18) relates the following incident:

*The Romans were leading Rabbi Yishmael and Rabbi Shimon to be executed. Rabbi Shimon told Rabbi Yishmael, "My heart bothers me that I do not know why I am being killed."*

*Rabbi Yishmael said to Rabbi Shimon, "Did it ever happen to you that a person came to you for a ruling or with a shailah, and you pushed him off until you finished drinking your 'kos' (tea or some other drink), or fixed your shoe or finished putting on your tallis? If so, then the Torah says, 'Im aneh s'aneh oso… — If you afflict him… My anger will be aroused and I will slay you with the sword and your wives will be widows and your children orphans'"* (Shemos 22:22-23).

*The pasuk Rabbi Yishmael cited repeats the word meaning affliction — "aneh." The Mechilta there explains the repetition of the word means not only a major affliction, but a minor affliction as well. After Rabbi Yishmael directed Rabbi Shimon to consider this question, Rabbi Shimon answered him, "You have comforted me."*

For a *tzaddik* on the level of Rabbi Shimon, there was comfort in understanding why he warranted death. He understood that for him, causing someone to wait even a moment for the opportunity to clarify an issue that was troubling him — for someone to feel that he wasn't important enough to receive the great man's attention — was a grievous failure. On our own level, we can learn from this *Mechilta* the extraordinary importance of giving our attention to those who call upon us.

In an earlier lesson, we discussed the example set by Rabbi Zeev Rothschild, in taking up the cause of those who had no one to advocate for them. This selfless dedication also showed itself in the care he took to make sure no one was left hanging; no one who put in a call to Reb Zeev had to clamor for his attention.

Leon Goldenberg, CEO of Goldmont Realty, worked with Reb Zeev to save Shalom Torah Centers, a *kiruv* school in New Jersey that had fallen into a difficult financial situation. He recalls that the only time Reb Zeev interrupted a meeting was to take a call from an individual experiencing a difficult time. At the end of each day, Reb Zeev would answer each and every email before he would go to sleep. This was all the more remarkable because Reb Zeev was one of the founders of the *k'vasikin minyan* of Beth Medrash Govoha in Lakewood, which *davens* at the earliest possible time of morning.

Reb Zeev would not allow the possibility that someone who called him for help would feel unwanted or neglected. However, so many well-meaning people let this happen without even realizing they are doing so. Someone who is in a sensitive emotional state because his life is not going well can interpret a delayed response or no response as, "What are you worth? Who are you?"

In our times, causing people to wait for a response has become almost a norm to be expected. "If you need me, you call me. If I need you, I'll call you." People feel that we should realize that they are busy and if we want to reach them, we must take the initiative to keep calling. For Rabbi Shimon, making someone wait a few minutes while he finished his tea or tied his shoelaces had disastrous consequences.

For us, on our level, the standards are not that strict; we lack that level of sensitivity. However, we have to be aware that when someone calls upon us, they are waiting anxiously for our response. The right way to do chessed is to alleviate their anxiety at the first available moment.

This doesn't mean we have to present an instant solution. People begin to feel better the moment someone calls them back, even if the message is that they will not be able to take steps to help them until some later time. Just knowing that they're being acknowledged and that their situation matters to the other person gives them comfort.

If we make it our business to do this, as Reb Zeev did, we will find that *middah k'neged middah,* Hashem will do the same for us. He'll answer our call when we need Him. We'll never have to wonder if we matter, and we'll never have to wonder if He's listening.

# Non-Stop Chessed;
# Non-Stop Protection

We know from *Chazal* in *Parashas Noach* (see *Rashi, Bereishis* 6:13) and from many horrific episodes of our history that when Hashem lets loose the powers of destruction because of the abundance of sin in the world, the good may be swept away with the evil. However, in the most sweeping act of destruction ever decreed — the flood in the times of Noach — one family was saved. Everyone and everything on earth was destroyed, and yet Noach's family and the animals they brought aboard the Ark with them emerged unharmed by this world-wide destruction. In today's terms it would be as if one family on all the earth survived a nuclear war.

Clearly, whatever was protecting them had to have been the most powerful protection ever conceived. The *Midrash Shocher Tov* (*Tehillim* 37) reveals what this was, and when we learn this Midrash, we may find ourselves shaken by its implications.

The Midrash explains how Avraham Avinu, our paradigm of chessed, learned the importance of this mitzvah. It relates that

Avraham met Shem, the son of Noach, and asked him by what merit he was saved from the flood. Shem explained that the occupants of the *teivah* merited to be saved because of the *tzedakah* they gave. Avraham responded with surprise. To whom could they have given *tzedakah*? There were no poor people on board. Shem explained that the care and feeding of the animals and birds on the *teivah* was their *tzedakah*. In fact, the *Midrash Rabbah* relates this as well.

However, there is more. Shem goes on to explain the full extent of their chessed: It went on day and night. They did not sleep, but rather, consistently took care of the animals, feeding the diurnal ones during the day and the nocturnal one at night. This was the merit that kept Noach and his family alive. In fact, one time, when Noach arrived a bit late to feed the lion, the animal almost killed him; he became vulnerable because there was a gap in his chessed.

From Shem's answer, Avraham Avinu deduced the following: If Noach's family was saved from the world's worst disaster in the merit of feeding animals, this was a sure sign of how much Hashem cherishes chessed. Moreover, if Hashem so dearly loves and protects those who care for animals, how much more so would He love and protect those who care for people — *bnei adam* created in Hashem's image. Based on this, he determined that if he wanted Hashem to protect him from danger, he should dedicate his life to taking care of Hashem's children. Immediately, he equipped himself for the mitzvah of *hachnassas orchim,* stocking his home with food and drink, and opening his tent to passersby all day and night.

From this Midrash, we learn that protection comes from doing chessed consistently. The Chofetz Chaim discusses this concept in *Sefer Ahavas Chessed,* where he says that to be saved from *chevlei Mashiach* — the upheavals preceding the coming of Mashiach — a person must be *osek* in Torah and *gemilus chassadim.* This means "toiling" in these mitzvos, which means making them our constant priority, being busy with them at all times. Doing chessed is a mitzvah for which we earn exceptional merit, but toiling in chessed is our constant protection in times of trouble.

If we keep this in mind, we will grab an opportunity to do chessed whenever it comes our way. We already discussed the *Zohar's* teaching that if someone, *chas v'shalom*, is subject to a harsh decree, and Hashem loves this person, He sends a poor man to his door. If the person grabs the opportunity to help this poor man, he can avert the decree.

But the *Zohar* says this will happen "if Hashem loves him." Although Hashem loves us all, what happens if for some reason, Hashem does not feel that the individual who is subject to the decree warrants to be spoon-fed his chessed opportunity? The answer is that the person needs to seek opportunities himself. He should look for people who need help and extend himself to help them. In this way, a person can lift the *middas hadin* from himself.

This advice might seem beyond the reach of some people because they are not among others on a regular basis. Some people work at home. Many women have days preoccupied with caring for children and keeping their household functioning. Some elderly people are retired and don't go out often. Where will these constant opportunities for chessed come from?

As we've learned in several lessons throughout this book, the *Rambam* says that the greatest chessed — to give a compliment — is always at our fingertips. This is the greatest way to fulfill the mitzvah of *v'ahavta l'rei'acha kamocha* because this mitzvah requires us to do for others that which we want done for ourselves, and that which every human being most desires is recognition.

Therefore, even someone who rarely leaves home has access to constant opportunities for chessed. A husband or wife can give each other a magnanimous boost with a few words of appreciation. A parent can build a child's sense of self-worth with frequent doses of praise. Workers become happy and loyal when their bosses notice and compliment their hard work. If we can find 7, 10, even 20 opportunities a day to say a kind word to someone, we can acquire the *zechus* to be saved from destructive forces. We can keep ourselves afloat even in the most troubled seas.

# For This I Was Saved

A true incident:

*A young woman was trying with all her emotional and spiritual strength to avoid falling into despair. She was well past the age at which she thought she would be a wife and mother. One after the other, her younger siblings preceded her to the chuppah and became busy with their children and households while her life seemed stuck in a rut.*

*The most painful times for her were Yamim Tovim, when her siblings and their families would gather at her parents' house. As much as she loved her adorable nieces and nephews, she could not deny the pang she felt as she watched the young families interacting. Wanting to be part of the action, she would often prepare a light supper for the small children so their parents could get them into bed before the seudah. Nevertheless, she wasn't the Mommy. She wasn't the one to tuck them in at night. She wasn't the one giving her parents all the nachas, and the pain of her situation was hard to bear.*

*The one satisfaction she had in life was her teaching career. She was a devoted and talented teacher who poured all her energy into bringing Torah to life for her girls. She loved them and they loved her in return.*

*One Succos, this young woman's grandfather came to join the family for Yom Tov. He was a Holocaust survivor, but he never spoke about his experiences. The memories were simply too painful to bring to the surface of his mind. The family respected his wishes and never brought it up.*

*On this particular Yom Tov, the grandfather came home from Simchas Torah davening and sought out this single granddaughter.*

*"You know who I saw in shul?" he asked. "I saw your principal's husband. He told me that it's unbelievable how many neshamos you're touching in your classes. He says you do an incredible job."*

*Then he said something completely unprecedented and unexpected.*

*"I don't talk about the War," he said. "All my siblings, everyone died. So many people died. But Hashem was with me through the concentration camp, and He saved me. And now I know why. It was to have a granddaughter like you — a granddaughter who builds Yiddishe neshamos."*

*These words instantly penetrated the young woman's heart and salved the pain. She wrote about the experience in a magazine, revealing that she was still unmarried, but that her grandfather's words changed her entire outlook on herself and her value. She realized that she was indeed giving her family nachas and bringing them zechusim, no less than the siblings who were raising their families.*

We learn from this story just how mistaken we are when we think of praise as "just words." One of the best investments we can make in our chessed is to think about how we might use a few encouraging words of praise to uplift someone who is down. Let them know what an impact they have — how something they did was a great help, or something they said turned out to be just the right advice, or how well they understand a certain topic or perform a certain skill. A little praise — something real and specific, not general or untrue — can change everything. The woman in the incident above did not only feel better for a minute or a day, but from that moment on.

Rabbi Akiva's students provide us with an example of the flip side of this principle. We know that *Sefiras HaOmer* is a period in which we observe certain aspects of mourning due to the death of these 24,000 students, who would have become the leading lights of Torah in their generation. We cannot fathom the loss of people such as this, the direct students of the great Rabbi Akiva. They could have flooded the world with knowledge of Hashem! However, they died of a plague, as we learn from *Chazal*, because they did not treat each other with proper respect.

Because they lived on a level we cannot even imagine, their flaw was without a doubt something that would not even register today. However, if *Chazal* record this information, they mean for us to learn from it that failing to give honor and respect to another person is serious business.

Expounding on this, the Chofetz Chaim discusses the *Zohar* on *Parashas Metzora*. It teaches that a person is liable for the punishments associated with speaking *lashon hara* if he says nothing negative at all, but simply fails to say something positive when he is in the position to do so. **He failed to say something to make someone feel good when he is in the position to do so.**

We can understand this *Zohar* on a deeper level when we consider the story of the young woman above. What if her grandfather had thought these beautiful, inspiring thoughts about his granddaughter but had left them unsaid? The lifeboat that has been taking her through the ups and downs of her life would never have been created. She would have been left to flounder about, looking for something to keep her going amid a storm of pain and doubt. This is like holding life-saving medicine in our pocket and neglecting to give it to someone who needs it.

As Rabbi Akiva's students prove to us, refraining from *lashon hara* is not enough. We have to show respect for each other, recognize each other's attributes and build each other up. "What you are doing with your life," this grandfather said, "is so important to me. Hashem saw that it was worth saving me just so that you would be born and come into this world and inspire Jewish *neshamos.*"

We can do something similar: It may not be as dramatic and memorable, but it can be just as important. When we tell our parents, children, spouse, workers, teachers, students, neighbors and friends that we're lucky to have them — and why — we are helping them build the lifeboat that will carry them over the rough waters that come along. The *Zohar* is urging us, "When you have something good to say, don't hold back!"

# 70

## There's Only One Solution

Since the devastating outbreak of COVID-19 in 2019, followed by several horrific tragedies in 2021 that hit the Jewish community hard, the sense that "Mashiach must be around the corner" is being voiced by everyone from second graders to great-grandparents. Although we believe that the coming of Mashiach will bring a time of perfect peace, with Hashem recognized by all as the Ruler of the World, we also know from numerous sources that the times leading up to the ultimate *Geulah* will be fraught with dramatic, unusual events.

It's frightening! Even in the times of the Gemara, *Chazal* discussed the dangers that would face the generations living during the times of *chevlei Mashiach*, the "birth-pangs" of Mashiach. In *Sanhedrin* 98b, the students of Rav Elazar ask him what people living in the times of *chevlei Mashiach* could do to protect themselves. His answer: *"Ya'asok b'Torah ub'gemilus chassadim* — You should toil in Torah and in acts of chessed."

Centuries later, according to an account by Rav Boruch Ber Leibowitz (found in the preface to Volume 4 of *Birkas Shmuel*) a delegation came to the Chofetz Chaim to ask him how the Jewish people could protect themselves from the troubles besetting them. The world had become so dangerous. World War I wreaked horrific destruction on the Jews and World War II was lurking around the corner. How could a Jew stay safe?

The Chofetz Chaim said, "If you gather all the *gedolei hador* and ask them what we should do to be saved from the *tzaros* in Klal Yisrael, they will not be able to give you an answer. Even if you go back two generations, three generations — all the way back to the time of the *Rishonim* — they won't be able to tell you what to do to be saved from the *tzaros* in Klal Yisrael. Do you know why? It's because *chevlei Mashiach* has already started, and all of Klal Yisrael's *tzaros* in our times are part of *chevlei Mashiach*. Therefore, you are wasting your time looking for ways to be saved from *tzaros*. There is just one answer, which the *Tanna* Rav Elazar gave his students, and that is to toil in Torah and acts of chessed. There's no other answer."

As mentioned in the introduction, the Chofetz Chaim adds that the word "*osek*" is significant. We understand that a person who learns for 10 minutes a day with little concentration cannot be said to be toiling in Torah. By the same measure, a person who haphazardly does chessed with no passion, forethought, or energy, cannot be said to be toiling in acts of kindness. The toil, he says, is what saves us. But to be "*osek*" implies being occupied with an activity as a businessman is with his business. What happens to people who don't seem to have enough "business opportunities" to keep them busy with chessed? How can they earn their protection? The answer, as the following conversation illustrates, might be right in front of our eyes.

> *A man was speaking to his friend about the financial pressures he was facing. COVID-19 had ruined his business, Pesach was around the corner and he was committed to supporting two of his sons-in-law with $1,200 a month each to enable them to remain in kollel. Not only did he have to buy food for Pesach, but he had to buy plenty of it, because these two sons-in-law and their*

*families would be coming for the sedarim. Normally, all of this would be manageable for this man, but with his business in shreds, the pressure and worry were mounting. He didn't want to renege on his commitments and up-end the lives of the two couples, and yet... what could he do?*

This man had brothers and sisters who were better off financially than he was. He also had friends and neighbors who had not suffered as much impact on their incomes. Someone who is *osek* in chessed looks around and says, "It's been a hard year. How is my brother making it? How is my friend making it? What can I do to help?" He doesn't wait for the person to come to him with his hand out but rather, he makes the other person's needs his "business." When all of Klal Yisrael is operating such a business, we will have done the only thing we *can* do to weather the *chevlei Mashiach,* which will bring us to the birth of a beautiful, renewed, redeemed world.

# 71

## Find a Chance to Give

In a magazine article, a son wrote a sad and thought-provoking account about his father, which is summarized here. It opens our eyes to an often-hidden need in the realm of chessed:

*The man's father spent a successful career as a Rav. For decades, he worked to strengthen Torah knowledge and mitzvah observance in America, at a time when Orthodox Judaism was at a low ebb. Besides a Rav's regular duties of conducting weddings and funerals, he wrote articles for Jewish publications and gave powerful speeches to inspire the community. His passion for a Torah-true mesorah made a noticeable impact.*

*After several decades, during which he served as the Rav of two different communities, he was pushed into an early retirement. At the time, he was in his 70s and still had plenty to offer. His son recalls that his father would sit in his study and look over the notes he had made for his speeches and articles. "No one asks me to speak anymore. No one wants my derashos," he commented. "Everyone used to value my opinion, but no one asks for it now."*

*The son related the heartbreak of seeing his father — still a brilliant man with a burning desire to disseminate Torah — relegated to the sidelines. He had done so much for Orthodox Judaism in America, and now, the world was passing him by.*

This article leaves us to wonder; how many people are wasting away because no one offers them an opportunity to give what they have to give? Being needed is a vital part of being respected. We feel valuable because people need what we bring to the table. Our opinions, experience, talents, and knowledge cannot instill us with self-esteem if they are not brought out into the world, transformed from potential into accomplishments.

This is true at any age, but it is especially true of people who have a long list of achievements to their credit and are now, for some reason, sitting on the sidelines. Sometimes the best way to do chessed is to find out what the other person has to give and provide him with an opportunity to give it. The following story, heard on the Chazak Inspiration telephone line during the height of the Covid-19 pandemic, illustrates the good we can do by asking someone to do for us:

*A recently widowed woman described how she faced the prospect of her first Pesach alone — not only without her husband, but without anyone. Because of the quarantine and the danger Covid-19 posed to a woman her age, she would not be having guests; neither would she be a guest of any of her children. She would be making her own seder and spending the long Yom Tov days in isolation.*

*Next door to her, however, a young mother thought about all the exciting pre-Pesach learning her children had missed as a result of the schools being closed down. They would be coming to the seder without any of the preparation and excitement that was so essential to the experience.*

*As she thought about the problem, an idea came into her head. Her next-door neighbor, the recently widowed woman, was a talented, highly experienced teacher. Maybe she could somehow teach the children about Pesach. The mother called her neighbor and asked if she would do it, provided they could come up with a Covid-safe way to connect her with the children.*

*The widow was thrilled to take up the offer. She quickly began gathering materials to teach and inspire her little class. The children — both boys and girls — sat in the widow's yard while she took a seat on the porch. The teacher began doing what she had done so expertly in the past — inspiring children with the majesty of yetzias Mitzrayim. The children's parents were thrilled with the knowledge and enthusiasm they brought to the seder.*

*The widow, who recorded the story for Chazak, reported that her Pesach was an entirely different experience because of her few days spent teaching the children. It went from being a dreaded prospect to a beautiful experience, because nothing makes a person feel more alive than giving to others.*

Most of the time, chessed involves doing something for others, not asking others to do something for us. However, when someone is standing on the sidelines feeling useless, the best thing we can do for that person is to say, in effect, "You're needed! Could you please do this for me?" Every person can look around and see someone — relative, neighbor or friend — who would love to feel that they're still "in the game" in some way. With a little thought, we can make it happen — and everyone benefits.

The *Chovos HaLevavos* says, "*lo mitoch machshevoseinu ela mitoch ma'aseinu* — not by our thoughts, but rather, by our deeds." This is how Hashem judges a person; our good intentions are laudable, but if we have the ability to bring them into action and don't, then the thoughts do not amount to much. If we each brainstorm with our family for five minutes, we will almost certainly be able to think of someone to whom we could give the joy of giving. It might be just what he needs.

# Fragile Hearts

Most people do not want to be the cause of others' suffering. Who would want to think that someone is lying in bed awake, mulling over something we said or did and feeling pained because of it? As this story of the Beis Yisrael illustrates, if we don't want to cause such a situation, we have to think a little harder about our interactions:

> The Beis Yisrael, the fourth Gerrer Rebbe, emigrated to Eretz Yisrael at the start of World War II. Every Friday night, he would make a l'chaim tisch, which also attracted people from outside the Gerrer chassidus. At the tisch, the gabbai would call up by name those who were honored by receiving a l'chaim from the Rebbe, or shirayim — portions of the Rebbe's food. The person would then go forward and take his portion.
>
> The custom followed by Ger was to call the person up by his name, without any title, such as Rav or Rosh Yeshivah. One Friday night, a Litvishe Rosh Yeshivah decided to attend the tisch, something he did infrequently. When the gabbai called him to

receive a l'chaim from the Rebbe, he naturally called him up without his title.

Much later in the evening, when the tisch ended and most people had gone home, the Rebbe turned to his gabbai and expressed a concern. The Litvishe Rosh Yeshivah had only been appointed to his position recently. The words "Rosh Yeshivah" were no doubt sweet to his ears, and perhaps he had been slightly hurt to have been called up without the title. The gabbai told the Rebbe not to worry, because this was the Gerrer custom, applied equally to everyone, and the Rosh Yeshivah therefore had nothing about which to feel hurt.

"Yes, but he doesn't frequent the tisch," the Rebbe answered. Indeed, the Rebbe's sharp eyes noticed the faces in the crowd, and he knew who was a newcomer. When the conversation ended and the gabbai walked away, the Rebbe noticed another chassid who had been nearby and had overheard the Rebbe's comments. "I want you to go to the Rosh Yeshivah's house," he told the man. "Tell him that you overheard the Gerrer Rebbe talking about how badly he feels that he didn't have him called up by his title."

"I'll gladly go," said the chassid, "but it's late. He's probably sleeping."

"He's not sleeping," came the Rebbe's sure reply.

Despite the late hour, the chassid did as the Rebbe asked. He knocked on the man's door and only a moment later, the Rosh Yeshivah appeared. The chassid relayed the Rebbe's message and he saw the Rosh Yeshivah's face brighten. Then he returned to report back to the Rebbe.

"Nu?" the Rebbe asked him. "Who has the ruach hakodesh, me or you? Was he still up? Did he feel bad?"

The chassid told the Rebbe that the Rosh Yeshivah was still awake, and that his face lit up when he heard the message. Apparently, he had been bothered by the incident, as the Rebbe assumed.

"But it wasn't ruach hakodesh that told me he felt bad," the Rebbe said. "The Torah is so careful about the aveirah of onaas *devarim,* and the Torah is Hashem's words, the absolute truth. If it says that people are vulnerable, you can assume they are. If it is possible that someone is expecting a certain measure of respect and he doesn't get it, you can assume he feels bad. The Torah is telling you, be very careful of people's feelings."

With his penetrating mind, the Beis Yisroel was able to see this. But we, too, have to internalize this message because often, no one will tell us outright that we've hurt them. The Rosh Yeshivah in this story would never have let anyone know he was hurt; that would be beneath his dignity. Likewise, if a relative isn't invited to speak at a *sheva berachos,* or to recite a *berachah* under the *chuppah,* if a neighbor isn't invited to a *simchah* — even if these decisions are perfectly logical or they are just an oversight — we have to assume that those who are left out feel at least a bit insulted, and the Torah wants us to realize this and act accordingly. It's true that there are only so many *berachos* under the *chuppah* and people have only so much patience for speeches, but if we care about the other person's honor, we'll find a way to make him know he's important in our eyes.

Along similar lines, a small slight can even hurt someone who knows we care about him. This is something that happens in families. Objectively, spouses are usually certain that they are important to each other, as parents are to their children and children are to their parents. Even so, it takes very little to mar that secure feeling.

For instance, imagine parents who have a nice, warm relationship with a married daughter. However, because of the size of the daughter's family, she cannot bring them for Shabbos to her parents very often. Furthermore, her hectic Fridays often leave her with no time for a quick "good Shabbos" phone call. Because of this, her parents are hurt. They know she's a well-intentioned, loving daughter, and yet when they hear friends talking about their Erev Shabbos phone calls from their children, and their table filled with grandchildren, the parents feel a sting of neglect.

We might think the parents could solve the problem easily by telling their daughter that they'd be happy to hear from her on Erev Shabbos. However, they won't do that because to their way of thinking, if the move isn't coming from her, motivated by her own feelings of love and respect, it isn't meaningful. They won't tell her that they are hurt.

Without going into the right and wrong of this situation, we need to learn something from it. People are vulnerable. Hearts are fragile. The strong, confident person you see standing next to you in shul, the parents who seem to have life under control, the wealthy relatives who are connected to every big name in Klal Yisrael — even a newly appointed Rosh Yeshivah — all have a human heart, and the Torah tells us that we are obligated to handle them with care.

# 73

# The Badchan's Serious Business

hat is the value of putting a smile on another person's face? Can telling a joke or a funny story add anything to our account in *Shamayim,* or is it just a distraction from our serious *avodas Hashem*? That question is answered in the Gemara (*Taanis* 22a).

*Rabbi Baroka, one of the Amoraim, would often encounter Eliyahu HaNavi in the marketplace. During one of those encounters, Rabbi Baroka asked Eliyahu to point out who in the marketplace was a ben Olam Haba — a person destined for Olam Haba.*

*At first, Eliyahu didn't see anyone who fit the description. Then he noticed someone and pointed him out. Rabbi Baroka stopped the person and asked him, "What is your occupation?" The man told Rabbi Baroka to come back the next day. When Rabbi Baroka returned the next day, Eliyahu pointed out two other people. The Amora approached the two men and asked about their occupation, and the men replied, "We are badchanim. When we see someone depressed, we cheer him up. Alternatively, when we see two people quarreling, we try to make peace."*

We might read this story and think, "Well, that's very nice for those two men, and for *badchanim* in general, but it doesn't apply to me because I am not a *badchan*." However, that misses the point: It wasn't their profession that gave them the merit for *Olam Haba*. Rather, it was the goal to which they devoted themselves — cheering up people who were downcast. That is something anyone can emulate, no matter what his profession might be. That makes a person a *badchan*, and a *ben Olam Haba*.

As inspiring as this story is, the *Toras Chaim* (*Sanhedrin* 90a) presents a question that many people might have. Doesn't the Mishnah tell us that every Jew has a portion in *Olam Haba*? How was it that in an entire marketplace, Eliyahu HaNavi could only identify two people who met this description?

The explanation the *Toras Chaim* gives us (based on a *Tosafos*) is eye-opening. He confirms that indeed, every Jew has a portion in *Olam Haba*. However, most of us do not travel an express train from this world to *Gan Eden*. Unfortunately, the soul needs to separate itself from the impurities it amassed during the person's lifetime. Certain processes that occur in the grave and in *Gehinnon* accomplish this cleansing so that the soul can thrive in the spiritual world. Even before a person's passing, the troubles he endures in his lifetime can accomplish some of this.

However, the *Toras Chaim* says, Rabbi Baroka wanted to know who in the marketplace was destined for the "express train," bypassing all the painful stops along the way to *Olam Haba*. Eliyahu pointed out the *badchanim* — people who make others happy, who bring joy to those who are downcast. Such a person is a *ben Olam Haba* while he is still alive. He doesn't require any purification to qualify for *Olam Haba*. He is already worthy as he walks, talks and breathes in this world.

What is the other side of this? It is the despair we learned about in the story of Choni Hame'aggel, who awoke after 70 years of sleep and found himself unrecognized and alone in the world. His plight, says Rava, illustrates the meaning of the words, "*oh chavrusa, oh misusa* — either a friend or death." *Rashi* expounds that this teaches us that a person would prefer not to be in this world if he cannot have friendship and respect from others.

If loneliness and depression are comparable to death, then cheering someone up is comparable to saving a life, and opportunities to do this are all around us. Not everyone has the *zechus* of saving someone's life physically, but anyone can give a fellow Jew a new lease on life in this manner. We might think, "He'll smile for a minute and then be right back where he was," but that is an underestimation of the power of that minute. It can ignite a spark of hope. It can give the person the feeling that his life is worthwhile, which gives him energy to address what's troubling him. It erases his feeling of being invisible and makes him feel noticed and valued.

We discussed earlier how Rav Shach would tell his students that they need not look for chessed opportunities outside yeshivah. He could not imagine how they did not notice fellow students who were lonely or sad. If someone was looking for a chessed to do, he advised, they should take five minutes out of their supper time, or even from their learning, to tell a depressed boy a good joke and bring a smile to his face.

There is a father of a successful yeshivah *bachur,* who, when speaking to his son Erev Shabbos, asks the boy not only how his learning is going, but he also asks, "Are you looking out for a *bachur* who needs a good word? Someone who needs some friendship?" The father stresses this especially at the start of a new *zman,* when new students enter the yeshivah. They may feel out of place, missing their old familiar yeshivah and friends. Even if they learn well, they may not yet have established their reputation among their new peers. In such situations, a friendly interaction with a fellow student definitely has the power to make a difference.

Of course, this is true anywhere — homes, offices, neighborhoods, families. Does the new *chassan* or *kallah* feel at ease with the in-law siblings? Does the new neighbor feel welcome? Does the new employee know where to go and what to do? And obviously, there are dozens of other reasons people can feel ill at ease or depressed, and our effort to bring a smile to their faces is, as we've learned, one of the most crucial things we can do for them and for ourselves. May we all be *zocheh* to be *badchanim,* and with that, to merit — without pain and suffering — our *chelek* in *Olam Haba.*

# Think Ahead

Our great *talmidei chachamim* earn their reputations based on their genius in learning. Their genius in chessed may be less known, but it is equally a part of their greatness. Rav Avraham Genachovsky was a shining example of this fact. Two stories portray the wisdom and forethought that made his chessed great.

The first story was told by one of his students after the Rav's passing:

> The talmid had made an appointment to see Rav Genachovsky one Shabbos afternoon at the Rav's home in Bnei Brak. At the appointed time, the student arrived at the Rav's door and, in a moment of mindlessness, rang the doorbell. Immediately, he realized what he had done, and his stomach churned inside him with shame. However, he knew that it would be worse to turn around and go home, as much as he wished he could disappear.
>
> He waited a few moments, but no one came to the door. He knocked and waited again, but still, no one appeared. Every few minutes, he knocked again, knowing that the Rav would certainly be there.

*After about 10 minutes, dressed in pajamas and a robe, Rav Genachovsky opened the door.*

*"I'm so sorry! I hope you haven't been waiting long," he said. "I was in such a deep sleep."*

*The talmid later heard from someone in the Rav's family that he never donned pajamas during the daytime. Only for this occasion, so that he could pretend that he didn't hear the doorbell and thus spare his student embarrassment, did he come to the door in the middle of the day in pajamas and a robe.*

Not only did this *gadol* perceive the shame a student might feel, but just as keenly, he knew that an accomplished *talmid chacham* also needs to be treated with sensitivity to his dignity. A different student witnessed the following example:

*On Erev Yom Kippur, the Minchah davening was coming to an end in Rav Genachovsky's shul. In moments, he knew, everyone in the shul would be flocking around him, seeking berachos. However, his eye was set on someone sitting toward the back of the shul — a distinguished talmid chacham.*

*Before the tefillos had even ended, the Rav abruptly strode to the place where the talmid chacham was sitting and asked him, "Could you please give me a berachah that I should have a gemar chasimah tovah?"*

*"No, no, why should you ask me for a berachah?" the talmid chacham replied.*

*"Why? Because you're a chashuve talmid chacham," he answered. "I would very much like to have a berachah from you."*

*The talmid chacham complied. Moments later, the davening ended and as Rav Genachovsky walked through the shul, everyone followed him. They lined up and waited to get their berachah for a good year.*

*The student who related this story saw very clearly what had happened. Rav Avraham Genachovsky understood that the talmid chacham would have felt disparaged when he saw the entire shul line up to receive the Rav's berachah. Instead of allowing that to happen, he protected the other man's pride. He would be able to think to himself, "They all want Rav Genachovsky's berachah, but Rav Genachovsky wants mine!"*

These stories are a lesson in the heights of chessed a person can attain. We may not all have the capacity for this "genius" in chessed, just as few of us have Rav Genachovsky's genius in Torah. However, we can strive to do at our own level what he did so brilliantly — to think ahead. What will our actions or words cause another person to feel? What can we do to make sure that we are not the cause of someone else's pain? This is the ultimate expression of *"ashrei maskil el dal"* — how fortunate are those who tend to the needy with wisdom, because *middah k'neged middah,* Hashem will protect their dignity in turn.

# 75

## Teshuvah in an Instant

How far are we supposed to go to do a chessed? There might not be one specific answer, but as this story illustrates, the farther we go, the farther Hashem goes for us.

Rav Moshe Dovid of Chortkov, a grandson of the Rema, was the Rebbe of the Chortkove dynasty. This was a branch of the Ruzhiner *chassidus,* whose hallmark was a demeanor of dignity and royalty.

Throughout the year, the Rebbe would distribute money to the poor of the city, and there were many in need. One year, before Yom Tov, he ran out of funds. He sent for his teenaged son, Reb Yisroel, who would one day become the Rebbe and the renowned rebbi of Rav Meir Shapiro.

Rav Moshe Dovid instructed his son to go around the city knocking on doors, collecting *tzedakah* for the Yom Tov needs of the poor. The Rebbe's *gabbaim* were aghast. How could the Rebbe send his son, the future leader of Chortkov, on such a humiliating mission as knocking on doors for contributions? The Rebbe explained with a story about his grandfather, the Rema, whose famous commentary on the *Shulchan Aruch* has made him the rebbi of Klal Yisrael:

In Krakow, where the Rema was the Rav, there lived a man known as Moshe the Shikkur (drunkard). He worked minimal hours and spent most of his week collecting money for his weekly Erev Shabbos indulgence — a supersized serving of shnapps that would put him into a fog. In this condition, he would walk into Kabbalas Shabbos, each week confirming his reputation once again.

One week, as he began to enter the tavern to buy his drink, a woman called to him. "Moshe the Shikkur," she said, "here you are using your money to buy a drink when I am so poor that I don't have Shabbos candles to light or a challah to make hamotzi on."

Moshe was torn. He looked forward to his drink all week. He spent all week collecting the money for it. But here was this woman who needed the money. A battle ranged inside him for a few moments and at last, he handed her the money. Depressed, he headed home and lay down on his bed. He fell asleep and never again opened his eyes.

The chevrah kaddisha was called, but there was no time before Shabbos to prepare Moshe for burial. They brought him to a place near the shul designated for bodies to be kept, intending to give him a proper burial as soon as possible after Shabbos. Few people knew of Moshe's passing.

Shabbos came in, and as the Rema sat learning that night, Moshe walked into his home. "Rebbe," he said to the Rema, "I'm here to tell you that there's a grievance against you in Heaven."

"Moshe, I know you drink on Erev Shabbos and maybe you want to play a joke on me, but I'm in the middle of learning."

"I'm not making a joke," Moshe insisted. "I'm dead. I died right before Shabbos. I'm coming from Shamayim with a message for you. If you don't believe me, go look next to the shul where they keep the bodies. You'll see me there."

The Rema went to the designated spot and saw one body there, covered with a tallis. He peeked underneath and there, indeed, lay

Moshe. The holy Rema didn't lose his composure over the strange circumstance, but simply returned to his home to question Moshe about his mysterious visit.

"You just passed away," the Rema said. "You haven't had your funeral yet. You're Moshe the Shikkur. But you are of such high status that you've already been allowed to come from Shamayim to give me a message? How is that?"

"I will tell you. It's because I gave away my last few coins — money I needed for a drink — to a poor woman." He told the Rema the story and explained that this deed wiped away all his sins. "I went straight to Gan Eden," he said. "I died right away so I wouldn't have time to ruin my clean slate."

He then went on to give the Rema the message from Heaven: "You are being faulted for not going door to door collecting money for the poor people in the city, like the woman I helped. How could a situation such as hers exist in your city?"

The Rema answered that he collected from the wealthy. "But you don't go to the poor. You don't knock on every door," Moshe rebuked. The Rema said that from then on, he would do so.

Concluding the story, Reb Moshe Dovid of Chortkov said, "Now you know why I'm telling my son, Reb Yisroel, to knock on doors. I don't want there to be any complaints in Heaven against us."

This amazing story shines a brilliant spotlight on the intense power of one act of chessed. A man who was a drunkard his entire life, who put all his time and energy into begging money to buy himself one drink a week so that he could spend Friday night in a fog, wiped his entire slate clean with one moment of kindness. He didn't save the world. He didn't give millions. He didn't build a yeshivah or donate a sefer Torah. He battled it out with his yetzer hara and gave his shnapps money to a woman in need.

Beyond that lesson, we learn that there is no shame in raising money for tzedakah. In the eyes of Shamayim, going door to door was considered proper for someone as venerated as the Rema, and in

Chortkov, it was considered a proper endeavor for the future Rebbe of a regal dynasty. This tells us that we should not hesitate to reach out to others to help those in need, and equally important, that when people come to our door collecting for the poor, we should know that they are doing exactly what Hashem wants of them.

May our chessed wipe our slate clean, and — unlike Moshe the Shikker — may Hashem grant us the opportunity to keep it clean with many more acts of chessed.

# 76

# A Ray of Light

Wе often struggle to keep Hashem in focus even when we're enjoying all His gifts and His light is shining into our life. How much harder is it to see His goodness when we're lost in the dark! However, just as the stars are only visible to us against the darkness of the night sky, sometimes the darkness provides the backdrop for the most extraordinary rays of light.

The tragedy that took place in Meron on Lag B'Omer, 5781 was a never to be forgotten moment of darkness for Klal Yisrael. Just as we emerged from the worst of Covid, and people dared to gather again for *simchos* and *avodas Hashem,* this misfortune, which took 45 Jewish souls, plunged Klal Yisrael into a time of mourning. We wondered how much more we could handle.

But there were rays of light as well, and these let us know that Hashem was with us in our pain. Here is one remarkable story of two people's kindness — a father and a son each making the effort to go that "extra mile" for *kibbud av v'eim* — and the priceless reward it reaped:

Moshe Walkin, a 21-year-old bachur from Lakewood, was learning at Yeshivas Mir in Yerushalayim. A few days before Lag B'Omer, his close friend ran to him bursting with excitement. "You're not going to believe it!" he said. "I got a few VIP passes to pour the oil for lighting the Toldos Aharon bonfire in Meron!"

Every year on Lag B'Omer, Meron is the site of a huge gathering in honor of the yahrtzeit of Rabbi Shimon bar Yochai, who is buried there. Tens of thousands stream in from all parts of Eretz Yisrael and abroad to pray at his kever and take part in the joyous singing and dancing that goes on throughout the night and day. Bonfires are a key feature of the event, and the Toldos Aharon bonfire is the final one lit.

Moshe and his friends would be up-front and close to the center of the action. They would be able to pour the oil that the Toldos Aharon Rebbe would light!

The boys reserved an apartment in Meron and thought about little else but their thrilling upcoming adventure. However, Moshe got a call from his father, Rabbi Aharon Walkin, that would change the plan. Reb Aharon had been putting in a concerted effort to obtain all the permits needed during those times of Covid-restricted travel to come to Yerushalayim and pay a long overdue visit to his elderly father. He would be arriving right before Lag B'Omer and he wanted his son to come with him to visit his zeidy.

Moshe was disappointed. Instead of spending the night with his friends in Meron, he would be spending it with his father and Zeidy in Yerushalayim. He would miss the once-in-a-lifetime experience of pouring the oil on the Toldos Aharon bonfire. However, Moshe knew what his priorities had to be. He told his father about his arrangements for Meron, adding, "But of course I'll stay with you, Totty."

On Erev Lag B'Omer, at 5 p.m., Reb Aharon arrived at Ben Gurion airport. He took a cab directly to his father's apartment in Yerushalayim, where he and Moshe spent several hours. At about

*10 p.m., Reb Aharon told Moshe that he would drive with him to Meron to catch the remainder of the celebration.*

*However, by the time they arrived in Meron, several hours later, the police were stationed along the road turning everyone back. "No one is allowed into the area," they were told. The Walkins had no choice but to return to Yerushalayim. They awoke the next morning to the shocking news. The combination of overcrowding and limited exits had resulted in causing the people to lose their balance, fall upon and crush each other. The epicenter of the tragedy was the Toldos Aharon bonfire, and the two friends with whom Moshe was supposed to share the experience — Duvi Steinmetz and Yossi Kohn— had perished in the crush.*

The Torah gives us two ways to merit *arichus yamim*. One is the mitzvah of *kibbud av v'eim*. As Reb Aharon so eloquently stated as he pondered the immensity of the miracle he had experienced, it took two hefty doses of this mitzvah to save Moshe's life. "For me, leaving Lakewood to go visit my father in Eretz Yisrael was very hard to arrange. For my son, he had to give up this once-in-a-lifetime opportunity. He had his VIP badge, and everything was all set up. It was with magnificent *mesiras nefesh* that he did *kibbud av v'eim* for me. With these two *zechusim*, he merited to be saved."

No matter what happens, we have to look for the ray of light Hashem will always show us. In our present times, we often see it against the darkness, but we will soon arrive at the time when Hashem's light will forever drive the darkness away.

# 77

# *My Way or the Highway*

One person finds a story touching; another finds it dull. One person feels uplifted by a certain *niggun*; it gives another person a headache. One person is inspired by a speaker; another is checking his watch.

These are normal human differences. However, many people find it hard to honor those differences. They feel free to downplay, dismiss or even discourage the other person's sources of inspiration. Somehow, they believe that bursting the other person's bubble and instructing him on the "right" way to connect to Hashem is their obligation.

The following incident, told by Rav Zalman Nechemia Goldberg, during his *hesped* for his illustrious father-in-law, Rav Shlomo Zalman Auerbach, guides us in a different direction:

> One Rosh Hashanah, a warm-hearted chassidish baal tokei'a, began crying as he prepared to blow shofar. The baal makri — the one who calls out the sounds before the baal tokei'a blows — observed him disapprovingly. "I don't understand," said the baal makri. "Before you do the mitzvah of taking the lulav and esrog,

*do you cry? Before you go into the succah, do you cry? Why are you crying now, before you do the mitzvah of tekias shofar?"*

*Rav Zalman Nechemia told this story to Rav Shlomo Zalman on Rosh Hashanah, curious to know how his father-in-law would respond — and he was soon to regret telling the story. Rav Shlomo Zalman was troubled to his core. "A Jew feels inspired to do a mitzvah. He's feeling very close to Hashem. He's shedding some tears. How dare that Rav take away his inspiration from him!" Rav Shlomo Zalman exclaimed. "If someone's way is to cry before tekias shofar and someone else's way is not to cry, what does it matter? How dare he take away the feeling for the mitzvah that this person felt?"*

*Rav Zalman Nechemia worried that he had ruined Rav Shlomo Zalman's entire Rosh Hashanah, so greatly was he disturbed by the story.*

The point that pierced Rav Shlomo Zalman's heart was that one person took it upon himself to dampen another's most precious asset — his spiritual fulfillment. While there are certainly improper ways to serve Hashem, there are many proper ways. If someone has found what moves him, to diminish it or taunt him for it is a cruel deed. It is like pointing out the flaws in the *kallah* to the new *chassan*. He sees perfection. He's happy, energized, excited to build a life with this person. What can be gained by telling him that she's not all she seems to be?

This story, witnessed first-hand, portrays a wiser, more sensitive approach:

*A particularly perceptive person was approached by a man whose personality was simple and sincere. The sincere man told the wise man, "Did you ever hear a shmuess from Rabbi X? I listen to him all the time. I learn so much from him. I really believe he has ruach hakodesh! Don't you agree?"*

*The wise man said, "Of course!"*

*His friend beamed with satisfaction. This man, whose opinion he valued, also held in high esteem the speaker who inspired him so greatly.*

*In telling this story several years later, the wise man commented, "Do I know if Rabbi X has ruach hakodesh? I have no idea. But if this man is inspired in his avodas Hashem because he believes this person has ruach hakodesh, how dare I take that away from him!"*

The wise man knew something we can all instill within ourselves to avoid deflating another Jew's *avodas Hashem.* If someone believes in a certain Rebbe or Rosh Yeshivah, if he derives inspiration from a certain teacher, if he prefers a certain type of learning, if he enjoys a particular style of *davening,* how we feel about these things, as Rav Shlomo Zalman said, is irrelevant. We all struggle to find our inspiration and motivation to keep growing, and when someone has found it, the greatest chessed is to encourage him as he makes his way up the ladder of spiritual growth.

# 78

## *Preventive Medicine*

Around 20 years ago in Lakewood, a young man in his late 30s collapsed and died of a heart attack. The town was much smaller then, and everyone felt the impact of the tragedy. People in Beth Medrash Govoha launched a campaign to help the widow and orphans of this man so that they could meet their expenses.

As the collectors were making their rounds, there was one *yungerman,* a generous, kind-hearted person, who told the collector something uncharacteristic. "I'm not giving anything to this," he stated. The person standing next to him looked at him in shock: How could he not give to a young widow and her orphans?

"Let me explain," the young man said. "I spoke a short while ago to a wealthy man here in town and he told me that this person who just died was under overwhelming financial stress. For three days before his heart attack, he hadn't eaten. He had no appetite. The wealthy man told me, 'I knew about this situation, and I cannot in good conscience say, "our hands did not spill this person's blood." I knew and I didn't do anything. Now I am going to give this family a lot of money.'

"So, I see that this family is being taken care of, and that's how it should be. Orphans and widows come first in halachah. It's beautiful how everyone is running to give. But obviously, that's not where I'm needed. What I want to do now is find out who else is struggling. I'm sure I must have some relative, someone I know who I can help out so that the mother in that family does not turn into a widow, G-d forbid, and the children do not become orphans."

About five years ago, this yungerman, who was earning a respectable *parnassah,* recalled this conversation and said that he still lives by this motto. At the time, there was a family that had lost its breadwinner, not to a stress-induced heart attack, but to an illness. During the illness, the family had been unable to pay their mortgage, and this yungerman was paying it. Once the man passed away, however, activists became involved and raised money to pay the mortgage and other expenses.

The young man therefore stopped giving to this cause; others were filling the need. He turned his attention instead to finding the next desperate family "hiding in plain sight," doing their best to keep up appearances while they struggled to carry an overweight financial burden. "When there's no widow and no orphans, if someone is struggling, they're on their own. That's where I look to give my *maaser* money. It's preventive medicine, to forestall a situation that can lead to widows and orphans."

It's important to keep in mind that this man's "motto" is only valid when the widows and orphans are already receiving everything they need, because they take priority in halachah. When these tragedies strike, the community rises to the occasion, and contributing to such a family's welfare is a *tzedakah* priority.

However, this young man provides a different perspective. We have to keep our ears tuned to the silent cries of people who will never ask us for help, but who need it desperately. They're behind on their mortgage and tuition. They have an unpaid balance at the grocery store. They're inundated with overdue bills, late fees and debt payments. They won't come to us because they are ashamed and embarrassed, or perhaps they're holding onto hope that matters will improve before they are forced to put out their hand. So we must find a way, while protecting their dignity, to help them.

This is a point not only for individuals, but for organized *tzedakos* as well. While each has its own mission and bylaws, sometimes there's leeway to answer a need that's not in their target area. When they're approached to pay a grocery bill or a month's mortgage payment, it's worthwhile to consider, "Can we do it? Is there any reason why not, even though it's not our mission'"?

If we can imagine the stress and despair churning in the heart of someone who is drowning in expenses, we can imagine the feeling of freedom and happiness he feels when his plight is alleviated. "*Ashrei maskil el dal* — Fortunate is the one who understands the needs of the poor," says Dovid HaMelech. What beautiful merit comes to those who turn their chessed in this direction!

# Experience Is the Best Teacher

The wealthy know they must give to the poor. The strong know they must help the weak. The healthy know they must care for the sick. But do they know what it feels like to be in the recipient's position?

One year, right before *Kol Nidrei*, the Minchas Elazar, the Munkaczer Rebbe, told a story that addressed this question in an unforgettable way:

The Chernobyler Maggid was known for his significant efforts in the mitzvah of pidyon shevuyin — freeing those who were jailed. During that time in Europe, many false charges were lodged against Jews as a means of harassment, and there were frequently people who had been ripped from their families and left to waste away in a dank prison cell. The Maggid would find these people and raise money to get them released.

Then one day, the Maggid himself was arrested on a fabricated charge that someone had brought against him. After two days in jail, he was allowed visitors.

One of the visitors who came to him was a woman he had never before encountered. She had a question. It was based on the Gemara (Bava Kamma 50a) about a man named Nechunia, who would dig wells so that those on their way to the Beis HaMikdash on the Yamim Tovim would have access to water for their needs.

"Nechunia's daughter fell into a well," the woman said, "and people came to Rav Chanina ben Dosa for advice. He told them not to worry. Everything would be alright. When the girl was still not rescued, they came a second time, and he reassured them again. They went to Rav Chanina a third time. Rashi explains that at this point, they no longer believed the girl could still be alive. However, Rav Chanina answered them, "Don't worry. She's already out." They later found out that the girl had been saved by a miracle. They asked Rav Chanina how he knew what the outcome would be. Was he a navi? He answered that he didn't need to be a navi. It was clear to him that someone who exerted himself to dig wells for the Jews coming to the Beis HaMikdash would not lose his daughter in a well. Hashem does not pay back the very mitzvah in which he toiled with a tragedy. That's what the Gemara says.

"Therefore, I have a question for you, Rebbe. How can it be that you, who exert yourself so greatly for the mitzvah of pidyon shevuyin, are sitting in jail?"

The Maggid couldn't answer her question.

"Well, I will tell you, she said. "As much as you do for people who are imprisoned, you would do even more if you actually felt their pain. But it's impossible for anyone to feel someone else's pain completely if they have never experienced it themselves. Since you do this mitzvah at such a high level, Hashem wanted you to be able to perfect it. Sitting in jail, for just a short while, is the only way. Since you've now felt that pain, you will soon be released."

She walked away and her prediction came true. The Munkaczer Rebbe said this woman was Rochel Imeinu.

This story can give us a whole new perspective as to how we interpret the pain we go through in life. No one wants pain and we pray that no Jew should suffer, but the fact is that troubles come. And when they do, they may very well be a hint pointing at something we can accomplish for others.

For example, if someone has a child who had difficulty getting into school, he has in him a potentially powerful motivation for helping some other parent get his child into school. He also has gained an understanding of what is helpful and what is not. Likewise, if someone has been ill, or has a family member who has been ill, he knows in a much clearer way how much and what kind of help is needed.

Even when the underlying situation is a *simchah,* we can learn from the stresses and strains we encountered in our own *simchah.* For instance, money might be an issue. Fitting in all the errands with the rest of the full schedule might seem impossible. Also, we might be more conscientious about sending back a return card if we've sat there, two days before a wedding, unable to give the caterer a count of expected guests.

When we've passed through a stressful or painful time, we can do more than say, "*Baruch Hashem,* that's over!" We can take the lessons we've learned from the experience and use them to perfect our chessed — to know what needs to be done and how to sensitively and wisely do it. We can remember how we felt and let that guide us on how to help others without lowering their dignity, or how to show interest and concern without being intrusive.

We hope to be spared any kind of pain, but if troubles do come our way, may we gain wisdom from them that can assist us in helping others on a whole new level.

# What They Need

In Yerushalayim, a young woman suddenly lost her husband and was left with a houseful of young orphans. Inconsolable, she sat at home behind a locked door and refused to admit any visitors coming to comfort her during shivah.

Someone informed Rav Shmuel Auerbach about the situation, since he was known to come to the aid of widows in mourning, even if he did not know them. Despite warnings that the woman was refusing guests, on the last night of shivah, he came to her door. Naturally, she was not going to refuse entry to someone of the Rav's stature, and so, she admitted him into her house where she had been mourning alone all week. There were no other visitors present.

He sat down in front of her and said, "I am jealous of you."

She looked at him in surprise. "Jealous?" she repeated.

"Yes. Let me tell you something," he said. "I don't have any children. My wife, who was a wonderful tzaddekes, has passed away. I am all alone. When Shabbos or Yom Tov comes, no one is calling me on the phone and saying, 'Totty, can you please come visit?'

"Right now, you have a burden of mind-boggling proportions

*with all these children. But let's look a little further down the road. Your children are going to grow up and get married. They will be fighting over you. Who has the zechus to have Mommy for Shabbos? They'll be arguing, 'I want her!' 'No, you had her last week. Now I want her.'"*

*Those who knew this widow said Rav Shmuel's words changed her entire demeanor. She was truly comforted.*

Once again, we have to marvel at the wisdom that fuels a great person's chessed. Some people seem to know exactly what to do or say to break through what may seem to be an irreversible case of despair. We saw this earlier with the Chofetz Chaim, who spent the entire Yom Kippur night speaking to Rav Hershel Kamnitzer, who later told the story to Rav Shach. Rav Hershel was at the time a 60-year-old man who had never been married and had health issues that precluded his ever marrying. The Chofetz Chaim saw him sitting alone in shul after everyone else had gone home. The *tzaddik* sat next to him and spoke to him throughout that holy night, not with words of Torah or *mussar,* but a warm, personal conversation that helped Rav Hershel see the value in himself and his life.

However, it would be a mistake to believe that having insight into what another person needs is a skill reserved for great Torah figures. The Torah gives all of us the fundamental mitzvah upon which chessed is based, which we have identified many times throughout this volume: *"v'ahavta l'rei'acha kamocha."* Further, we've noted that the *Rambam* and the *Ramban* concur that this is a mitzvah of action. We fulfill the mitzvah by doing for our friend what we would want done for ourselves in similar circumstances.

This may be simple enough when the person's need is physical. If he's hungry, we feed him. If he's in debt, we give him money or try to raise money for him. But what do we do for someone whose heart is aching? Where do we find the right words?

We have to listen carefully to the person, so we understand fully what is on his mind. We have to listen without inserting ourselves into the picture, thinking, "What's the big deal? I've gone through much worse things," or "If he only had *emunah,* he wouldn't be in such distress," or some other thought that minimizes the other person's situation. While any of these thoughts may be true, thinking them will not bring into one's heart the right approach to helping the person. First, we have to feel what he feels. No one can tell another person what he should feel.

As we listen, we have to think, "What would help me right now if I were in his shoes?" We might want to offer long-term solutions, but people in despair don't feel the energy and confidence they need to adopt a solution. Instead, they will think, "You don't get it," and we will think, "What can I do? He doesn't want to be helped!"

In fact, the person does want to be helped. He wants to feel loved and valued and understood. With that, he can feel worthy of Hashem's goodness and see a time down the road when his situation will get better. That's when he's ready to work on solutions. Those who truly act *"kamocha"* with people who are in despair are not mind-readers. They are just people who put their egos aside and live with the other person in his pain. "I feel for you. I believe in you. I believe things will get better."

The *Ramchal* asks, why did Hashem create the world? He answers, *"olam chessed yibaneh* — the world is built on chessed." Hashem created the world to have a recipient for his chessed. Therefore, when we seek to do the mitzvah of "follow in Hashem's way," doing chessed for others is the greatest way to fulfill it.

Additionally, we can never forget what our chessed does for us, personally. As the Baal Shem Tov explains, according to the precept of *middah k'neged middah,* when we alleviate another person's pain, Hashem alleviates ours.

# 81

## Your "Self" Is Your Gift

Some words are so eye-opening that a person remembers exactly where he was when he heard them. That is the case regarding words I heard from Rav Matisyahu Salomon as I was driving along, listening to a tape he had recorded years earlier, while he was still *mashgiach* of the Gateshead Yeshivah. He cited a *Rambam* that made an indelible impression on me. It was from *Hilchos Dei'os* (6:3), and it stated that the ultimate way to fulfill the Torah's mitzvah of *gemilus chassadim* is "*l'shabei'ach chaveiro b'devarim* — to compliment your friend."

We already understand from the *Rambam*, that the mitzvah of chessed is to do for others what we want done for ourselves, and since we all want praise, praising others fulfills the mitzvah of chessed. However, this does not explain why he considers it the optimal way to do so. We might think, "It's just words! Aren't deeds more important than words?"

But let's think more deeply into the value of these specific words — words of praise. As we've learned in several lessons throughout this *sefer*, words that convey our recognition of another person are a lifeline. The Gemara's account of Choni HaMe'aggel (*Taanis* 23a), who *davened* to be taken from the world when he awoke from a 70-year sleep to a world that did not recognize and respect him, illustrates the point. As the Alter of Slabodka told us, a person who has no recognition from others cannot live. His *neshamah* departs from his *guf.*

No other chessed — except for the actual physical saving of a life — has this component. For example, imagine a mother has a sick child and must spend a great deal of time at doctors' offices and hospitals. If someone offers to prepare dinner for her family, this is a great chessed to her. If the person calls later and says, "Sorry, I can't do it," the woman will be disappointed. However, she won't feel so worthless that she wishes she could leave this world.

Similarly, if someone is hitching a ride on a rainy day and no one stops for him, he might be disappointed or even resentful. However, his will to live will not ebb away because he has to walk in the rain.

Nothing causes anguish to a person as feeling irrelevant or worse yet, disliked. His very identity is suffering. Therefore, says the *Rambam*, the greatest chessed is to restore this person to life, which we do by showing him friendship and recognition. This fact puts incredible positive power in our hands, because just by giving of ourselves, we can revive another human being's heart.

*Bachurim* in yeshivah and girls in high school and seminary have a unique opportunity to grasp this ultimate chessed. They are surrounded by fellow students, among whom are inevitably those who feel inferior and left out. As we mentioned in an earlier lesson, Rav Shach once spoke with a student who considered visiting an old-age home to do chessed, telling him that the yeshivah itself was a "goldmine of opportunities to do chessed," where he could seek out a few of the boys who were not feeling good about themselves and offer his friendship. The *bachur* could utilize 10 or 15 minutes of his free time to engage in a friendly conversation, and in doing so, fulfill a Torah mitzvah in the optimum way.

Girls, too, need only look around them in school to notice those who are often overlooked. In many schools, Sundays are a day girls go out together to shop or to each other's homes to study. There are the established groups of friends and then, there are the outsiders. The emotions an outsider feels are like those of someone flailing around in the ocean, trying hard not to go under.

We can guide our daughters, most of whom love to do chessed and are more than happy to stock the Bikur Cholim pantry or help a mother of a large family prepare for Shabbos, to reset their chessed priorities. **Connecting with girls who are left out is "ICU-level" chessed — life and death — compared to anything else they can do.** Parents and teachers can teach girls that with respect for a girl's dignity and a dose of common sense, they can extend a lifeline to such a girl and invite her to join the circle of friends.

The new girl may not quite fit in. She might have some personality quirks that the others find draining to deal with. However, this is where giving of ourselves comes in. A Jew is willing to be a little uncomfortable, to have less than the optimum level of enjoyment, for the sake of saving another person from feeling that life is not worth living. Every person, young or old, craves acceptance and can be taught to relate to the pain of being left out. And of course, every person has value, positive traits and talents to contribute; we often find that the person we never thought of including is someone who has plenty to offer.

Yeshivah *bachurim* and high school girls who learn to notice and reach out to those who are overlooked are developing a strength that will guarantee them the greatest blessings in life. They are fulfilling the mitzvah of loving their fellow Jew at the highest level, and *middah k'neged middah,* Hashem will make sure they are never overlooked or left out.

82

# Be My Guest

I t's the week after Pesach and you've just served about 20 people per meal, for eight Yom Tov meals, two Shabbos meals and a few Chol HaMoed meals as well. You're looking forward to a quiet Shabbos. No fancy side dishes, no company. Then an old friend who has moved out-of-town calls and says he and his family will be visiting for a few days and need a Shabbos meal. Could you accommodate?

Before anyone makes a decision on this question, he should take a closer look at the list of pros and cons. Here is a Gemara that figures prominently into the equation:

*I Melachim* (Ch. 13) tells of a *navi*, identified by *Rashi* as Ido HaNavi, who went to warn Yeravam about serving *avodah zarah*. A *navi sheker*, false prophet, wanted to provide Ido with hospitality, to fulfill the mitzvah of *hachnassas orchim*. With great effort, he took his donkey and chariot and went out to find Ido and invite him to his home to eat. Although Ido was told by Hashem not to go back and eat at this false prophet's home, various circumstances — including lies told by the *navi sheker* — led him to accept the invitation.

At this point, Hashem came to the *navi sheker* and gave him the true power of prophecy. The Gemara (*Sanhedrin* 103b) draws from this episode an illustration of the priceless value Hashem places on the mitzvah of *hachnassas orchim*.

According to strict justice, the *navi sheker* was liable for the death penalty. He even lied to convince Ido to come to his house. However, on the other side of the balance was his desire to feed Ido, which, says the Gemara, brings the presence of the *Shechinah* into his home. *Hachnassas orchim* turned him from someone worthy of death to someone worthy of the power of prophecy.

The above story amplifies one we discussed earlier, regarding Michah the idol-worshiper. In that case, the smoke of Michah's idolatrous sacrifices arose so close to the *Mishkan* in Shiloh that it mingled with the smoke of the pure *korbanos* coming from the Altar there, resulting in horrific contamination. The *malachim* wanted to kill Michah but Hashem would not allow it, simply because Michah always kept bread available for passersby. On that merit alone, he was spared the punishment due to him. *Rashi* (*Sanhedrin* 103b) explains that people who feed others are so precious in Hashem's eyes that He looks away from their sins.

The crux of the mitzvah is feeding people who need a meal or snack. However, it does not mean we must have 20 people at our Shabbos table every week. We can tap into the power of *hachnassas orchim* just by offering a packaged cookie or danish and a water bottle to the *tzedakah* collectors who come to our door. Having refreshments on hand for passersby has life-saving potential, as we just learned directly from the Gemara.

A further point to consider is this: Not only did Hashem not permit the *malachim* to kill Michah, He did not take away Michah's portion of *Olam Haba*. Here was an individual who had the audacity to carry an idol across the *Yam Suf*, clinging to a false god while one of Hashem's greatest miracles was taking place right before his eyes. Then he set up his temple a mile and a half from the *Mishkan* and burned his sacrifices is a way that contaminated the holy offerings ascending.

The Gemara asks why many categories of sinners whose deeds are far less egregious are said to lose their portion in *Olam Haba,* and yet Michah, an idol-worshiper, is not on that list. The Gemara answers that because Michah was careful to keep bread on hand for passersby, Hashem reserved his portion for him.

In our daily lives, these stories can influence the way we greet and treat the people around us. Giving food to people, putting out some pastries or cookies in shul and making food available to hungry Jews are all ways to earn this exceptional merit. Even when a *tzedakah* collector comes to the door with a story that doesn't sound quite right, there's a mitzvah to offer him something to eat. He may not be poor or the situation he says he's in may not be as dire — although the vast majority of cases are legitimate — but feeding him is a mitzvah apart from giving him money. On that count, we cannot lose.

*Hachnassas orchim* is a powerful mitzvah that carries such a priceless load of merit. Why not grab it?

# Shalom Protects Us All

Throughout *Tanach*, we see that the Jewish people needed to fight many wars, but we also see that they are not naturally soldiers. They win only when Hashem commands them to fight, when He says, "This is a cause I want you to fight for." When Hashem stands behind them, they don't need to be mighty warriors. He brings them victory. On the other hand, when they strike out on their own, when they decide for themselves what is a righteous cause worth fighting for, they inevitably go down in defeat.

Nothing has changed since then. Many people still feel entitled to decide what is a righteous cause and to go to war for it, and those wars — the *machlokes* that keeps us in *galus* — never bring victory. *Machlokes* robs individuals, families, communities and Klal Yisrael of the *berachos* that only *shalom* can bring. The greatest chessed we can do for ourselves and each other is to live *b'shalom*.

The *Midrash* (*Bereishis Rabbah, Parashas Noach,* §38) teaches this lesson through a comparison of the *dor hamabul* with the *dor haflagah*. It asks which generation was worse. The obvious answer would seem to be the *dor haflagah* because the people were waging a direct war against Hashem. They were engaging in the ultimate *avodah zarah,* imagining that their own power and might could not only reach, but conquer the Heavens. However, the *dor hamabul,* in addition to *avodah zarah* and immorality, sinned against each other. They engaged in stealing and robbery, which people can only do if they've completely disregarded their fellow man's well-being. Stealing means, "I come first and who cares what happens to you!"

This *Midrash* presents a paradox: The *dor haflagah* was in essence like a nation committing treason against its king — the worst possible crime — yet it was spared, while the *dor hamabul* was utterly wiped out. Why did Hashem spare them? The *Midrash* answers that the *dor haflagah* had a special merit; they were at peace with each other. They worked together in unity, and even though their goal was wrongful, their *shalom* saved them. *Rashi* in *Parashas Noach* (*Bereishis* 11:9) relates this Midrash and explains that it illustrates the degree to which Hashem despises *machlokes,* and the greatness of *shalom.*

In a small way, we can relate to this seemingly astounding idea. Imagine a household with many children. The mother is busy in the kitchen and the children are playing so nicely, quietly and cooperatively in the playroom. Even if she knows they are making a major mess, she thinks, "Let them be. They're being so good and playing so nicely together." On the other hand, let's imagine the children have taken it upon themselves to clean the playroom for Shabbos and they're squabbling endlessly about who should do which job. The mother is bound to rush in there and scold them. Their "mitzvah" loses its appeal when it is accomplished with anger and fighting.

This, essentially, is what the Midrash is telling us: Not that it's acceptable to sin as long as we do it with *achdus,* but that our *machlokes* takes away the protective power and *berachah* that our mizvos merit, while our *achdus* can protect us from the full impact of our sins. *Machlokes* leaves us exposed while *achdus* gives us shelter.

The Midrash continues by quoting a comment from Rebbi: Rebbi said that "when Klal Yisrael worships idols but there is peace among them, then Hashem says, 'I leave them alone,' and the Satan (i.e., the *malach ha'maves*) will have no control over them. But if there is *machlokes* among them, even if there is no *avodah zarah*, the Satan has permission to prosecute the Jews, *Rachmana litzlan.*"

The Midrash supports this idea with the following *pesukim.* The first (*Hoshea* 4:17) says "*Chavur atzabbim Efraim hanach lo.*" The simple translation of this is "Ephraim is joined (*chavur*) to idols (*atzabbim*); let him alone." Hashem appears to be washing His hands of the tribe of Efraim, stating that they are so connected to *avodah zarah* that the *navi* need not waste his time rebuking them. They won't listen.

The Midrash, however, presents a mind-boggling interpretation. The word *chavur* is from the root *chibbur,* joining together, and the verse signifies that Efraim is joined together in *shalom.* Therefore, the Midrash continues, *atzabbim* — even though they worship *avodah zarah,* Hashem says '*hanach lo* — leave them alone.' I am not going to destroy them. The *malach ha'maves* will not have power over them."

The second *pasuk* that the Midrash addresses (ibid. 10:2) says, "*Chalak libam* — When their hearts are separated, *atah yeshamu* — now they will be desolate" — they will be held responsible for their sins and punished. The message of the verse, says the Midrash, is that when people's hearts are divided from each other, when they are immersed in *machlokes,* they will suffer the full recompense for their sins, even if they do not worship *avodah zarah.*

This is a stark message. The *malach ha'maves* needs Hashem's permission to do its job, and when we are *b'shalom,* he is not given the power to harm us. The frightening "other side of the coin" is that when we are divided, when we disregard each other's dignity and feelings in order to win our battles, we lose that protection and bring troubles upon ourselves.

As we mentioned at the beginning of this lesson, most people do not set out to be *baalei machlokes.* Instead, they convince themselves that they have a righteous cause and are fighting *l'sheim Shamayim.* We have to examine our motives very carefully. Before we take a stand against a fellow Jew, we should check with a Rav to ensure that our cause is actually righteous and that there is no peaceful way to accomplish it.

How quickly we can fall into factions became frighteningly clear in the difficult period when Covid was rampant all over the world. In some communities, wearing masks was seen as a sign of social responsibility and concern for each other's health. In some communities, it was seen as useless and unnecessary. Instead of this becoming a question each person would discuss with his own doctor and Rav, it became a flash point.

The one certainty, however, is that the Torah's ways are "*darchei noam* — the ways of pleasantness," and any discussion between people regarding mask-wearing should have been conducted privately and respectfully. I heard an eye-witness story about a shul in Brooklyn where the *mispallelim* were careful to wear masks. When one person in the shul disregarded the rule, someone screamed at him in front of the entire shul, that he was being disrespectful. The person screamed back, "That's right! *I'm disrespectful!*"

This kind of exchange displays a massive blind spot. Masks don't protect anyone, just as armies don't win wars. If we want to see our efforts succeed, we need Hashem on our side. Embarrassing a Jew in front of an entire congregation is an act of *machlokes* which, we have just learned, gives the *malach ha'maves* control of the situation. In that case, a million masks will not help.

In all matters, we must do our *hishtadlus*, but ultimately Hashem is our only protection. Fighting a "holy war" against our fellow Jew can never bring us what we are seeking. As the final Mishnah in Mishnayos teaches us, "*Lo matza HaKadosh Baruch Hu kli machzik berachah elah hashalom* — Hashem did not find a vessel for His *berachos* other than *shalom*." Pursuing *shalom* is the greatest chessed we can do for ourselves, our family and the world, because only with *shalom* do all His other blessings flow.

# Going "Above and Beyond"

I n Lesson 82, we learned about the power of *hachnasas or-chim*, which is credited for protecting two people — Mi-chah, the idol-worshiper and a *navi sheker* who deceived Ido HaNavi — from the full force of the justice they warranted. Could this mitzvah's power be any greater?

It can, as any mitzvah can, when the person doing the chessed loves the mitzvah so much that he or she seeks out opportunities and better ways to do it. We see this idea applied to *hachnasas orchim* specifically in the *haftarah* of *Parashas Vayeira*, which conveys the story of Elisha and the Shunami woman.

As the *pasuk* (*II Melachim* 4:8) in the *haftarah* tells us, the Shu-nami woman, who was childless, was known as a "great woman." The *Zohar* in *Parashas Beshalach* states that she was greater than any other woman in her generation, for the simple reason that she performed *hachnasas orchim* with *simchah* and desire for the mitzvah. Her love of chessed was so deep that, according to the *Midrash Rabbah,* she invit-ed Elisha to stay in her house even before his reputation was known. Her desire was not just to have the honor of the *navi's* presence — to be able to say, "a great man stays in my home." Rather, her intention was to do good — to feed and shelter a traveler.

The *Zohar* focuses on the praise that specifically applies to a woman seeking to accommodate guests. That is because usually, the burden falls upon her. She is the one to wash the linen, make the bed, cook the food and ensure that the room is clean and comfortable. While many kindhearted Jewish women are willing to do all this, it's the rare person who seeks out extra work and expense. The Shunami woman did not wait for guests at her door; she went out to seek visitors to the city in need of hospitality. She not only accommodated Elisha, but even had a room built especially for him.

Because of her hospitality, Elisha blessed her that she would have a child, and she did. However, the child died. Elisha then returned and brought the child back to life. This child was Chavakkuk HaNavi. Thus, all the wisdom Klal Yisrael merited to be granted by this prophet was the product of one woman's *ahavas chessed*.

This segment (*II Melachim* 4:1-37) presents us with a powerful image of the esteem in which Hashem holds the mitzvah of *hachnasas orchim*, and the immense magnitude of its value when it is done with *simchah* and *ahavah*. Not only did this mitzvah bring the Shunami woman a child, but it brought her a son who would be a *navi* for Klal Yisrael.

We can apply this rule to any chessed; it is always worth many times its value when we do it willingly, with a true desire to be an agent of goodness and assistance for a fellow Jew in need. That is the "greatness" ascribed to the Shunami woman, and it can be our source of greatness too. When we look around us and think, "What is needed? How can I help?" and then act to fulfill the need, we are opening the door to the *berachos* and *yeshuos* we need in our own life.

Beyond this power of *ahavas chessed*, the Midrash says that *hachnasas orchim* is a special *segulah* for having children. It works in tandem with a *berachah* to activate its power and bring about the miracle for which the person is praying. Not only do we see this force at work with the Shunami woman, but also with Sara Imeinu, who was Avraham

Avinu's full partner in the legendary *hachnasas orchim* that made him the paradigm of this mitzvah. Through her constant, enthusiastic effort in seeing to the needs of many guests entering the four open doors of Avraham's tent, she became worthy of becoming the mother of Yitzchak, and ultimately, of the Bnei Yisrael.

Charged by the power of *ahavas chessed, hachnasas orchim* brings about *yeshuos* that are above the norms of nature. If this is the case, then surely it also protects us from harm of all kinds. Going "above and beyond" to bring guests into our home and care for their needs with happiness and thoughtfulness will ensure that Hashem cares for us "above and beyond" as we live out our years as His guest in His world.

# The Most Beautiful Fruit

The Tepliker Rav was one of the notable *poskim* of Yerushalayim. It was to him that Rav Shlomo Zalman Auerbach turned many times for clarification when Rav Shlomo Zalman was writing his *sefer, Meorei Eish,* in which he discusses the subject of electricity — at the time, a new and complex topic of halachah.

With the Tepliker Rav's reputation for the highest levels of Torah knowledge, it was no surprise that from Yom Kippur to Erev Succos, long lines of people formed at his door wishing to show him their *esrogim*. The Tepliker Rav not only knew *esrogim* but treasured the mitzvah and always purchased for himself the most beautiful *daled minim* available.

Therefore, shock waves were set off when on the first day of Succos, the Tepliker Rav asked someone, "Could you please give me your *esrog* as a present?" He phrased his request this way because halachah dictates that on the first day of Yom Tov, a person may only fulfill the mitzvah with *daled minim* that he owns. The man understood the request, but was incredulous that the Tepliker Rav didn't have an *esrog*. How could that be?

He gave the Rav his *daled minim* and later, set out to discover the story behind the strange request. Here is what he found out:

> On Erev Succos, the Tepliker Rav's apartment had quieted down. The lines were gone and the Rav sat quietly learning. Suddenly, he heard shrieking coming from somewhere in the apartment building. It sounded like someone was in trouble. He leaped out of his seat and ran out the door into the hallway. There, he saw an open door and could perceive that the screaming was coming from within that apartment.
>
> He knocked on the door. "Is everything OK? Is anyone hurt?" he asked.
>
> The woman of the house was hysterical. "It's so important to my husband to get a good esrog," the woman explained "He bought the most expensive one the dealer was selling, and he warned all the children to stay away from it. He just left the house to do a few last-minute Yom Tov errands. My son took the esrog and began to play with it and it fell. A piece broke off. The esrog is ruined, and I can only imagine what my husband is going to do when he finds out!"
>
> "There's nothing to worry about," the Rav told the woman. "Wait right here." He ran to his own apartment and came back with his own esrog.
>
> "Listen to me well," he told the woman. "Here's a beautiful esrog, but your husband obviously is not going to be misled into thinking it's his. Give me the broken esrog. I'll dispose of it. Take this new esrog and tell him as follows:
>
> "Tell him that I came to see his esrog because I heard it was so beautiful. I looked at it carefully and I admired it, but I found a shailah that might have made it invalid. So, I took an extra esrog that someone gave me as a gift — a very special esrog — and gave it to him as a gift."

That is how the Tepliker Rav found himself without an *esrog* on Succos, and from this we learn what our priorities should be. Having a beautiful *esrog* is a worthy goal, but it's not the only mitzvah in the Torah. It doesn't supersede everything else. When faced with the choice between having a magnificent *esrog* or doing an exquisite act of chessed, the Rav knew which to choose.

Along the same lines, there is a story of the Chofetz Chaim that took place while he was temporarily living in Russia during World War I. The community there needed *daled minim,* but they were impossible to obtain. Finally, one set was procured for the Chofetz Chaim, and on the first day of Succos, he used his *daled minim* and then gave everyone in shul a chance to do so as well. They were then returned to the Chofetz Chaim for use during *Hallel,* but he did not perform the customary shaking of the *lulav* during the *Hallel.*

Later, the Chofetz Chaim was asked why he did not take the opportunity to use the *daled minim* during *Hallel,* since everyone had already fulfilled the mitzvah with it. He answered that while shaking the *lulav* and *esrog* during *Hallel* is a beloved and important *minhag,* it is still a *minhag.* If some of the men in shul would have felt bereft watching the Chofetz Chaim do what they could not, he explained, he would be transgressing a Torah prohibition against causing another pain. A *minhag* does not have the status of something for which a person can transgress a Torah mitzvah; therefore, he refrained.

A similar story is told about Rav Dessler: When his wife passed away, he began making *Kiddush* with a different *becher.* One of his children asked why he made this change. He explained that as a wedding gift, his father-in-law had given him the original *becher,* which fulfilled the *halachic shiur* of most *poskim,* but was not the *shiur* of the Chazon Ish. Rav Dessler used that *becher* throughout the years of his marriage. Eventually he became the *mashgiach* of the Ponevezh Yeshivah in Bnei Brak, which was the domain of the Chazon Ish. At that point, he felt he should rightfully change to the Chazon Ish's *shiur,* but he did not wish to risk hurting his wife's feelings by putting aside the *becher* that her father bought him. Once she was no longer living, he switched to a larger *becher.*

As we have discussed earlier, *minhagim and chumros* are precious, wonderful ways to elevate our *avodas Hashem,* and we must take them seriously. However, unlike mitzvos, if there is a pressing need, we are allowed to be lenient, and the greatest, most pressing need a Jew has is to avoid hurting someone's feelings. It was pressing enough for the Tepliker Rav to give away his beautiful *esrog* and not have one of his own, ensuring peace in a family.

To be sure, putting aside a *minhag* is not something to be taken lightly. We have to determine that our situation meets the criteria for a pressing need that allows us to be lenient. This is not something we should decide for ourselves, but rather, it is a question for a Rav. Our part is to develop the *seichel* to know that the question should be asked; we should not just plow ahead with our way of doing things, numb to the fact that someone else will suffer as a result. May we all find the sensitivity and *seichel* (common sense) to serve Hashem in a way that pleases Him most — by protecting the feelings of others.

# More Than a "Nice Thing to Do"

Before we sit down to a Shabbos meal, we must make *Kiddush.* Before we eat the challah, we must wash our hands. We know what to do and when to do it. These are mitzvos and we know how to fulfill these commandments.

But what about the mitzvah of "*V'ahavta l'rei'acha kamocha*"? Let's imagine that a person knows he has a lonely, widowed grandmother. Does he know when he has to call her and what he has to say to make her feel loved? Or perhaps a man finds when he comes home at the end of the day that his wife is exhausted and having trouble getting the children to bed. Does he know where to step in and what help would be useful to her?

Some things we cannot look up in the *Shulchan Aruch.* In our eyes, therefore, they become optional — nice if we do them, but not a sin if we don't. "Where is it written that I have to sweep the kitchen floor?" "Who says it has to be me to call my grandmother. I'm so busy. Why can't my sister do it?"

Because we regard chessed as an entity that is lacking substance, we underestimate just how definitive an obligation it is. The following

Gemara (*Avodah Zarah* 17b) enlightens us and may even come as a rude awakening:

> *Rav Chanina ben Teradyon, whose name is familiar to us as one of the Ten Martyrs of whom we speak in the Yom Kippur Mussaf, was captured by the Romans along with Rav Elazar ben Perata. Rav Elazar ben Perata's name is not as well known, and we will soon see the reason.*
>
> *The Gemara doesn't state the reason they were captured, but we can assume that it was for teaching Torah and performing mitzvos in defiance of the Romans' rule. The trial they faced was bound to have only one ending — the execution of the defendants.*
>
> *As they discussed their situation, Rav Elazar ben Perata said to Rav Chanina ben Teradyon, "You are lucky. You were only arrested on one charge. You can find some way out of it, give some kind of justification, and you might stay alive. For me, there are five separate charges. There is no way I am going to overcome all of them. I'm not going to get out of this alive."*
>
> *However, Rav Chanina ben Teradyon didn't see the situation this way. He told Rav Elazar ben Perata that in fact, he was the lucky one. "You will be acquitted, and woe is me, with one charge against me, I will be executed."*
>
> *"Why?" asked Rabbi Elazar ben Perata.*
>
> *"Because you toiled in Torah and you also toiled in gemilus chassadim," answered Rav Chanina. "whereas I only toiled in Torah, without gemilus chassadim."*

The Gemara then amplifies the message: "As Rav Huna said, anyone who is *osek* in Torah but doesn't also toil in chessed, it is as if he has no Hashem." What does this mean? How could he be considered a non-believer? *Rashi* explains that this is not the meaning. Rather, it means *lehagen alav* — Hashem gives him no protection. Rav Chanina ben Teradyon understood that his failure to toil in chessed was going to remove Hashem's protection from him and leave him vulnerable to the Roman's evil intentions. Rav Elazar ben Perata had a "bullet-proof vest," and Rav Chanina did not.

With this explanation, however, the Gemara asks a new question. Rav Chanina ben Teradyon was a *gabbai tzedakah*. He collected money and distributed it to the poor. He was certainly doing chessed. However, the Gemara explains that at his level, he did not do as much as he could do. Therefore, he is not identified as *"osek"* in *gemilus chassadim*.

As we discussed earlier regarding the Gemara's advice for weathering *chevlei Mashiach*, being *osek* in Torah and chessed means that we use whatever time and resources we have available for Torah and chessed to fulfill these purposes. If we're only using half of what Hashem has given us to give to others, we're not being *osek*. It is as if someone has given us $10,000 to invest in our business and we use $5,000 of it to buy new furniture.

The aforementioned Gemara illustrates the frightening result of failing to take the mitzvah to do chessed as an ironclad commandment from which we must not cut corners. Rav Chanina ben Teradyon, who was a *gabbai tzedakah*, but according to his level wasn't a toiler in chessed, had no protection. In contrast, the Gemara relates that Rav Elazar ben Perata was acquitted of all five charges, with the help of Eliyahu HaNavi. That is why his name is not as well known; he was not among the Ten Martyrs murdered by the Romans and mourned every Yom Kippur by all of Klal Yisrael.

Although the Mishnah (*Pe'ah* 1:1) relates that *"Talmud Torah k'neged kulam,"* nevertheless, to be saved from *chevlei Mashiach*, as we have mentioned, we must be *osek* in Torah and *gemilus chassadim* — both together. Even the merit of great protection that comes from learning Torah is incomplete without toiling in chessed.

Practically speaking, what does this idea require of us? Are we supposed to give up our jobs and devote ourselves to raising money or visiting the sick? Obviously, people have to live their lives, raise their families, pay their bills and so forth. Being *osek* is a mind-set that directs us, whenever there's a need and an opportunity to fill it, to do so.

For example, during the Covid lockdown when people were secluded in their homes, we might have thought that chessed could be put on hold for a while. There was no place to go and nothing to do! But someone who was *osek* in chessed thought, "I still have a phone. I can still call people," and used that resource to connect with those who might have been struggling with loneliness and fear.

We know that even during the darkest periods of the Holocaust, when people had nothing to give each other but an encouraging word, there were those who were *osek* in chessed. They saved lives by noticing who was on the verge of giving up and igniting a spark of hope in them. There's always something we can give when we are aware of the needs of others and stand ready to help them. This is the way we must look at chessed if we want the protection it provides. May we all merit that protection!

# 87

## You Know Who

"I know a man — he's a maggid shiur and his wife is a teacher — and they're having a hard time financially. Now that Pesach is coming up, I don't know how they're going to make it. Would you help me raise some money for them?"

This is a request someone made of me about 10 years ago, and I have never forgotten the powerful lesson this episode taught me. I agreed to help the man raise money and began contacting people I thought could give a substantial donation.

As I described the situation to one such man, he said, "How do you know they need money?"

"I know," I answered. "I've heard things from a few people that make it obvious."

"You know, I have a brother-in-law who is a maggid shiur and his wife is a teacher," he said. "Maybe they need money. Maybe I shouldn't look around for other people to help and just give the money to my own family."

"You're absolutely right," I agreed. "If you think that your brother-in-law might need help, go find out."

*But the man wasn't sure how he would find that information. I offered to look into it for him, and he gave me his brother-in-law's name. It was the name of the man for whom I was collecting!*

The halachah in *Yoreh Dei'ah* (*Siman* 251, *Se'if* 3) states clearly that we are obligated to give *tzedakah* to relatives first. In fact, the Vilna Gaon explains, based on the *Sifri,* that this is a *mitzvah d'Oraisa.* The *Shulchan Aruch* even provides a prioritized list of relatives, beyond the obvious requirement to support the children in our home. The order begins with parents, then married children, and then siblings. We are obligated by the Torah to distribute our *tzedakah* to our relatives who are in need, before giving any other *tzedakah.*

An important point from the above story, besides understanding our priorities in giving, is that the person to whom I was speaking was a *baal tzedakah.* He gave generously to many causes, but it never dawned on him that maybe his own brother-in-law was in need. It took someone calling him and describing the family to awaken him to the possibility that his own brother-in-law was in this situation.

This might seem surprising. However, I heard from a *gabbai tzedakah* that in nine out of 10 cases, if people are not sure how someone is managing, he isn't managing. Whether he is a rebbi, or he is a person with a regular job in the business world, if he's supporting married children, has a mortgage and debts, is paying tuition, car insurance and so on, he is either living uncomfortably close to the edge or he is sinking. The story above proves the point.

Once we understand this point, however, there is still another important step to take. As we saw with the *baal tzedakah* in the story, people are not comfortable delving into someone else's financial situation to find the facts. A person needs tact and a little creativity. The first step could be to call any of the children's schools and explain that you would like to help pay the tuition if the family has fallen behind. By finding out how much a family owes, a person can ascertain a picture of the family's overall finances. We can assume that people who owe a great deal of tuition are having trouble paying other bills as well.

By remembering the story above, we can remind ourselves of its two crucial points. Number one is that helping our relatives first is the halachah. All *poskim* agree that before donating to a yeshivah, a chessed organization, a *kollel*, the poor of our hometown and the poor of Eretz Yisrael, halachah tells us, "family first," and the Vilna Gaon holds that this is *d'Oraisa*. Rav Moshe Feinstein (*Igros Moshe* 1:144) and the Chazon Ish (quoted by Rav Chaim Kanievsky in *Derech Emunah, Hil. Matnos Aniyim* 7, 104; *Tziyon Halachah* 247) specify that this means at least half of our *tzedakah* should be distributed to family members if they are in need.

The second point is that if we are marveling at how a family is able to manage all their expenses on their tight budget, we should stop marveling and start inquiring. People who are in our lives day in and day out — our siblings, our cousins, perhaps even our own parents — might be experiencing constant stress just beneath the surface of the façade they show us. A little bit of interest and caring can go a long way to ensuring that when we give our *tzedakah*, we have our priorities straight. Not only will we be easing the suffering of those we care about most in life, but we will ensure that the full merit of our mitzvah will be available for us to enjoy forever.

# Better Than Honor

As we learned, the *Shulchan Aruch* (251:3) states that in giving *tzedakah*, our relatives must be our first priority. But from where does this ruling derive? The source is *Parashas Re'eh* (*Devarim* 15:11), which says that there will always be poor people, and therefore, "you shall surely open your hand *to your brother*, to your poor one, and to your needy one in your land."

The simple explanation of this verse, says the Vilna Gaon, is that *tzedakah* must first be given to "your brother" who is poor. Upon this, he bases his opinion that giving to family members first is a *mitzvah d'Oraisa*.

Rav Moshe Feinstein (*Igros Moshe* 1:144) rules that halachah requires us to give the majority of our *tzedakah* to needy relatives. Technically, that might mean giving away all our *tzedakah* to relatives, but Rav Moshe stops short of that proposition because it could mean that people will no longer support other *tzedakos*, which would be a *chillul Hashem*. That is because when the collectors are getting "no" after "no" as they try to solicit funds, they do not realize that people are giving their money to relatives. In their view, everyone is being tightfisted. Therefore, Rav Moshe sets the idea at "the biggest portion" and the Chazon Ish sets the proportion at half and half.

As a consequence of this rule, someone could give a million dollars to *tzedakah,* but if he hasn't given half of it to any relatives who are in need, he has not given properly. It's not a matter of how much he gives; this person is giving generous amounts. Rather, the issue is how he has apportioned his giving, and if relatives in need are not receiving at least half of the money, his mitzvah is flawed. While he still receives merit for his giving, it is not all it should be.

This leads to another scenario. Imagine a person decides to give $200,000 to a yeshivah to help pay for a new *beis medrash.* Meanwhile, he has a nephew in that yeshivah whose parents are behind in tuition. The fact that he is giving $200,000 to the yeshivah does not erase the fact that he should first have given part of that money to erase his nephew's tuition debt. Since he gave the money to the yeshivah without first taking care of his relative's needs, he hasn't utilized *tzedakah* funds properly — even to the yeshivah!

We might find this shocking. A person gives $200,000 to a yeshivah and there's something wrong — a flaw, a blemish — on his beautiful mitzvah. This is only because he has transgressed the mitzvah of caring first for "your brother," as the Torah requires.

However, people do not always find this obligation easy or appealing to fulfill. Giving big donations to *yeshivos* and organizations garners great recognition and expressions of gratitude. Often, the donation becomes public knowledge, adding to the donor's status and prestige. Giving to a relative, on the other hand, must be done quietly so as not to cause him embarrassment. It might even need to be done anonymously. Sometimes, instead of a thank you, the recipient resents the giver.

Therefore, we have to appreciate the strength of people who rise above these challenges, as in this true story:

> *A chassidishe young man told me that he is one of many brothers, almost all of whom are struggling financially. One brother,*

*however, is quite wealthy, and he supports most of the siblings. He pays all their tuitions and helps supply each family with their everyday needs.*

*"My brother told me that many times, when a chassidishe Rebbe comes to town, he is offered the privilege of hosting him," said the young man. "But he turns it down. And do you know why? He says that when a Rebbe stays at a person's house, the host is naturally expected to give large contributions to the rebbe's mosdos. But along with that comes the prestige of being the host and having everyone in the community flock to his home. He said he has an overwhelming yetzer hara for this honor, but he realizes that according to halachah, his first obligation is to help his family."*

This is a beautiful example of someone who understands what the Torah wants of him. May we be *zocheh* to follow his example and give *tzedakah* in a way that pleases Hashem.

# The Surprise Ending

Is that child who sits alone at recess really just an introvert who prefers reading to being with others? Or is she doing her best to keep her mind off the stabbing pain she feels? The following true story provides us with a clear picture:

*Malky\* was a highly intelligent little girl, but by third grade, she was already feeling that she didn't quite fit in with her classmates. This was made painfully obvious to her by Atara, an aggressive and charismatic child who made it her business to taunt Malky. The situation grew worse in fourth grade as Atara's arsenal of insults grew more sophisticated.*

*By fifth grade, school life was intolerable for Malky. She would daven for a rainy day because then, recess would be indoors. Her teacher would sit at her desk grading papers and Malky would sit nearby, feeling protected from Atara, who would not dare do her bullying within the teacher's hearing.*

*Finally, as sixth grade approached, hope dawned for Malky. The middle school had parallel classes, and she would be switching into a new class where she could start afresh. Throughout the summer, she was bursting with excitement at the prospect of* finally being freed from constant bullying. However, on the first day of sixth grade, her hopes were shot down like a bird from the sky — Atara was in her new class.

Telling the story as an adult, Malky says she still does not know how such a mistake happened. Her mother had been on the phone for hours with the principal, trying to ensure that Malky would be freed from her terrible plight, but there she was, once again under Atara's reign of terror. Matters continued to get worse until Malky began to lose her desire to live. In her 11-year-old eyes, three more years with Atara was a lifetime — too much for her to endure.

Then Mrs. Steinfeld entered the picture. She was a grammar teacher who taught a few periods each week. Before Chanukah, Mrs. Steinfeld introduced the Secret Friend project. She asked each girl to write down the name of one girl on a piece of paper and make it her mission to make that girl happy.

One Sunday, Malky received a phone call from a popular girl in the class who invited her to come to her home to study together. Immediately, Malky assumed that she was the girl's Secret Friend chessed project and she refused to go. However, her mother forced the issue, literally lifting her up, putting her in the car and taking her to the girl's house. When she rang the doorbell and the girl opened the door, the house was dark. Suddenly, the lights went on. The room was bright with banners and balloons. A few more very popular girls in the class were there, and in unison, they shouted, "Happy birthday!"

"We heard your birthday's tomorrow," one of the girls told her. "our dream is to make someone a surprise birthday party." That Sunday, Malky says, she experienced techiyas hameisim — a dead child came to life.

Malky ended her story with a simple tribute: "Where are you Mrs. Steinfeld? You saved my life." And indeed, Mrs. Steinfeld along with these warm-hearted girls changed Malky's self-image from "a discarded no one" to "the guest of honor." (Adapted from a true story printed in The Voice of Lakewood.)

As we have shown numerous times, this is chessed at its finest. This is the *Rambam's* definition of the ultimate way to fulfill the *mitzvah d'Oraisa* of *v'ahavta l'rei'acha kamocha*, because if we want to do for others what we want done for ourselves, then we must strive to do what we *most* want done for us. We want to be respected and acknowledged, to know that our life matters, because if our life doesn't matter, we have no reason to live.

For the price of a few balloons and cupcakes, these girls turned Malky's life around. We cannot let people in her situation, whether they are children or adults, drift into despair. Sometimes we are sitting at a wedding, and everyone is talking to the people sitting near them, but one person is sitting quietly, nibbling on pickles and coleslaw. The person to his left is talking to the man on his other side. The person to his right is talking to the one sitting on *his* other side. This person feels invisible, even if he knows everyone at the table. We have to be aware. We cannot let this happen to people. As the *Rambam* tells us, there is no chessed we can do — no money we can donate, no organization we can support — that better fulfills what Hashem wants of us.

# A Bit of Yourself

The Satmar Rebbe often told the following story of the Divrei Chaim of Sanz that illustrated the trait which, in his view, qualified a person for the title "Rebbe."

*A man came to the Divrei Chaim and told him, "I am a chassid of your son, the Shinover Rav (Rav Yechezkel Shinover)."*

*"Why are you his chassid?" the Divrei Chaim asked him. "There are so many other rebbes. What do you find special about my son?"*

*"His davening is awesome to see," said the man. "He is a true servant of Hashem."*

*"True, but many other rebbes also daven with tremendous kavannah."*

*"But also," said the man, "he is an incredible talmid chacham."*

*"Also true," the Divrei Chaim agreed. "But so are many other rebbes. Why have you chosen my son over all the others?"*

*The man started to become flustered. He wasn't sure how to answer. At last, he was able to pinpoint the trait that drew him to the Shinover Rav.*

*"I will tell a story that answers the question," he said. "Once, a poor man came knocking at the Shinover Rav's door for tzedakah. It was freezing cold outside and the ground was covered with snow. After the Shinover Rav gave the man some money, he looked down at the man's feet and saw that he had no shoes. Instead, his feet were wrapped in rags. The Rav took off his own shoes and gave them to the man."*

*This answer pleased the Divrei Chaim. "Someone who takes something from himself and gives it to someone else, now that's a Rebbe!" he exclaimed.*

It all started with Avraham Avinu. In *Parashas Vayeira*, the Torah relates that on the third day after his *bris milah*, at the height of the day's especially intense heat, he sat outside his tent on the lookout for guests. Although the timing was inconvenient and quite difficult for him, his desire to do the chessed of *hachnassas orchim* overcame the obstacles. He took from himself; he sacrificed his comfort and convenience to be of service to passersby in need of food and rest.

Avraham Avinu's chessed is still our paradigm, and our *gedolim* exemplify it for us. One story about Rav Elya Svei illustrates this. His illustrious *talmid*, Rav Yitzchok Isbee, was in the hospital suffering from the illness that took him from the world at the young age of 45. His illness truncated a stellar career in which he was able to exert significant positive influence on his community of Agudas Yisrael Bais Binyamin of Avenue L and the greater Flatbush community.

Rav Elya Svei came to visit. There, he met Rebbetzin Isbee, the daughter of Rav Dovid Kronglas. She said to Rav Elya, "Please give me a guarantee that my husband will have a *refuah sheleimah*."

"I can't give a guarantee," said Rav Elya. "But I can tell you that I have already fasted *taaneisim* for him to have a *refuah sheleimah*."

Rav Elya was by then an older man. His days were filled to capacity tending to the needs of Klal Yisrael while also preparing and giving *shiurim* and serving as Rosh Yeshivah. Nevertheless, he felt the need to give something of himself for his *talmid*, more than thoughts and words — even the decidedly powerful words of his *tefillos*. He backed his prayers with a deed, something that said, "I will take a share of your suffering."

In a similar vein, after the passing of Rav Shmuel Auerbach, someone close to him revealed the special way he gave of himself. Whenever one of his *talmidim* married, he and his rebbetzin would fast on the wedding day and go to the *Kosel HaMaaravi* to *daven* that they would merit building a *bayis ne'eman b'Yisrael*. They backed their prayers by lovingly giving from their own comfort and convenience.

Although *davening* for someone, remembering their name during *Shemoneh Esrei* or saying *Tehillim* for them is still a beautiful and worthwhile chessed, the lesson here is that there is a higher level. Moreover, it's accessible to all of us. We may not be ready to fast for someone else's troubles, but we can all step out of our comfort zone and say "yes" when it might not be the most convenient time for us. When someone who needs to talk calls, we can put aside what we were planning to do and give him our attention. When someone needs a ride to a destination that's not exactly on our way, we can gladly provide it. When someone asks us to pick up an item while we're out, we can find the 15 minutes to do the favor.

Putting ourselves out for someone is not only a praiseworthy thing to do, but it benefits us as well. As we have observed numerous times throughout this volume, Hashem treats us *middah k'neged middah*. This means that when we are the ones asking a favor of someone, and that person is thinking, "Oh no, not now, I don't have the time for this," Hashem can send him that little spark of inspiration that makes him think again: "Sure, why not help him out? Can't I spare a half-hour?"

While everyone has the power to make his own choices, the Vilna Gaon tells us that Hashem puts thoughts into people's heads. He derives this from the *pasuk*, "*Rabbos machashavos b'leiv ish va'atzas Hashem hi sakum* — Man's thoughts are many, but Hashem's counsel is what prevails" (*Mishlei* 19:21). Why, he asks, does the *pasuk* refer to thoughts first as *machashavos*, and then as *eitzah*? He answers that *machshavos* are the thoughts we generate in our own minds. *Eitzah,* however, is "advice." It's the thought of another's mind, which that person instills into us.

*Mishlei* is telling us that no matter what thoughts a person generates in his own mind, Hashem's *eitzos* — the advice He wants us to heed — will override them. For example, Hashem will put into one's mind the thought to accept a certain child into his school, or to hire a certain person for a job. When we stand by our friend's side, Hashem's *eitzos* will override the thoughts of those who wish to do us harm. When we are kind to others, we claim our place in a world of kindness.

91

# *Drive Away Trouble*

The Gemara (*Gittin* 52a) relates that, on a steady basis, the Satan harassed a husband and wife. The Gemara asks why the Satan chose these two people to provoke. It answers that they would argue with each other every Friday evening, in the period of *bein hashemashos*. Because there was *machlokes* in their house the Satan had an open door by which to enter their home.

The story continues with Rav Meir, who knew through *ruach hakodesh* that the Satan was able to move into their house because they would argue every week on Erev Shabbos. Rav Meir therefore visited their home on Erev Shabbos, and he kept the peace between them. He came back the next week and did the same. By the third week, the Gemara says, he had succeeded in bringing complete *shalom* to these people. He then heard the Satan say, "Woe is to that man that Rav Meir drove him out of the house." He was referring to himself, pitying himself for being driven away from his comfortable spot in this home by Rav Meir's successful peace-making.

The immediate message of the Satan's remark is that he and peace cannot coexist in one place. Where peace comes in, he must depart. Only because the two people argued with each other did the Satan find a welcoming environment. Their *machlokes* was his oxygen. When Rav Meir quelled their *machlokes* the Satan was forced to leave. Shalom deprived him of his "oxygen."

While *machlokes* draws the Satan, *shalom* draws blessing. We learn this from a famous *Chazal* that compares the success of Dovid HaMelech's army to that of Achav's army. In *Yerushalmi* (*Pe'ah*, Ch. 1), among many other sources, we learn that in the generation of Dovid HaMelech (some say Shaul HaMelech), the army sustained many casualties when they went out to battle. In contrast, in the times of Achav, when *avodah zarah* was rampant, the soldiers would return home victorious and unharmed.

In all the accounts of this phenomenon, only one cause is cited for the difference: the level of *shalom* and *achdus* prevalent during each period. In Dovid HaMelech's times, *lashon hara* and *machlokes* flowed. Because of this, Hashem's protection in battle was compromised. Achav's generation, however, was united. Although they were united in their worship of *avodah zarah,* the very fact that they were at peace with each other was enough to draw Divine protection.

As we discussed in Lesson 83, we see the same dynamic at work when we compare the generation of the *mabul* (flood) to the *dor haflagah* (generation of dispersion). *Midrash Rabbah* on *Parashas Noach* explains that Noach's generation was immersed in robbery, which indicates that people acted against each other's interests, with no concern about the other person's rights or well-being. That generation had to be destroyed completely. The *dor haflagah,* however, worked together to build the Tower of Bavel. They were united, although the goal of their unity was to challenge Hashem. Therefore, Hashem allowed them to live, and punished them only by dispersing them and causing them to speak many different languages.

*Chazal* are teaching us in many different ways that our best efforts at *avodas Hashem* can be ruined by a lack of *shalom*, and conversely, our gravest mistakes can be mitigated by peace. No one wants to leave the door unlocked for the Satan, or to invite disaster into his life. We all want *berachah*. That is why *Rabbeinu HaKadosh* (Rav Yehudah Ha-Nasi), who compiled the Mishnayos, zeroes in on this one vital point. The final Mishnah concludes with this lesson: Hashem's *only* vessel for *berachah* is *shalom*.

In the most practical way, we see that this is true. No matter what *berachos* Hashem bestows on us — health, wealth, family, *nachas* from our children — we cannot feel the full happiness of it when our hearts are soured by *machlokes*. Only with *shalom* does all the good Hashem wants to give us and all of Klal Yisrael come to fruition.

# 92

# Just a Drop

A well-known *mechanech* in Eretz Yisrael tells of his efforts to help a student who was gradually leaving the path of Torah:

*The boy had one foot out the door of the yeshivah, and the mechanech was struggling to draw him back. When nothing he did seemed to help, he arranged an appointment for the boy to meet with Rav Shmuel Auerbach.*

*Before the day of the appointment, the mechanech apprised Rav Shmuel of the boy's situation and everything that had been done up until that point. When the time came for the meeting, Rav Shmuel welcomed the boy into his office, but did not make any mention of what had precipitated the meeting. Instead, the gadol said, "Could you do me a favor? I have a difficult Gemara here and I need some help. Can you sit down and learn it with me?"*

*He took down two Gemaras, and Rav Shmuel learned with the boy for about an hour. In telling the story, the mechanech related that when the learning was finished, the boy's eyes were filled with* tears. *"You are the first person who treated me like an equal,"* he told Rav Shmuel. *"You are the first one who was interested in what I have to say. You gave me back some kavod, and whatever the Rosh Yeshivah will advise me, I will do."*

We truly do not understand the power we hold in our hands. Rav Yaakov Meir Shechter spoke about a boy he was working with who had become *mechallel Shabbos*. "I'm not making excuses for someone giving up the mitzvos," Rav Yaakov Meir said, "but listen to what this boy told me. He said, 'When I was in yeshivah, if I would have gotten even one drop of *kavod* — one drop in an ocean — I wouldn't have left. I would still be *shomer Shabbos* today.'"

Obviously, the boy still had *bechirah* and could choose a better path, but there is a point that must penetrate out minds and hearts; people need respect. As Rav Moshe Shapiro used to repeat from the Alter of Slabodka, if a person felt that he was totally worthless, his *neshamah* would depart from his body. The need for *kavod* is like the need for oxygen. There is no life without it.

Explaining further, Rav Moshe Shapiro quotes the *Baal HaMaor's* insight into the words of *Mizmor Shir Chanukas Habayis l'Dovid* (*Tehillim* 30), which we say every day in *Pesukei d'Zimrah*. The *perek* ends *"le'maan yizamercha chavod* — So that my *neshamah* will sing." Therefore, the *Baal HaMaor* writes in his introduction to his commentary on *Shas*, this *pasuk* is equating the *neshamah* with *kavod* — one and the same.

Ideally, a person's *kavod* comes from his innate sense of self-worth, but if this is insufficient, he still needs to sustain his *neshamah*. He needs to inculcate that *kavod,* that respect, from somewhere else.

A *talmid* of Rav Moshe Shapiro recalled that Rav Moshe used to say that if someone were to squeeze every drop of self-respect out of a person, one of two things will happen. Either the person would die, as the Alter from Slabodka says, or he will imagine a new identity for himself, one in which he is respected. His mind will snap. He will think he is Mashiach or Emperor Napoleon. Because he *must* have *kavod* to go on living, he will either stop living or stop being himself.

Unfortunately, there are many people who are "dying for *kavod*," not to feel superior but just to feel esteemed, valued, worthy, respected. Most of us know someone like that, and we might wonder how anything we could do would have any significant impact on him. We see it as putting a small band-aid on a gaping wound. However, this is not an accurate way to regard it, because when someone feels no *kavod,* the smallest drop makes a difference. It's like a small dot of color on a black sheet of paper. With that dot, the sheet is no longer all black.

Every person has the ability to inject one drop of *kavod* into someone. It is the means Hashem has given us to perform a miracle we might never believe we could perform — to be *mechayeh hameisim,* to bring a person back to life.

# Great Isn't Always Good

There are many people who have much to offer Klal Yisrael and they are intent on giving all they can. That may seem like the path to greatness, but sometimes, it's a path to pain, as this story from Rav Sholom Schwadron portrays:

*There was a certain mashgiach in a yeshivah in Eretz Yisrael who needed to travel to America to solicit for the yeshivah. His regular mussar shmuessen would be suspended in his absence. The talmidim wanted to fill the gap, and so, they obtained the mashgiach's permission to invite Rav Sholom Schwadron to speak.*

*Rav Sholom realized that the yeshivah students would benefit from hearing motivating, inspiring words to fuel their efforts in Torah and yiras Shamayim. He also knew that he was more than capable of giving them what they needed. However, one issue troubled him and left him unsure if he should accept their invitation.*

*Rav Sholom decided to discuss his dilemma with Rav Yechezkel Levenstein, the renowned Ponevezh mashgiach.*

*"This mashgiach gave the bachurim permission to ask me to give shmuessen," he told Rav Chatzkel. "On one hand, I understand*

*that I should do it because the students need to hear mussar. But on the other hand, I'm worried because I know that I'm a more captivating speaker than their mashgiach, and he might find out that the students are enjoying my shmuessen more than they enjoy his. The mashgiach's feelings will be hurt, and in that case, maybe I shouldn't do it."*

*Rav Chatzkel answered with this advice: "We have a kabbalah that if we could rebuild the Beis HaMikdash, but rebuilding it will cause pain to another Jew, we don't rebuild it. Therefore, you should not speak in that mashgiach's place."*

Of course, we cannot make specific decisions in our own life based on stories; we need to ask our own *shailah*. We see from this story, though, that no matter how lofty the goal we are setting out to accomplish, we must weigh it against the feelings of those who will be affected by what we do. We must realize that there is a *shailah* to be asked.

A second story reinforces this point:

*The son-in-law of Rav Aryeh Levin, Rav Shmuel Aharon Yudelevitz, was known as a tzaddik and brilliant talmid chacham. On Yom Kippur night, he was attending a shul whose Rav had recently passed away. Therefore, there was no one to give the derashah a Rav usually gives after Kol Nidrei — a derashah whose purpose is to open hearts to teshuvah. Many in the shul turned to Rav Yudelevitz and asked him to fill the void. However, he refused. They repeated the request several times, but each time he remained steadfast, until at last Maariv began.*

*On the way home, one of his children asked him why he refused to speak and inspire people to do teshuvah on Yom Kippur night.*

*"I could have done it," he said. "But it would not have been worthwhile if the Rav's widow would have shed just one tear upon hearing someone other than her husband, giving the speech. That would outweigh the tears of a hundred people crying in teshuvah. One tear of a widow in pain would push away any benefit my speaking could bring."*

In *Parashas Shemos,* we see how deep this idea goes. Moshe Rab-beinu resisted Hashem's assignment to rescue the Jewish people from Egypt. First, he claimed that the people would not believe him and therefore, would not follow his leadership. Next, he claimed that his speech impairment disqualified him from the job. Finally, he argued that Hashem should send Aharon, his older brother.

*Rashi* says that this argument lasted for seven days, but the final reason was the real reason for Moshe's reluctance. He did not want to step over the head of his older brother and risk hurting his feelings. This was an issue in his eyes even though the mission was to save the Jewish people and his marching orders were coming straight from Hashem!

Moshe was being asked to do a great thing. Rav Sholom Schwad-ron was also being asked to do a great thing, as was Rav Yudelevitz. We learn from them that the greatness of the mission is only one side of the question. The other — "Will I be hurting anyone?" — is the other, equally important side, because causing anyone pain would override the good they might do.

# The Day Amalek Leined

One year on the Shabbos of *Parashas Zachor*, Rav Sholom Schwadron, the famous *maggid* of Yerushalayim, witnessed this scene:

*A bar mitzvah was taking place in shul. After the bar mitzvah bachur capably leined the parashah, the time came to read the maftir portion of Parashas Zachor. Because hearing this parashah in its complete and correct form is a mitzvah from the Torah, many shuls do not permit a bar mitzvah boy, whose status as a gadol may not be fully established, to be the one to lein it.*

*In this shul, however, there was no firm policy. The boy had prepared the leining and was about to go ahead when the shul's regular baal korei went to the bimah and stopped him.*

*"I don't know for certain that you are a gadol," the baal korei told the boy.*

*"I am!" the boy answered.*

*"Well, you don't have a beard," the baal korei answered. "So it isn't 100 percent certain."*

*The argument continued until the bar mitzvah boy burst into tears. The baal korei moved him aside and leined Parashas Zachor.*

In telling this story, to which he was an eyewitness, Rav Sholom Schwadron said the *baal korei* should have gone to another *minyan* to hear *Parashas Zachor* again if he was concerned that he hadn't fulfilled the mitzvah. He could even have quietly advised others to do the same, without the boy's knowledge.

To embarrass the *bar mitzvah bachur* in order to ensure hearing *Parashas Zachor* from someone whose adult status is beyond doubt, said Rav Schwadron, was a grave miscalculation. He expressed his opinion in these stark terms: "That year I heard *Parashas Zachor* read by Amalek himself."

This is a powerful indictment. The *baal korei's* intention was surely *l'sheim Shamayim;* he only wanted to be sure that he was fulfilling the mitzvah correctly. However, as the *Chovos HaLevavos* teaches, "*Lo mitoch machshevoseinu, ela mitoch ma'aseinu* — We are judged not by our thoughts, but by our actions." A person can intend to serve Hashem with his action, but instead, perform a deed worthy of Amalek.

The Gemara (*Bava Metzia* 59a) gives us a picture of how serious a matter this is: "It is better for a person to throw himself into a fiery furnace than to embarrass another person in public." If this is the case, then certainly we have to realize that before we stand up and create a public issue with another person, we have to think it over a thousand times.

We must understand that when we are trying to fulfill a mitzvah at the expense of someone else's *kavod*, we are standing in front of an open door to *Gehinnom*. The Gemara (*Bava Metzia* 58b) relates that a person who humiliates someone in public does not have a portion in *Olam Haba*. Therefore, no matter what we are trying to accomplish, we must make sure we do not accomplish it through the destruction of another person's pride. On top of the rubble we thereby create, we cannot build anything worthwhile or lasting. Even when there's a mitzvah in front of us, and we have five different indications in halachah that we are supposed to exercise stringency in performing it, those five indications do not outweigh the sin of embarrassing someone.

May we always realize this and internalize it when it counts. When the time for a mitzvah arrives, and we are on fire to perform it with all the *chumros,* may we have the wisdom to stop and look around us for a moment, and see if there is someone who we perceive to be "standing in our way." If so, we need to realize that when we run this person down, we are plunging ourselves into the fire of *Gehinnom.* It is far better, says the Gemara, to plunge ourselves into a furnace, in an effort to avoid inflicting pain on someone.

This is an awareness we need to build. It is a paradox, because the very strength of our desire to serve Hashem can fuel words and actions that take us far in the opposite direction. The message is clear; when we're "on fire," we need to avoid getting caught up in our passion and make sure it's the right kind of fire. And if we're not sure what to do, we should ask a true *daas Torah.*

# Something to Add

In 1948, Yerushalayim was under siege and bombs were exploding in the streets. One night, Rav Isser Zalman Meltzer told his wife, "I have to go out to take care of an emergency." Defying the curfew and risking his life, he left the house. His wife waited fretfully until he returned an hour later, his face radiating pure simchah.

"What happened? Where did you go?" his rebbetzin asked.

"My sefer, Even HaEzel on the Rambam, is ready to go to print," Rav Isser Zalman said. "In it, I quote two of my brothers-in-law on explanations of a Rambam. When I was reviewing the sefer for the final time before sending it to the printer, I realized that my third brother-in-law, who is a very respected talmid chacham, isn't quoted anywhere in the sefer. If the sefer came out and he saw my two other brothers-in-law quoted while there's nothing from him, he might feel hurt.

"I couldn't wait for morning because I have to give it in to the printer, and then it's too late to make changes. I decided it's worth risking my life to go and make sure that he should not feel slighted.

*"So, I went to the house, and I asked him for an explanation on a particular Rambam. He gave me a good explanation, and I can now quote him in the sefer."*

This is a special message for us, especially when our families gather for a Shabbos or Yom Tov. During these times, when families are together, we can easily slip into showing favoritism to one son, son-in-law, brother or brother-in-law, and the others feel it.

Rav Isser Zalman was willing to risk his life to make sure that one brother-in-law did not feel passed over in favor of the other brothers-in-law. He knew that no matter how great a person's stature, he feels pain at being left out. The most brilliant lawyer, the wealthiest businessman, the great Rosh Yeshivah — no matter who they are and what they've accomplished, they all need to feel they have a place at the table.

Furthermore, faking it doesn't help. People are intuitive. If there's a conversation going on and it changes course when someone new joins the group, that person is aware that his contribution to the topic that was being discussed isn't considered worthwhile. We might look at people and think they're not learned enough or smart enough to have something to add. We may be wrong, or we may be right about that, but we will always be wrong if we relegate people to the sidelines, and we'll always be right if we bring them into the conversation. Thinking about this is a worthwhile preparation for any Yom Tov or Shabbos when our families will be around the table together. It's a time to build bonds and warmth, not, *chas v'shalom*, resentment. May we have the wisdom to navigate this delicate territory smoothly.

# 96

# The Chessed of Showing Up

There's a prevalent custom when people make a wedding of displaying an invitation in a public place. The printed invitation usually includes a hand-written note stating that everyone is invited to attend. In fact, the *sefer Likkutei HaRim* records many invitations for the weddings of the children and grandchildren of the Chiddushei HaRim, on which he himself wrote such a note. Most are phrased, "I'm asking all the *chassidim* to come participate in my *simchah* in order to fulfill the mitzvah in the Torah of *v'ahavta l'rei'acha kamocha.*"

As we've discussed in many of our previous lessons, the mitzvah of *v'ahavta l'rei'acha kamocha* is a mitzvah of action. Whatever we would like someone to do for us, we should do for others. When we make a *simchah,* we want people to come and participate; therefore, it is a *mitzvah d'Oraisa* of *v'ahavta l'rei'acha kamocha* to participate in someone else's *simchah.*

That idea holds true for any act of chessed. However, the Chiddushei HaRim points out that *simchas chassan v'kallah* has an additional distinction. On one of the invitations included in the *sefer,* he asks why *Chazal* made this a distinct mitzvah if it is already included in *v'ahavta l'rei'acha kamocha*. The reason, he says, is that this particular mitzvah instructs us how to fulfill the mitzvah of *v'ahavta l'rei'acha kamocha* properly.

Why this mitzvah? There are many *chassadim* that *Chazal* could have used as the paradigm. The power of this mitzvah is based on the idea that the greater our desire to have others do a certain act of kindness for us, the greater is the mitzvah to do it for them.

This leads to a point: Our greatest desire is for friendship, and when people join us in our *simchah*, we recognize this as an act of friendship. They've given up their evening and prioritized our *simchah* over anything else they might have done in that time, even if it was only to get to bed early. They've driven — sometimes long distances. They've put on their *simchah* clothes, perhaps found a babysitter. They've come to our *simchah* even though it's the third one that week. That's a friend! And for any human being, that's the greatest treasure.

Furthermore, most acts of chessed are driven by our compassion for a person who is in need. Our sympathy and empathy are aroused. We see that someone needs our help, and as good Jews, we rise to the occasion. However, we might easily overlook the chessed of participating in a *simchah* because after all, the *baal simchah* is on top of the world. He's not needy. Furthermore, a few hundred other people are likely to be there, making our presence seem that much less important. If we view it this way, however, we are vastly underestimating how precious our own expression of friendship is to the *baal simchah*, whether he's a relative, neighbor, coworker, or friend.

I recently heard from a very wise person something that I never realized. He said, "I made a *simchah* and Zelig did not attend. I consider him a close friend and I felt bad he could not share in my good fortune. I missed him but he must have had a good reason. This taught me to go the extra mile. *Iy"H* when he or anyone else makes a *simchah* I'll try my best to participate."

The main point is not how bad someone might feel if we fail to participate in his *simchah*. Rather, it is the opportunity to make others happy when we do participate. One acquaintance told me, "You know why I try my best to come to people's *simchos*? Because I was also once a *baal simchah*, and I saw how much it meant to me that people showed me their friendship. I realized that it mattered to me, that I wanted people to join my *simchah*, and therefore, I should *shlep* to them."

This is what the Chiddushei HaRim is telling us: *Chazal* are teaching us how to fulfill the mitzvah of *v'ahavta l'rei'acha kamocha*. When we make a *simchah*, we want people to participate, to show that they consider us a friend. We want our relatives to show that they're not just related by blood, but by care and connection.

Of course, we have to be *dan l'kaf zechus*, and make it our business not to take offense when others cannot attend our *simchos*. However, we would want them to give us a phone call, to show that they share in our happiness because they are our friends. When we give others what they want most in life — friendship and recognition — we fulfill *v'ahavta l'rei'acha kamocha* at the highest level, as *Chazal* teach us to do.

# 97

## Open Door Policy

There's a knock on the door. The homeowner takes a quick look at his security monitor and yells from the next room, "Come in!"

What does this tell us? Would he call "Come in!" if he suspected that the person at the door was there to rob his house? Or if it was the mailman or the local cop on the beat? When we open our door to someone, we're acknowledging that they're connected to us. Furthermore, we are making them feel connected. We're saying, "You're someone I will share my space with."

This may not seem like a very important feature in the wide world of chessed, but the *Zohar* teaches us otherwise through a discussion on a dispute among the *Tannaim* in *Masechta Sanhedrin* regarding whether the people of Sedom will be among those brought back to life in *techiyas hameisim*. The *Zohar* relates that one *Tanna* asks another *Tanna* whether Sedom's inhabitants, who were totally wiped out and sent to *Gehinnom*, have any merit that will enable them to be revived. The other *Tanna* answers that the issue can be settled by examining the precise *middah k'neged middah* of Hashem's justice.

He then describes three factors upon which the justice for the people of Sedom will ultimately rest. The first is that they refused to satisfy the pleas of the poor for food. Since they did not revive the *nefesh* of those begging for food, *middah k'neged middah*, Hashem will not revive their *nefesh* in *techiyas hameisim*. Secondly, they did not give *tzedakah*, and therefore, Hashem removed them from this world.

The third point is less obvious but provides us with an insight that can prove priceless. The *Zohar* says that not only did they refuse to give food to poor people, and not only did they fail to give *tzedakah*, but in addition, they did not allow visitors to their city to walk its streets. They closed the pathways of the city to non-residents. Therefore, says the *Zohar*, Hashem sealed off the pathways to *rachamei Shamayim*, Heavenly mercy, sealing their fate in this world and in the World to Come.

Incredibly, this *Zohar* is saying that all the cruelty Sedom's inhabitants exhibited in their first two sins did not create a permanent roadblock to *techiyas hameisim*. Only the roadblock they themselves erected against strangers, guests and newcomers walking the streets of their city cut them off from any kind of spiritual future.

This should awaken us to the merit we can attain when we open the door to our home to let someone in, or open the door to our car to give someone a ride, or leave our accustomed seat in shul open to let a guest have a place. As we break down barriers and roadblocks in this world, *middah k'neged middah* we open the path to *rachamei Shamayim* in the next world.

Not only does this *Zohar* let us in on a whole new reservoir of merit, but it shows us that there is more value than we realize in the chessed we already do. For example, giving someone a ride is a chessed; we're easing his way, saving him a long walk or a half-hour of waiting around in the heat or the rain for someone to pick him up. This is great because we are doing for someone else what we would want done for us. But on top of that, and no less valuable, is the fact that we are opening our car door and inviting him to sit with us in our domain.

Similarly, the food, bed and companionship we give a guest is a beautiful chessed, but simultaneously, there is another chessed taking place. We have brought him into our home. We're not stopped by concern that he'll spill wine on our tablecloth or cause us to have to cook extra food and wash extra linens. Even more precise a correlation to the situation in Sedom is our willingness to let others cross our property or allow children to fetch a stray ball that's landed into our yard.

The more we say to our fellow Jew, "You are welcome in my world," the more merit we have for Hashem to say to us, when He brings us to the majestic time of Mashiach, that we are welcome in His perfected World of *Geulah*. And until that time, we can open the paths of *rachamei Shamayim* to lead us in peace through the world in which we live.

# Going Public

Years ago in Eretz Yisrael, a person claimed to be possessed by a *dybbuk*. Some *gedolim* said the person was indeed possessed, while others said that it was a case of mental illness. People lined up behind the two factions and the debate became widespread and heated.

Not long after this news broke, Rav Gamliel Rabinowitz, addressed one aspect of the situation, which was based on an eyewitness story that a man had told him:

*The man was part of a group of people who were debating about the dybbuk. One of those in the group became enraged. He stood up and began screaming at another man, "You believe this? You think this is real? Anyone who believes this is a naïve fool!"*

*The person against whom he was railing was clearly embarrassed. The man who told me the story said that at that moment, he had one thought, "Whether the dybbuk is real or not, I have no idea. But one thing I do know. I do know that because of this topic of a dybbuk, someone lost his chelek in Olam Haba. I do know that the Mishnah (Pirkei Avos 3:11) says that 'Hamalbin pnei chaveiro b'rabbim* — *If someone embarrasses someone in public, ein lo chelek l'Olam Haba* — *he has no share in Olam Haba."*

"The person who told me this story was very smart," Rav Gamliel added. "What he said is true."

The *Pri Megadim* (in his *Matan Secharan Shel Mitzvos* §5) rules that embarrassing someone in "public" in this context means in front of three people — two bystanders and the person who is being embarrassed. That means that if four people are together, and one of them humiliates another while two other people witness the humiliation, the perpetrator is guilty of embarrassing someone in public. That's all it takes to commit an act that removes a person from a future in *Olam Haba*. Whether he does it in front of a packed auditorium or a few people, it meets the definition of "public." Furthermore, I have never found an *acharon*, or a *posek*, who disagrees with the *Pri Megadim* on this point.

Rav Chaim Brisker advised that anyone who believes he might have a case in which the Torah allows a person to embarrass someone in public must ask *daas Torah*. One possible instance might be a rebbi dealing with certain behaviors in a student. But even where there seems to be justification, or even a necessity to speak publicly, the decision cannot be taken likely, said Rav Chaim, because the question is not just one of halachah — which itself deserves serious consideration — but of his entire stake in *Olam Haba*. He must proceed with the utmost caution. If he must criticize someone, he should do it in private unless *daas Torah* advises him that this specific issue requires a public response. Without that assurance, he is risking *Olam Haba*.

The frightening truth about this concept is that people often speak harshly to someone without a second thought about who else is hearing the words. For example, someone recently told me of an instance in which she was among a group of women when one, who was a bit older than the others, began strongly demeaning another woman in the group. The rest of the group appeared shellshocked. No one stood up for the victim.

The woman who told the story said that later, she texted the victim and told her that she knew the things being said were not true, and she felt for the woman's humiliation. "I want you to know," the victim texted back, "that my poor husband is going to have to put up with my crying to him the entire night after I experienced such embarrassment."

The one who caused this embarrassment may not realize how grave her transgression was. She might think, "I said what needed to be said. Someone had to say it," or whatever justification she might have in her mind. But the truth is, this is a woman who is in dire need of *teshuvah* and *mechilah,* because she did something that literally removes a person from his *chelek* in *Olam Haba.* She could easily have prevented the entire episode by speaking to the woman in private if she felt she had something worthwhile to impart.

Embarrassing someone needlessly is not an option in giving rebuke. Rachel Imeinu shows us, through the sacrifice she made to protect her sister's dignity, the exceptional importance of protecting others from this type of suffering. Rachel was supposed to marry Yaakov. It was her moment, but she gave it to her sister Leah and shared the *simanim* Yaakov had established with her to ensure that Lavan would give him the right daughter. She could have been the happy *kallah* that day, but she couldn't bear to cause her sister humiliation.

Nevertheless, when humiliation happens, the victim can turn it around into an outstanding source of goodness for themselves or someone else. The story above has just such a conclusion, which I will share.

> The woman who was embarrassed had been having difficulty getting her daughter into an elementary school. The woman who texted her said, "You know, now that you were so embarrassed in public, it will be a kapparah for you and you'll get your daughter into school."
>
> "Well, it so happens that we have an interview tomorrow for another school," said the woman. "We'll see what happens."

*After the interview, the friend received another text telling her, "My daughter was not acting properly during the interview. I doubt if she'll be accepted." But the next day, the woman received a call inviting her daughter to join the coming year's class. "It really was a kapparah!" the mother said.*

People who are humiliated in public and do not respond are also known to have the power of *berachah*. There are many stories of people running after someone who is quietly slinking away after enduring derision, begging that person to give them a *berachah* to have children, with a successful outcome. Often this is after many years of fruitless effort and doctors saying nothing more can be done.

However, this is a side-point, albeit an encouraging one for anyone who endures embarrassment. The main point, whose importance cannot be overstated, is that we must look around us before we speak and see fellow human beings, fellow Jews with hearts and souls and the same need for dignity as we have. And we have to do all we can to avoid being the person who crushes that dignity, because it is something from which Hashem does not look away.

# Something I Can Do

Sometimes, we see a disaster about to happen and there's nothing we can do but watch. We see that the car in front of us has stopped suddenly, but we're too close to avoid the fender-bender. We see the glass about to fall off the edge of the table, but we're not close enough to intercept it. It's a helpless feeling. But how much worse is it when the disaster we see unfolding is the destruction of someone's self-respect? This story, told by Rabbi Yitzchok Hisiger, illustrates that we're not always as helpless as we think we are:

> The crowd was settled into their seats waiting for the chuppah to begin. Meanwhile, behind the scenes, drama was unfolding.
>
> Someone approached the Debrecener Rav, who was to be the mesader kiddushin, and conveyed to him a vital, and thus far unspoken, bit of information. The chassan was on medication for a seizure disorder and had not disclosed this fact to the kallah or her parents. The Rav said he could not go ahead with the chuppah unless the kallah and her father were told about the condition and agreed to the marriage nonetheless.

The Rav broke the news to the kallah. "I need time to think about this," she said.

Meanwhile, the long wait was arousing concern among the guests. Some knew what was going on and dreaded the thought of the humiliation the chassan would suffer if the wedding was called off. But what could they do?

Rav Yosef Rosenblum was among the chuppah guests, and with his tremendous wisdom and sensitivity, he saw the impending disaster as clearly as someone might see a thunderstorm rolling in. But his instinct was not to run and find shelter; it was to push back the storm.

He saw a young man among the guests, a bachur who was himself a chassan, and he called him over.

"There's a major tragedy about to take place," he told the boy. He went on to explain the details.

Rav Yosef saw a way out. He knew the kallah's family and was aware that they struggled financially and worried a great deal about meeting their expenses. He surmised that the financial implication of the potential medical issue was weighing heavily in their decision, and that money could play a powerful role in ironing out the situation.

The bachur to whom Rav Yosef was speaking was marrying into a very wealthy family. He knew the young man's in-laws would be giving him far more money than he needed each month, and he would soon be joining their extremely successful business. Therefore, the Rav made a request of the boy: "I want you to go to the kallah and her father and tell them that if they go through with the chuppah, you are going to support this couple. You are going to give them support on a monthly basis for many years, for themselves, for their children — whatever they need."

"But how can I promise that?" the boy asked. "I'm not even married yet."

"I know what I'm asking you is not simple, but it's a matter of pikuach nefesh. If this matter comes out, it will be a huge public embarrassment and someone's life could be destroyed. We have to put ourselves out," the Rav explained. "I'm telling you, you are going to have berachah v'hatzlachah in all your parnassah, and it's going to work out. You have to do it."

The chassan agreed. He and Rav Yosef brought the proposal to the kallah and her parents and they consented to it. The chasunah went forward and the bachur who guaranteed their financial future became extraordinarily successful. He supported the couple and their family for many years. They are raising their family and have married off several children.

This remarkable story seems to fit within the purview of a *gadol hador* like Rav Yosef Rosenblum, for it demonstrates incredible insight and determination. However, the story speaks to us as well. There were probably several hundred people sitting in that *chuppah* room while a *shidduch* was breaking apart a few feet away, poised to plunge a young man into a tragic situation. Those who knew about it felt there was nothing they could do but wait. However, one person looked at the situation and thought, "There must be something I can do." He searched outside the box for an idea, and Hashem sent *siyata d'Shmaya* that allowed it to succeed. The lesson for us is, we cannot be content to be bystanders when someone's life is falling apart.

Sometimes the solution to an intractable struggle is relatively simple, as in the story that follows:

Many years ago, a young Lakewood woman lost her husband very suddenly. She was in her early thirties, already the mother of several children, and she was unable to cope with the loss. People came to her side and tried to provide comfort and support, but she could not regain her composure. She was not functioning.

Someone who did not know this woman personally, but was casually acquainted with one of her brothers-in-law, heard about her plight. He knew that a certain talmid chacham and tzaddik from Eretz Yisrael was coming to town to raise funds. He was known as one to whom people turned in times of trouble, because he was willing to sit with them and delve into their situation until he perceived the core of the problem. With that clarity, he provided guidance that was compassionate and precise. Therefore, this man thought that perhaps the tzaddik could help the young almanah.

The young man called the almanah's brother-in-law to ask if this idea seemed helpful. The brother-in-law readily agreed that it was worth a try, since no one had been able to soothe the woman's grief.

The connection was made. Despite the talmid chacham's packed schedule, he could not leave an almanah in distress if there was a chance that he could help her. Therefore, when he arrived in Lakewood, he went to visit the woman and spent hours speaking to her. In the three weeks he was in town, he went to meet with her five times, each time spending several hours in conversation with her. When he returned to Eretz Yisrael, he maintained contact with her.

The woman eventually remarried. Those who were close to her say that this talmid chacham literally saved her life.

We might not be amazed that a *tzaddik* had the right words, coming from his pure heart and deep wisdom, to revitalize the *almanah's* aching soul. The part of the story that should arouse our interest is that this young man, who was only peripherally familiar with the situation, was bothered enough by it to think, "Maybe there's something I can do." Someone's life was falling apart. He didn't know her; he only knew about the situation third-hand, maybe even fourth-hand, but he didn't shrug his shoulders and say, "That's so sad." Rather, he put on his thinking cap and said, "Let me try to help."

One caveat in taking on such a role is that when we're not connected to someone, we might misconstrue what would help him. Therefore, we should speak with someone who knows — a competent Rav or someone with insight into these matters — to make sure that the help we want to offer will actually help and not, *chas v'shalom,* hurt or insult our intended beneficiary.

Nevertheless, this should not deter us from feeling the urgency to act, to prevent the disaster we see unfolding in front of us. Even an unlikely idea is worth pursuing, because when we extend ourselves to help someone, Hashem sends us the *siyata d'Shmaya* to bring our effort to a successful conclusion.

# 100

# *Be Busy With What Counts*

O ne Erev Rosh Hashanah, Rav Shlomo Heiman, the legendary Rosh Yeshivah of Torah Vodaath, asked a few bachurim to please come to his house. The bachurim were in a state of high expectation. What mission, what words, would the Rosh Yeshivah have for them during this special moment right before the Yom HaDin?

Much to their surprise, the mission could not have been more mundane. "Could you please address these shanah tovah cards for me?" he requested. Immediately, Rav Shlomo noticed the disappointed looks on the boys' faces. He realized that they expected to be asked to do something grander than addressing envelopes.

"Am I doing the right thing to be busy right now, Erev Rosh Hashanah, addressing envelopes for shanah tovah cards?" he asked. "I don't know. Maybe I'm not doing the right thing. But I want to tell you bachurim something important. For you, this is definitely the right thing, because you are doing the Torah mitzvah of gemilus chassadim. You are doing the greatest thing possible to earn a zechus before Rosh Hashanah."

This is a remarkable perspective. Regardless of whether Rav Shlomo was doing the optimal thing, the moment he asked the boys to help him do it, they had a full, beautiful *mitzvah d'Oraisa* — no less than hearing the blowing of the shofar or putting on tefillin — and all the merit it brings. Someone needed help and they stepped up to provide that help. No other *segulah* they might have engaged in to bring them a favorable judgment on Rosh Hashanah could have been as powerful.

Let's imagine that someone asks his friend to be *sandek* at a *bris* on Erev Rosh Hashanah. The *sandek* is bound to feel that this is a wonderful *zechus* that Hashem has dropped into his hand. However, as we explained earlier, the *Pele Yoetz* says that this great merit of being a *sandek* pales in comparison to giving someone change for a dollar. This is because providing change fulfills the mitzvah of *v'ahavta l'rei'acha kamocha*. If we needed change, we would want someone to give it to us. Therefore, when we give someone change, we are fulfilling the mitzvah of *v'ahavta l'rei'acha kamocha*." Being a *sandek*, as important an honorific as that is, is not a *mitzvas asei d'Oraisa* of *gemilus chassadim*.

Therefore, Rav Shlomo taught his students this lesson: Nothing could be greater on Erev Rosh Hashanah than performing the mundane task of helping someone address *shanah tovah* cards, because doing so changes that mundane task into the fulfillment of a Torah mitzvah. A *segulah* does not provide this merit.

The challenge is to internalize this idea and keep it in mind when opportunities to do chessed arise. Imagine someone sitting on chair, reading an article about *segulos* a person can do for 40 days to merit a *kesivah v'chasimah tovah*. Just then, a neighbor knocks and the door and asks to borrow a hammer. The person who was poring over the article is disturbed — he's busy thinking about which *segulos* to try and now this neighbor comes along and he is compelled to go into his garage and hunt down a hammer. If this person had internalized an understanding of what chessed is, he would excitedly drop the article and run to find the hammer.

As the Chofetz Chaim explains in *Ahavas Chessed,* based on numerous sources, there is no greater *segulah* than the mitzvah of *gemilus chassadim.* We need to look for these opportunities, big and small — changing a dollar, giving a ride, helping someone fill out a form, loaning an item — and treasure each one as an easy, accessible opportunity to fulfill a Torah mitzvah.

101

# Office Hours

The famous *askan*, Rav Shlomo Lorincz, who worked closely with the Chazon Ish, the Brisker Rav and, later, with Rav Shach, expended boundless effort to help the *frum* community in Eretz Yisrael. In his autobiography, *Bemechitzasam*, he relates many remarkable personal stories of his interactions with these *gedolim*.

*Rav Lorincz, besides running his business, serving as a member of the Knesset, and advocating for the frum community, was an accomplished talmid chacham. He did his best to have a seder kavua, a set block of time each night for learning, but it was always interrupted by the non-stop stream of people coming to seek his help.*

*One day, he discussed his dilemma with Rav Shach. "Because I am in the Knesset, everyone thinks I can solve whatever problem they have," he explained. "In reality, it is only a very small percentage of people I can help. But they come to me at all hours and take up most of the time I set aside for learning. So I want to ask the Rosh Yeshivah if I can put a sign on my door that says when I will* be available to help people — say for a half-hour or 45 minutes each night — and that will be it."

Rav Shach normally answered Rav Lorincz's questions quickly, but this time he sat and thought for a few minutes. Finally, Rav Shach told him, "I can't answer you. But I will tell you what I do. I have the very same question. Now it's true, I'm a Rosh Yeshivah and I have time to learn during the day, which makes a difference. But, I have sedarim that I need to learn and I have to prepare shiurim.

And like you, I have people coming to me all day. And at night. And most of these people, I cannot help. (In his humility, Rav Shach did not recognize how many people benefited from his help.) But I never, ever make hours. I never close my door. When anyone comes in, even if I need to prepare a shiur for the next day or I'm in the middle of a difficult Tosafos that I need to finish, I never make hours and I never send someone away. That's what I do, but I can't answer for you."

Of course, when Rav Lorincz heard what Rav Shach said, he concluded, "My Torah learning is definitely not any more chashuv than Rav Shach's." He therefore continued his open-door policy.

This story reiterates a point we have made frequently throughout this sefer, a concept based on sources throughout Chazal (Sotah 8b, Sanhedrin 90a). That is that Hashem does everything middah k'neged middah — in a precise reflection of the way in which the person conducts himself.

We can envision this concept vividly through the famous vort of the Baal Shem Tov on the pasuk (Tehillim 121:5), "Hashem tzilcha — Hashem is your shadow."

The Baal Shem Tov explains that just as when a person moves the finger on his hand, his shadow follows his movement exactly, Hashem treats us exactly as we treat others. If we have rachamim on others whenever they need us, Hashem conforms precisely to our actions and unfailingly replies with rachamim to our pleas for help.

On the other hand, if we weigh and measure the situation — "Does he deserve my help? Has he ever helped me? Do I have time for him?" — then likewise, Hashem is our shadow; He weighs and measures our requests.

The *Mesillas Yesharim* (Ch.19) expounds on the Gemara (*Shabbos* 151b), "*Kol hameracheim al habriyos, merachamim alav min ha-Shamayim* — Whoever has mercy on people, [Hashem] has mercy on him from *Shamayim*." He adds that this is a matter of degree. The more mercy a person has on others, the more mercy he receives from *Shamayim*. But it's also a matter of self-protection; when we have *rachmanus* on others, we also have *rachmanus* on ourselves.

# 102

## "Come Back, We Miss You!"

We tend to look at people and categorize them: popular or unpopular, socially skilled or socially awkward, interesting or boring, normal or odd, with-it or out-of-it, smart or slow. Most people judge themselves to be somewhere along the spectrum of the positive categories: not the greatest, but normal and socially acceptable. Those we place in the negative categories, in our eyes, are unfortunate, but what can we do? Hashem gave them this *nisayon* and we don't have the power to turn them into more interesting, appealing people.

But someone who is attuned to chessed, and especially the chessed of extending friendship to those who need it, discovers that the "categories" we have in mind are not set in stone. By reaching out, we can light the spark that enables a person to shine brighter, as this true story portrays:

> *A high school girl from a prestigious family was struggling. While her difficulties initiated with academics, her poor performance soon led to social struggles as well. As the new school year approached, she begged her parents to send her to a different*

*school. They had many connections with influential people, and were close to many gedolim, but none of that helped them find a new place for their daughter.*

*A Rosh Yeshivah to whom they were close advised them to convince her to return to her original high school and bring her principal and teachers on board to work with her. However, the girl refused. People were telling the girl's mother, "Get her a job if she isn't going back to school. She can't just sit home doing nothing all day!"*

*The school year began, and this girl stayed home. Then, on Tzom Gedaliah, she received a call from a classmate.*

*"Could you please come back?" the girl asked. "We miss you so much! Tomorrow there will be a Yom Iyun with several speakers. It's a great day to come back to school. I hope you'll be there."*

*The girl hung up the phone and told her mother, "I think I'm going to go to school tomorrow because the girls really want me to come back."*

The friend who called this girl didn't think, "Too bad for her that she's so out of it and such a failure in school. But what can you do? Some people make it and some people don't." Instead, she thought, "This girl is suffering. What can I do to make her feel valued?" Maybe the girl will never become a star student or the most popular girl in class. However, by letting her know that her presence is missed, her fellow student restored her sense of her own value. Now, perhaps she is ready to work with her teachers to upgrade her skills. Now, she can develop the confidence that will help her socially. Now, the talents she has — perhaps not in academics, but in other areas — can have a chance to shine forth.

No one is beyond hope. There's no person who doesn't respond to a gesture of friendship. What a Rosh Yeshivah and an *askan* couldn't accomplish, a gesture of friendship accomplished. Like a leaf turns to the light and absorbs the energy of the sun, every human heart turns toward love, care and respect — and from this, every person can grow greater.

# 103

# Wield a Shield

The *Zohar* sheds light on an episode in our history that is so tragic it is recounted on Yom Kippur as a means to bring us to tears of *teshuvah.* That is the story of the *Asarah Harugei Malchus* — the 10 *Tannaim* killed by the Romans. Like everything Hashem does, these horrific murders had a just purpose, and as the *Zohar* explains, this was to serve as a *kapparah* for the 10 sons of Yaakov who sold their brother Yosef HaTzaddik into slavery and never received *mechilah* for their sin.

This explanation, however, raises a question: Why did the *kapparah* for this deed only come about centuries after the deed was done? The sale of Yosef happened much earlier (in *Sefer Bereishis*), yet the consequence waited until the Romans ruled Yerushalayim during the period of the *Bayis Sheini*. In the intervening centuries, Jews had entered Eretz Yisrael, conquered it, build the *Bayis Rishon*, gone into exile, returned and built the *Bayis Sheini*.

The *Zohar* answers the question with a lesson that can serve as a life-raft for us as we navigate the stormy seas of *chevlei Mashiach*. The *Shevatim,* says the *Zohar,* sold Yosef for the sake of Heaven. They believed this was what Hashem wanted them to do, and therefore, there was a certain *middas harachamim* — a measure of Hashem's mercy — that protected them. In their *zechus,* generation after generation of their offspring — the nation of Klal Yisrael — was spared punishment for the deed.

However, during the time of *Bayis Sheini,* the *middas hadin* — Hashem's attribute of justice—prevailed in the world. When justice is due, it does not simply vanish, says the *Zohar.* Rather, it waits for its time to strike, for a time when the shield of *rachamim* is lowered. We tend to think that because a sin fades into the past, all is forgiven and the justice due from it has faded as well; the court has dismissed the case and we can go on as if nothing has happened. However, the *Zohar* warns that a person does not know what outstanding debts might be waiting in his account for the bill to come due. We all need the *middas harachamim* to protect ourselves.

Rav Matisyahu Salomon explained this idea based on the Mishnah (*Pirkei Avos* 4:13), that *teshuvah* and *maasim tovim* are *kisris bifnei hapuranus* — like a shield in front of afflictions. He further clarified the essence of a shield; it is not an offensive weapon. It cannot destroy the sword that strikes against it. All it can do is protect, by deflecting the sword so that it cannot strike the person. In the same way, when afflictions are coming to attack a person, it is not within our power to strike them down. However, our *teshuvah* and *maasim tovim* can deflect them. They fend them off and prevent them from harming us.

A vital aspect of this protection is that we cannot put down the shield and expect it to continue helping us. In this light, it is worthwhile to review once more the story of Nevuchadnezzar's bout with insanity that is recorded in *Sefer Daniel* (Ch. 4).

The episode begins with Nevuchadnezzar's terrifying dream, which Daniel interpreted for him as a warning that he was going to lose his mind and believe himself to be an animal. Daniel then offered him a strategy to forestall this fate: If he gave *tzedakah* to the poor among the Jews, he could redeem his sins and postpone the onset of madness.

The king took his advice and set aside a time each day when poor Jews could come and receive charity from the king's treasury. This continued for 12 months. Then, one day, he became irritated by the noise of his daily visitors and told his servants to stop the practice. That very day, he lost his mind. The decree was waiting until the moment he lowered his shield.

This is a concept we cannot ignore. We know without a doubt that we are living in a time of *middas hadin*. Unfortunately, there are so many *almanos*, so many *yesomim*, so much violence and confusion. We have to forge a firm link in our minds between *middas hadin* and the protection chessed provides for us. We have to recognize the sword poised over us, and also realize that there's a shield in our hand. As the story of Nevuchadnezzar illustrates, every single day we do chessed and give *tzedakah*, we guard ourselves against afflictions.

The Gemara (*Shabbos* 151b) says, "*Kol hameracheim al habriyos, merachamin alav min haShamayim*" — Whoever is compassionate to [Hashem's] creations, compassion is shone on him from *Shamayim*." This heartening statement is balanced, however, by the follow-up: "*V'chol she'eino meracheim al habriyos, eino merachamin alav min ha-Shamayim*" — Whoever doesn't have mercy on people, then there is no mercy on him from *Shamayim*.

The *Mesillas Yesharim* (Ch. 19) expounds that the Gemara is teaching that Hashem's mercy comes to us measure for measure. The more we act with *rachmanus* for others, the more *rachmanus* He shows to us. If we do so in moderation, He does so in moderation. If we are generous, He showers us with abundant mercy.

In the *zechus* of the *rachmanus* we shower on others, may Hashem guide us through this time of *din* under the shelter of His protection, treat us with patience and forgiveness and permanently wash away all our sins. May we soon experience the *Geulah Sheleimah*, when we will see the world with perfect clarity and experience it as Hashem created it to be — a world built on chessed.